Learning Cocoa with Objective-C

Jonathon Manning and Paris Buttfield-Addison

O'REILLY®

Beijing · Cambridge · Farnham · Köln · Sebastopol · Tokyo

Learning Cocoa with Objective-C

by Jonathon Manning and Paris Buttfield-Addison

Published by O'Reilly Media, Inc., 1005 Gravenstein Highway North, Sebastopol, CA 95472.

O'Reilly books may be purchased for educational, business, or sales promotional use. Online editions are also available for most titles (*http://my.safaribooksonline.com*). For more information, contact our corporate/institutional sales department: 800-998-9938 or *corporate@oreilly.com*.

Editors: Brian Jepson and Rachel Roumeliotis
Production Editor: Rachel Steely
Copyeditor: Jasmine Kwityn

Proofreader: Becca Freed
Indexer: Lucie Haskins
Cover Designer: Karen Montgomery
Interior Designer: David Futato
Illustrator: Robert Romano

December 2012: Third Edition

Revision History for the Third Edition:

2012-12-07   First release

See *http://oreilly.com/catalog/errata.csp?isbn=9781449318499* for release details.

ISBN: 978-1-449-31849-9

[LSI]

Table of Contents

Preface. xi

1. Cocoa Development Tools. 1
    The Mac and iOS Developer Programs   1
        Registering for a Developer Program   2
        Downloading Xcode from Apple Developer   3
    Getting Around in Xcode   3
        The Xcode Interface   7
    Developing a Simple Objective-C Application   14
        Designing the Interface   15
        Connecting the Code   16
    Using the iOS Simulator   18

2. Object-Oriented Programming with Objective-C. 21
    Object-Oriented Programming   21
        Objects   22
        Inheritance   23
        Interfaces and Implementations   23
        Methods   24
        Messages   25
        Properties   26
        Protocols   29
        Class Extensions   30
    Memory Management   31
        Reference Counting   32
        Automatic Reference Counting   32
        Object Graphs in Objective-C   32
    The NSObject Lifecycle   33
        Allocation and Initialization   33
        Retain and Release   34

    Finalization and Deallocation   34

3. Foundation. **37**
    Mutable and Immutable Objects   37
    Strings   38
        Creating Strings   39
        Working with Strings   39
        Comparing Strings   42
        Searching Strings   43
    Arrays   43
        Fast Enumeration   46
        Mutable Arrays   46
    Dictionaries   47
    NSValue and NSNumber   49
    Data   50
        Loading Data from Files and URLs   50
        Serialization and Deserialization   52
    Design Patterns in Cocoa   54
        Model-View-Controller   55
        Delegation   56
        Key-Value Observing   57

4. Applications on OS X and iOS. **59**
    What Is an Application?   59
        Applications, Frameworks, Utilities, and More   60
        What Are Apps Composed Of?   61
        Using NSBundle to Find Resources in Applications   63
    The Application Lifecycle   64
        OS X Applications   64
        iOS Applications   66
    The Application Sandbox   69
        Application Restrictions   70

5. Graphical User Interfaces. **73**
    Interfaces in OS X and iOS   73
    MVC and Application Design   74
    Nib Files   74
        Structure of a Nib File   75
        Outlets and Actions   79
        How Nib Files Are Loaded   80
    Constructing an Interface   80
        Guidelines and Constraints   80

    Building an App with Nibs and Constraints   82
    Core Animation   84
      Layers   85
      Animations   85

6. Blocks and Operation Quotes. **89**
    Blocks   89
      Block Syntax   90
      Block Lifecycles   92
      Methods with Block Parameters   93
      Blocks and Memory Management   94
      Modifying Local Variables from Inside Blocks with __block   95
    Concurrency with Operation Queues   95
      Operation Queues and NSOperation   96
      Performing Work on Operation Queues   97
    Putting It All Together   98

7. Drawing Graphics in Views. **103**
    How Drawing Works   103
    The Pixel Grid   105
      Retina Displays   105
      Pixels and Screen Points   107
    Drawing in Views   108
      Frame Rectangles   108
      Bounds Rectangles   109
    Building a Custom View   110
      Creating the Project   110
      Filling with a Solid Color   110
      Working with Paths   113
      Creating Custom Paths   114
      Multiple Subpaths   117
      Shadows   118
      Gradients   122
      Transforms   126

8. Audio and Video. **129**
    AV Foundation   129
    Playing Video with AVPlayer   130
      AVPlayerLayer   131
      Putting It Together   131
    Playing Sound with AVAudioPlayer   135
    Working with the Photo Library   137

Capturing Photos and Video from the Camera   138
Building a Photo Application   140
The Photo Library   142

9. Model Objects and Data Storage. **145**
Key-Value Coding   146
Key-Value Observing   148
    Registering for Change Notifications   148
    Notifying Observers of Changes   150
Notifications with NSNotification   150
Preferences   151
    Registering Default Preferences   152
    Accessing Preferences   153
    Setting Preferences   154
Working with the Filesystem   154
    Using NSFileManager   156
    File Storage Locations   159
Working with the Sandbox   159
    Enabling Sandboxing   159
    Open and Save Panels   160
    Security-Scoped Bookmarks   160

10. Cocoa Bindings. **163**
Binding Views to Models   164
A Single Bindings App   164
Binding to Controllers   167
Array and Object Controllers   168
A More Complex Bindings App   169

11. Table Views and Collection Views. **175**
Data Sources and Delegates   175
Table Views   176
UITableView on iOS   176
    Sections and Rows   177
    Table View Controllers   178
    Table View Cells   178
    Implementing a Table View   182
NSTableView on OS X   184
    Sorting a Table View   188
    NSTableView with Bindings   189
Collection Views   190

UICollectionView on iOS   190

12. Document-Based Applications. 195
    The NSDocument and UIDocument Classes   196
    Document Objects in MVC   196
    Kinds of Documents   196
    The Role of Documents   197
    Document-Based Applications on OS X   198
        Autosaving and Versions   198
        Representing Documents with NSDocument   199
        Saving Simple Data   200
        Saving More Complex Data   202
    Document-Based Applications on iOS   206
        Representing Documents with UIDocument   206

13. Networking. 215
    Connections   215
        NSURL   216
        NSURLRequest   217
        NSURLConnection   218
        NSURLResponse and NSHTTPURLResponse   218
    Building a Networked Application   218
    Discovering Nearby Services   220
        Browsing for Shared iTunes Libraries   220

14. Working with the Real World. 223
    Working with Location   223
        Location Hardware   224
        The Core Location Framework   225
        Working with Core Location   226
    Geocoding   230
    Locations and Privacy   232
    Device Motion   233
        Working with Core Motion   234
    Printing Documents   239
        Printing on OS X   239
        Printing on iOS   240

15. Event Kit. 243
    Understanding Events   243
        Accessing the Event Store   244
        Accessing Calendars   245

    Accessing Events   245
    Working with Events   246
    Building an Events Application   247
    User Privacy   252

16. Instruments and the Debugger.................................... **255**
    Getting Started with Instruments   256
      The Instruments Interface   256
      Observing Data   259
      Adding Instruments from the Library   260
    Fixing Problems with Instruments   260
    Retain Cycles and Leaks   266
    Using the Debugger   269
      Setting Breakpoints   269
      Inspecting Memory Contents   273
      Working with the Debugger Console   273

17. Sharing and Notifications................................... **275**
    Sharing   275
      Sharing on iOS   277
      Sharing on OS X   280
    Notifications   281
      Push Notifications   281
      Sending Push Notifications   282
      Setting Up to Receive Push Notifications   284
      Receiving Push Notifications   286
      Local Notifications   287

18. Nonstandard Apps...................................... **289**
    Command-Line Tools   289
    Preference Panes   291
      How Preference Panes Work   291
      Preference Domains   292
      Building a Sample Preference Pane   293
    Status Bar Items   295
      Building a Status Bar App   295

19. Working with Text....................................... **299**
    Internationalization and Localization   299
      Strings Files   299
      Creating a Sample Localized Application   300
    Formatting Data with NSFormatter   302

    Formatting Dates with NSDateFormatter   302
    Detecting Data with NSDataDetector   304
      Testing a Data Detector   305

20. iCloud... **309**
    What iCloud Stores   309
    Setting Up for iCloud   310
    Testing Whether iCloud Works   312
    Storing Settings   312
    iCloud Storage   317

Index.. **325**

Preface

We've been developing for the Cocoa framework from when the Mac first supported it. Since then, we've seen the ecosystem of Cocoa and Objective-C development evolve from a small programmer's niche to one of the most important and influential development environments in the world. (In fact, as 2012 closes, Objective-C is the third most popular programming language according to the TIOBE index (*http://www.tiobe.com/index.php/content/paperinfo/tpci/index.html*), up from fifth most popular in 2011.)

Over the years, we've built a lot of large, complex iOS and OS X software, shipping it to millions upon millions of users along the way. We've picked up a deep understanding of the toolset, frameworks, and programming language, an understanding crucial to building the best possible software for iOS and OS X. Apple constantly changes things, as the recent introduction of the svelte iPad mini and the stretched iPhone 5 show, but the knowledge necessary to bend the development tools, frameworks and languages to your will stays fairly constant. This book will give you the knowledge, confidence, and appreciation for iOS and OS X development with Cocoa, Cocoa Touch, and Objective-C.

Audience

We assume that you're a reasonably capable programmer, but we don't assume you've ever developed for iOS or OS X, or used Objective-C before. We also assume that you're fairly comfortable navigating OS X as a user, and know how to use an iOS device.

Organization of This Book

In this book, we'll be talking about Cocoa and Cocoa Touch, the frameworks used on OS X and iOS, respectively. Along the way, we'll also be covering Objective-C, including its syntax and features. Pretty much every chapter contains practical exercises that you can follow along with. The early chapters cover general topics, such as setting up a development environment and coming to grips with the Objective-C language, while later chapters cover specific features of Cocoa and Cocoa Touch.

Here is a concise breakdown of the material each chapter covers:

Chapter 1, Cocoa Development Tools
>This chapter introduces Cocoa and Cocoa touch, the frameworks used on OS X and iOS. Introduces Xcode, the IDE that you'll be using while coding for these platforms. This chapter also covers the Apple Developer Programs, which are necessary if you want to distribute software on the Mac or iTunes App Stores.

Chapter 2, Object-Oriented Programming with Objective-C
>This chapter covers object-oriented programming, the programming paradigm used in Objective-C, as well as how Objective-C implements object-oriented programming. This chapter also covers memory management in Cocoa and Cocoa touch, which is one of the most important things to understand when developing for the Mac and for iOS.

Chapter 3, Foundation
>This chapter introduces the Foundation framework, which provides the basic data types (like strings, arrays, and dictionaries). This chapter also discusses the underlying design patterns on which much of Cocoa and Cocoa Touch are based.

Chapter 4, Applications on OS X and iOS
>This chapter discusses how applications are assembled and operate on Mac and iOS devices. In this chapter, we'll talk about the application lifecycle on both platforms, as well as how sandboxing affects application access to data and resources.

Chapter 5, Graphical User Interfaces
>This chapter demonstrates how user interfaces are loaded and presented to the user. This chapter introduces one of the most powerful concepts provided by Cocoa: *nibs*, which are predesigned and preconfigured user interfaces, and which can be directly connected to your code. This chapter also discusses Core Animation, the animation system used on OS X and iOS.

Chapter 6, Blocks and Operation Quotes
>This chapter introduces blocks, which are an incredibly flexible and useful addition that Objective-C introduces to the C language. Blocks are functions that can be stored in variables and passed around like values. This makes things like callbacks very simple to implement. This chapter also introduces operation queues, which are a straightforward way to work with concurrency without having to deal with threads.

Chapter 7, Drawing Graphics in Views

In this chapter, you'll learn about the drawing system used on both OS X and iOS, as well as how to draw custom graphics. The retina display is also covered, as well as how view geometry works.

Chapter 8, Audio and Video

This chapter covers audio and video playback using AVFoundation, the audio and video engine. You'll also learn how to access the iOS photo library and get access to the user's photos.

Chapter 9, Model Objects and Data Storage

This chapter covers a range of data storage options available on OS X and iOS. Key-Value Coding and Key-Value Observing, preferences, notifications, and filesystem access are all covered. In addition, you'll learn how to make security-scoped bookmarks, which allow sandboxed apps to retain access to locations that the user has granted your apps permission to use.

Chapter 10, Cocoa Bindings

This chapter covers Cocoa Bindings, a tremendously powerful system that allows you to connect your application's user interface to an application's data, without the need for intermediary "glue code."

Chapter 11, Table Views and Collection Views

This chapter covers table views (an effective way to display multiple rows of data to your user) and collection views, which allow you to display a collection of items to the user.

Chapter 12, Document-Based Applications

This chapter discusses the document systems on both iOS and OS X, which are instrumental in creating applications that work with multiple documents. Here, we discuss the differences in how the two platforms handle documents.

Chapter 13, Networking

Cocoa and Cocoa Touch provide very straightforward tools for accessing networked resources, and this chapter demonstrates how to retrieve information from the internet while keeping the application responsive. This chapter also covers the network service discovery system, Bonjour.

Chapter 14, Working with the Real World

This chapter covers a variety of technologies used to work with the physical world: Core Location, for getting access to the GPS; Core Motion, for learning about how the hardware is moving and oriented, and the printing systems on both iOS and OS X.

Chapter 15, Event Kit
> This chapter discusses the calendaring system used on iOS and OS X, and demonstrates how to get access to the user's calendar. We also discuss considerations for user privacy.

Chapter 16, Instruments and the Debugger
> This chapter covers Instruments, the profiler and analysis tool for Mac and iOS applications. An example of a crashing application is discussed, and the cause of the crash is diagnosed and fixed using the application. Additionally, this chapter covers Xcode's built-in debugger.

Chapter 17, Sharing and Notifications
> This chapter discusses how applications can share text, images, and other content with various other services like Twitter and Facebook, using the built-in sharing systems (which don't require your application to deal with authenticating to these services). Additionally, we'll cover both push notifications and local notifications, which allow your application to display information to the user without running.

Chapter 18, Nonstandard Apps
> Not every program you write will be an app that sits on the user's home screen, and this chapter tells you how to write three different kinds of non-traditional apps: command-line tools, menu bar apps, and preference panes.

Chapter 19, Working with Text
> This chapter covers the string localization system available on iOS and OS X. Here, we discuss data extraction from text using the built-in Data Detectors.

Chapter 20, iCloud
> This chapter discusses iCloud, the cloud data storage and syncing system provided by Apple. The functionality and requirements of iCloud are discussed, as well as demonstration apps for both OS X and iOS.

Conventions Used in This Book

The following typographical conventions are used in this book:

Italic
> Indicates new terms, URLs, email addresses, filenames, and file extensions.

`Constant width`
> Used for program listings, as well as within paragraphs to refer to program elements such as variable or function names, databases, data types, environment variables, statements, and keywords.

`Constant width bold`
> Shows commands or other text that should be typed literally by the user.

Constant width italic

Shows text that should be replaced with user-supplied values or by values determined by context.

This icon signifies a tip, suggestion, or general note.

This icon indicates a warning or caution.

Using Code Examples

This book is here to help you get your job done. In general, you may use the code in this book in your programs and documentation. You do not need to contact us for permission unless you're reproducing a significant portion of the code. For example, writing a program that uses several chunks of code from this book does not require permission. Selling or distributing a CD-ROM of examples from O'Reilly books does require permission. Answering a question by citing this book and quoting example code does not require permission. Incorporating a significant amount of example code from this book into your product's documentation does require permission.

We appreciate, but do not require, attribution. An attribution usually includes the title, author, publisher, and ISBN. For example: "*Learning Cocoa with Objective-C* by Jonathon Manning and Paris Buttfield-Addison (O'Reilly). Copyright 2013 Jonathon Manning and Paris Buttfield-Addison, 978-1-449-31849-9."

If you feel your use of code examples falls outside fair use or the permission given above, feel free to contact us at *permissions@oreilly.com*.

Safari® Books Online

 Safari Books Online (*www.safaribooksonline.com*) is an on-demand digital library that delivers expert content in both book and video form from the world's leading authors in technology and business.

Technology professionals, software developers, web designers, and business and creative professionals use Safari Books Online as their primary resource for research, problem solving, learning, and certification training.

Safari Books Online offers a range of product mixes and pricing programs for organizations, government agencies, and individuals. Subscribers have access to thousands of books, training videos, and prepublication manuscripts in one fully searchable database from publishers like O'Reilly Media, Prentice Hall Professional, Addison-Wesley Professional, Microsoft Press, Sams, Que, Peachpit Press, Focal Press, Cisco Press, John Wiley & Sons, Syngress, Morgan Kaufmann, IBM Redbooks, Packt, Adobe Press, FT Press, Apress, Manning, New Riders, McGraw-Hill, Jones & Bartlett, Course Technology, and dozens more. For more information about Safari Books Online, please visit us online.

How to Contact Us

Please address comments and questions concerning this book to the publisher:

O'Reilly Media, Inc.
1005 Gravenstein Highway North
Sebastopol, CA 95472
800-998-9938 (in the United States or Canada)
707-829-0515 (international or local)
707-829-0104 (fax)

We have a web page for this book, where we list errata, examples, and any additional information. You can access this page at *http://oreil.ly/Learning_Cocoa*.

To comment or ask technical questions about this book, send email to *bookques tions@oreilly.com*.

For more information about our books, courses, conferences, and news, see our website at *http://www.oreilly.com*.

Find us on Facebook: *http://facebook.com/oreilly*

Follow us on Twitter: *http://twitter.com/oreillymedia*

Watch us on YouTube: *http://www.youtube.com/oreillymedia*

Acknowledgments

Jon thanks his mother, father, and the rest of his crazily extended family for their tremendous support.

Paris thanks his long-suffering mother, whose credit card bankrolled literally hundreds of mobile devices through his childhood; an addiction which, in all likelihood, created the iPhone-, iPad-, mobile-obsessed monster he is today.

We'd both like to thank our editors, Brian Jepson and Rachel Roumeliotis—their skill and advice were invaluable to completing the book. Likewise, all the O'Reilly Media staff we've interacted with over the course of writing the book have been the absolute gurus of their fields.

A huge thank-you to Tony Gray and the AUC (*http://www.auc.edu.au*) for the monumental boost they gave us and others listed on this page. We wouldn't be writing this book if it wasn't for them.

Thanks also to Neal Goldstein, who deserves full credit and/or blame for getting both of us into the whole book-writing racket.

We'd like to thank the support of the goons at Maclab, who know who they are and continue to stand watch for Admiral Dolphin's inevitable apotheosis, as well as Professor Christopher Lueg and the rest of the staff at the University of Tasmania for putting up with us.

Additional thanks to Tim N, Nic W, Andrew B, Jess L, and Ash J, for a wide variety of reasons. Finally, very special thanks to Steve Jobs, without whom this book (and many others like it) would not have reason to exist.

CHAPTER 1

Cocoa Development Tools

Developing applications using Cocoa and Cocoa Touch involves the use of a set of tools developed by Apple. In this chapter, you'll learn about these tools, where to get them, how to use them, how they work together, and what they can do.

These development tools have a long and storied history. Originally a set of standalone application tools for the NeXTSTEP OS, they were adopted by Apple for use as the official OS X tools. Later, Apple largely consolidated them into one application, known as Xcode, though some of the applications (such as Instruments and the iOS Simulator) remain separate, owing to their relatively peripheral role in the development process.

In addition to the development applications, Apple offers memberships in its Developer Programs (formerly Apple Developer Connection), which provide resources and support for developers. The programs allow access to online developer forums and specialized technical support for those interested in talking to the framework engineers.

Now, with the introduction of Apple's curated application storefronts for OS X and iOS, these developer programs have become the official way for developers to provide their credentials when submitting applications to the Mac App Store or iTunes App Store—in essence, they are your ticket to selling apps through Apple. In this chapter, you'll learn how to sign up for these programs, as well as how to use Xcode, the development tool used to build apps for OS X and iOS.

The Mac and iOS Developer Programs

Apple runs two developer programs, one for each of the two platforms you can write apps on: iOS and OS X.

You need to have a paid membership to the iOS developer program if you want to run code on your iOS devices, since signing up is the only way to obtain the necessary code-signing certificates. (At the time of writing, membership in the developer programs costs

$99 USD per year, per program.) It isn't as necessary to be a member of the Mac developer program if you don't intend to submit apps to the Mac App Store (you may, for example, prefer to sell your apps yourself). However, the Mac developer program includes useful things like early access to the next version of the OS, so it's worth your while if you're serious about making apps. Downloading Xcode is free, even if you aren't a member of either developer program.

Both programs provide, among a host of other smaller features:

- Access to the Apple Developer Forums, which are frequented by Apple engineers and designed to allow you to ask questions of your fellow developers and the people who wrote the OS.
- Access to beta versions of the OS before they are released to the public, which enables you to test your applications on the next version of OS X and iOS and make necessary changes ahead of time. You also receive beta versions of the development tools.
- A digital signing certificate (one each for OS X and iOS) used to identify you to the App Stores. Without this, you cannot submit apps for sale, making the programs mandatory for anyone who wants to release software either for free or for sale via the App Store.

As a developer, you can register for one or both of the developer programs. They don't depend on one another.

Finally, registering for a developer program isn't necessary to view the documentation or to download the current version of the developer tools, so you can play around with writing apps without opening your wallet.

Registering for a Developer Program

To register for one of the developer programs you'll first need an Apple ID. It's quite likely that you already have one, since the majority of Apple's online services require one to identify you. If you've ever used iCloud, the iTunes store (for music or for apps), MobileMe, or Apple's support and repair service, you already have an ID. You might even have more than one (one of the authors of this book has four). If you don't yet have an ID, you'll create one as part of the registration process. When you register for a program, it gets added to your Apple ID.

To get started, visit the Apple site for the program you want to join.

- For the Mac program, go to *http://developer.apple.com/programs/mac/*
- For the iOS program, go to *http://developer.apple.com/programs/ios/*

Simply click through the steps to enroll.

You can choose to register as an individual or as a company. If you register as an individual, your apps will be sold under your name. If you register as a company, your apps will be sold under your company's legal name. Choose carefully, since it's very difficult to convince Apple to change your program's type.

If you're registering as an individual, you'll just need your credit card. If you're registering as a company, you'll need your credit card as well as documentation that proves that you have authority to bind your company to Apple's terms and conditions.

Apple usually takes about 24 hours to activate an account for individuals, and longer for companies. Once you've received confirmation from Apple, you'll be emailed a link to activate your account; once that's done, you're a full-fledged developer!

Downloading Xcode from Apple Developer

To develop apps for either platform, you'll use Xcode, Apple's integrated development environment. Xcode combines a source code editor, debugger, compiler, profiler, iPhone and iPad simulator, and more into one package, and it's where you'll spend the majority of your time when developing applications.

There are two ways to download Xcode. If you're running OS X Lion (10.7 or later), you can get Xcode from the Mac App Store. Simply open the App Store application and search for "Xcode," and it'll pop up. It's a free download, though it's rather large (the current version is about 1.7GB at the time of writing).

If you're running OS X Snow Leopard (10.6) or simply don't want to use the App Store, you can download Xcode from Apple's site. Doing this requires enrollment in either of the developer programs. Visit *http://developer.apple.com/xcode/* and sign in to your developer account to download the application. If you're running Lion and want to download directly, visit *https://developer.apple.com/downloads/* and search for "Xcode"—you can find the download link in the search results.

Once you've downloaded Xcode, it's straightforward enough to install it. The Mac App Store gives you an installer to double-click; if you've downloaded it directly, you get a disk image to open, which contains the same installer. Follow the prompts to install.

Getting Around in Xcode

Xcode is designed around a single window. Each of your projects will have one window, which adapts to show what you're working on.

To start exploring Xcode, you'll first need to create a project by following these steps:

1. *Launch Xcode.* Find Xcode by opening Spotlight (by pressing ⌘-Spacebar) and typing **Xcode**. You can also find it by opening the Finder, going to your hard drive, and opening the Applications directory. If you had any projects open previously, Xcode will open them for you. Otherwise, the Welcome to Xcode screen appears (Figure 1-1).

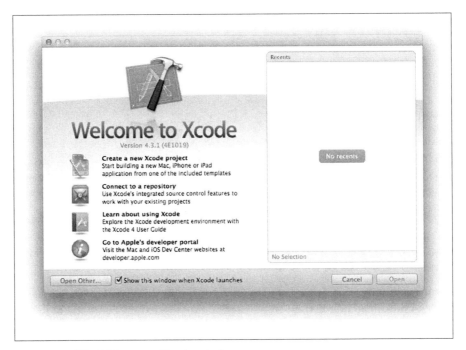

Figure 1-1. The Welcome to Xcode window

2. *Create a new project.* Do this simply by clicking "Create a new Xcode project" or go to File→New→Project.

   You'll be asked what kind of application to create. The template selector is divided into two areas. On the lefthand side, you'll find a collection of categories that applications can be in. You can choose to create an iOS or Mac project template, which sets up a project directory that will get you started in the right direction.

   Since we're just poking around Xcode at the moment, it doesn't really matter, so choose Application under the OS X header and select Cocoa Application. This creates an empty Mac application.

3. *Enter information about the project.* Depending on the kind of project template you select, you'll be asked to provide different information about how the new project should be configured.

At a minimum, you'll be asked for the following info, no matter which platform and template you choose:

The application's name

> This is the name of the project and is visible to the user. You can change this later.

Your company identifier

> This is used to generate a *bundle ID*, a string that looks like a reverse domain name. (For example, if O'Reilly made an application named MyUsefulApplication, the bundle ID would be `com.oreilly.MyUsefulApplication`.)

> Bundle IDs are the unique identifier for an application, and are used to identify that app to the system and to the App Store. Because each bundle ID must be unique, the same ID can't be used for more than one application in either of the iOS or Mac App Stores. That's why the format is based on domain names —if you own the site `usefulsoftware.com`, all of your bundle IDs would begin with `com.usefulsoftware`, and you won't accidentally use a bundle ID that someone else is using or wants to use because nobody else owns the same domain name.

The class prefix

> Class prefixes are two- or three-letter codes that go on the front of your classes and prevent your class names from interfering with existing classes.
>
> This means that a class called `String` with the class prefix of `LC` (for "Learning Cocoa") would be `LCString`. Apple's classes, for example, commonly use `NS` as their class prefix—their `String` class is `NSString`. Apple uses other prefixes as well.

Whether to use Automatic Reference Counting

> This controls whether your application uses the old-style manual memory-management method used prior to iOS 5.0 and OS X Lion (10.7.) You should almost always turn this on, as it saves a lot of headaches.

> This book assumes that all your projects will use Automatic Reference Counting, so make sure the checkbox is checked for all the projects you create for this book!

Whether to include unit tests

> Unit tests are separate blocks of code that are run at compile time to test the functionality of your code. They allow you to test parts of your code in isolation,

which lets you track down bugs more easily. Unit tests are extremely useful when you're doing anything more complex than small apps. We don't cover unit tests in this book, but there's an O'Reilly Breakdown Video (*http://shop.oreil ly.com/product/0636920016465.do*) that serves as a great resource.

 Though highly recommended, adding unit tests to your code is optional. For this reason, this book does not assume that you've added them to your projects.

If you're writing an application for the Mac App Store, you'll also be prompted for the App Store category (whether it's a game, an educational app, a social networking app, and so on).

Depending on the template, you may also be asked for other information (for example, the file extension for your documents if you are creating a document-aware application such as a Mac app).

Follow the steps below to create a new iOS application project named HelloCocoa, which will help familiarize you with the Xcode environment.

1. *Create a new Cocoa Touch application for iOS.* Create your new project by choosing File→New→Project or pressing ⌘-Shift-N. Choose Application from the iOS list, select Single-View Application, and then click Next. This creates an app that has only one screen (Figure 1-2).

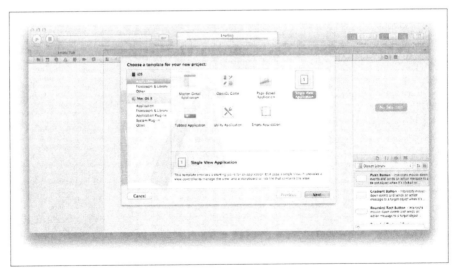

Figure 1-2. Selecting a single-view application for iOS

2. *Name the application.* Enter **HelloCocoa** in the Product Name section.

3. *Make the application run on the iPhone.* Choose iPhone from the Devices drop-down list.

> iOS applications can run on the iPad, iPhone, or both. Applications that run on both are called "universal" applications, which run the same binary but have different user interfaces. For this exercise, just choose iPhone.

4. *Set your company identifier.* Enter your site's domain name backwards. So our domain name, `oreilly.com`, would be entered as `com.oreilly`.

   If you don't have a domain name, enter anything you like, as long as it looks like a backwards domain name. `com.mycompany` will do.

> If you plan on releasing your app, either to the App Store or elsewhere, it's very important to use a company identifier that matches a domain name you own. The App Store requires it, and the fact that the operating system uses the bundle ID that it generates from the company identifier means that using a domain name that you own eliminates the possibility of accidentally creating a bundle ID that conflicts with someone else's.

5. *Click Next to create the project.* Leave the rest of the settings as shown in Figure 1-3.

6. *Choose where to save the project;* you'll be asked where to put it. Choose a location that suits you.

   Once you've done this, Xcode will open the project, and you can now start using the entire Xcode interface (Figure 1-4).

The Xcode Interface

As mentioned, Xcode shows your entire project in one window, which is divided into a number of sections. You can open and close each section at will, depending on what you want to see.

Let's take a look at each of these sections and examine what they do.

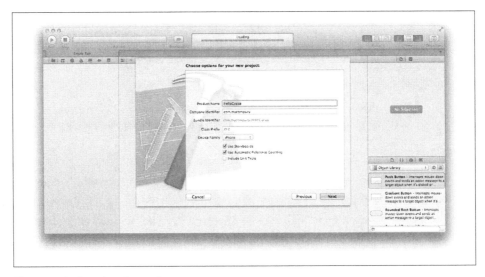

Figure 1-3. Creating the project

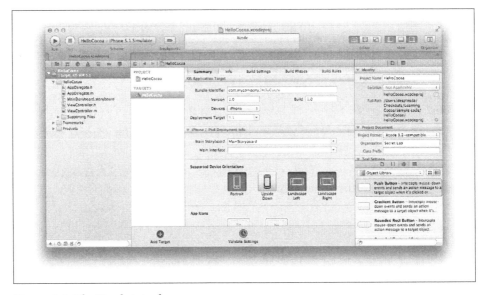

Figure 1-4. The Xcode interface

The editor

The Xcode editor (Figure 1-5) is where you'll be spending most of your time. All source code editing, interface design, and project configuration take place in this section of the application, which changes depending on which file you currently have open.

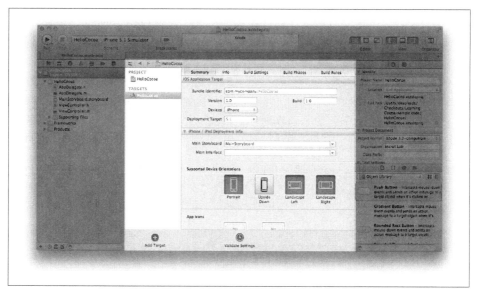

Figure 1-5. Xcode's editor

If you're editing source code, the editor is a text editor, with code completion, syntax highlighting, and all the usual features that developers have come to expect from an integrated development environment. If you're modifying a user interface, the editor becomes a visual editor, allowing you to drag around the components of your interface. Other kinds of files have their own specialized editors as well.

The editor can also be split into a *main editor* and an *assistant editor*. The assistant shows files that are related to the file currently open in the main editor. It will continue to show files that have that relationship to whatever is open, even if you open different files.

For example, if you open an interface file and then open the assistant, the assistant will, by default, show related code for the interface you're editing. If you open another interface file, the assistant will show the code for the newly opened files.

You can also jump directly from one file in the editor to its counterpart—for example, from an interface file to the corresponding implementation file. To do this, hit Control-⌘-Up Arrow to open the current file's counterpart in the current editor. You can also hit Control-⌘-Option-Up Arrow to open the current file's counterpart in an assistant pane.

The toolbar

The Xcode toolbar (Figure 1-6) acts as mission control for the entire interface. It's the only part of Xcode that doesn't significantly change as you develop your applications, and it serves as the place where you can control what your code is doing.

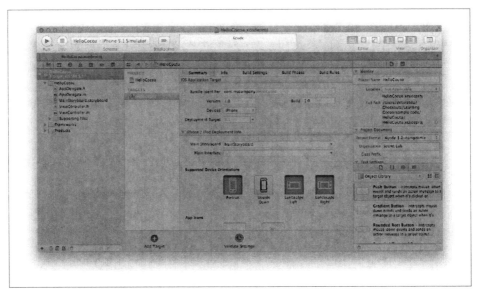

Figure 1-6. Xcode's toolbar

From left to right, the toolbar features the following items:

Run button

Clicking this button instructs Xcode to compile and run the application.

Depending on the kind of application you're running and your currently selected settings, this button will have different effects:

- If you're creating a Mac application, the new app will appear in the Dock and will run on your machine.

- If you're creating an iOS application, the new app will launch in either the iOS Simulator or on a connected iOS device, such as an iPhone or iPad.

  If you click and hold this button, you can change it from Run to another action, such as Test, Profile, or Analyze. The Test action runs any unit tests that you have set up; the Profile action runs the application Instruments (see Chapter 16); the Analyze action checks your code and points out potential problems and bugs.

Stop button

Clicking this button stops any task that Xcode is currently doing—if it's building your application, it stops, and if your application is currently running in the debugger, it quits it.

Scheme selector

Schemes are what Xcode calls build configurations—that is, what's being built and how.

Your project can contain multiple *targets*, which are the final build products created by your application. Targets can share resources like code, sound, and images, allowing you to more easily manage a task like building an iOS version of a Mac application. You don't need to create two projects, but rather have one project with two targets that can share as much code as you prefer.

To select a target, click on the lefthand side of the scheme selector.

You can also choose where the application will run. If you are building a Mac application, you will almost always want to run the application on your current Mac. If you're building an iOS application, however, you have the option of running the application on an iPhone simulator or an iPad simulator. (These are in fact the same application that simply changes shape depending on the application that is run inside it.) You can also choose to run the application on a connected iOS device, if it has been set up for development correctly.

Breakpoints button

The breakpoints button controls whether breakpoints are enabled. Breakpoints are points that you can place in your code that instruct the debugger to pause the app while it's running, allowing you to inspect the state of the program.

If the breakpoints button is on, the debugger will stop at any breakpoints that it hits. Otherwise, breakpoints are ignored.

Status display

The status display shows what Xcode is currently doing—building your application, downloading documentation, installing an application on an iOS device, and so on.

If there is more than one task currently in progress, a small button will appear on the lefthand side, which cycles through the current tasks when clicked.

Editor selector

The editor selector determines how the editor is laid out. You can choose to display either a single editor, the editor with the assistant, or the versions editor, which allows you to compare different versions of a file if you're using a revision control system.

View selector

The view selector controls whether the navigator, debug, and detail views appear on screen. If you're pressed for screen space or simply want less clutter, you can quickly summon and dismiss these parts of the screen by clicking each of the elements.

The navigator

The lefthand side of the Xcode window is the *navigator*, which presents information about your project (Figure 1-7).

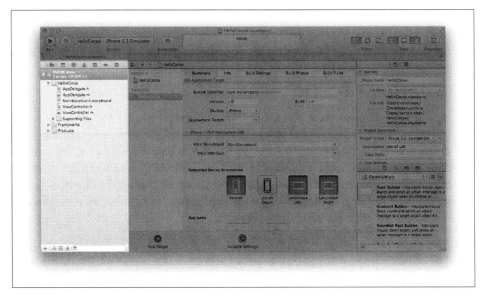

Figure 1-7. The navigator pane

The navigator is divided into seven tabs:

- The *project navigator* gives you a list of all the files that make up your project. This is the most commonly used navigator, as it determines what is shown in the editor. Whatever is selected in the project navigator is opened in the editor.

- The *symbols navigator* lists all the classes and functions that exist in your project. If you're looking for a quick summary of a class or want to jump directly to a method in that class, the Symbols navigator is a handy tool.

- The *search navigator* allows you to perform searches across your project if you're looking for specific text. (The shortcut is ⌘-Shift-F.)

- The *issue navigator* lists all the problems that Xcode has noticed in your code. This includes warnings, compilation errors, and issues that the built-in code analyzer has spotted.

- The *debug navigator* is activated when you're debugging a program, and it allows you to examine the state of the various threads that make up your program.

- The *breakpoint navigator* lists all of the breakpoints that you've currently set for use while debugging.

- The *log navigator* lists all the activity that Xcode has done with your project (such as building, debugging, and analyzing). Because logs don't get deleted, you can go back and view previous build reports at any time.

Utilities

The utilities pane (Figure 1-8) shows additional information related what you're doing in the editor. If you're editing an interface, for example, the utilities pane allows you to configure the currently selected user interface element.

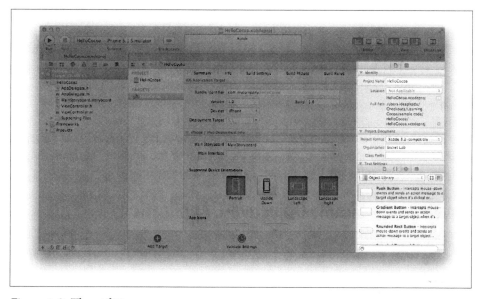

Figure 1-8. The utilities pane

The utilities pane is split into two sections: the inspector, which shows extra details and settings for the currently selected item, and the library, which is a collection of items that you can add to your project. The inspector and the library are most heavily used when building user interfaces; however, the library also contains a number of useful items such as file templates and code snippets, which you can drag and drop into place.

The debug area

The debug area (Figure 1-9) shows information reported by the debugger when the program is running. Whenever you want to see what the application is reporting while running, you can view it in the debug area.

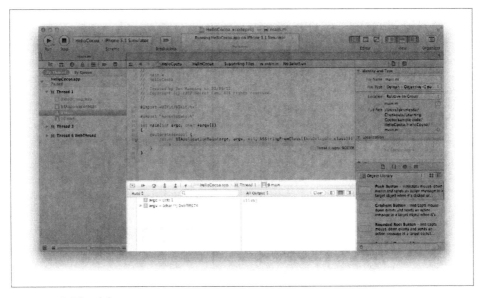

Figure 1-9. The debug area

The area is split into two sections. The left section shows the values of local variables when the application is paused; the right section shows the ongoing log from the debugger, which includes any logging that comes from the debugged application.

Developing a Simple Objective-C Application

Let's jump right into working with Xcode. We'll begin by creating a simple iOS application and then connect it together. If you're more interested in Mac development, don't worry—the same techniques apply.

This sample application will display a single button that when tapped, will pop up an alert and change the button's label to Test!. We're going to build on the application we created in the section "Getting Around in Xcode" (page 3), so make sure that you have that project open.

It's generally a good practice to design the interface first, and then add code. This means that your code is written with an understanding of how it maps to what the user sees.

To that end, we'll start by designing the interface for the application.

Designing the Interface

When building an application's interface for iOS, you have two options. You can either design your application's screens in a *storyboard*, which shows how all the screens link together, or you can design each screen in isolation. This book covers storyboards in more detail later; for now, this first application has only one screen, so it doesn't matter much either way.

Start by opening the interface file and adding a button:

1. *Open the main storyboard.* Because newly created projects use storyboards by default, your app's interface is stored in the file *MainStoryboard.storyboard*.

   Open it by selecting it in the project navigator. The editor will change to show the application's single, blank screen.

2. *Drag in a button.* We're going to add a single button to the screen. All user interface controls are kept in the *object library*, which is at the bottom of the Details pane on the righthand side of the screen.

   To find the button, you can either scroll through the list until you find Round Rect Button, or type **button** in the search field at the bottom of the library.

   Once you've located it, drag it into the screen.

3. *Configure the button.* Every item that you add to an interface can be configured. For now, we'll only change the label.

   Select the new button by clicking it, and select the Attributes inspector, which is the third tab to the left at the top of the Utilities pane. You can also reach it by pressing ⌘-Option-4.

   Change the button's Title to **Hello!**

 You can also change the button's title by double-clicking it in the interface.

Our simple interface is now complete (Figure 1-10). The only thing left is to connect it to code.

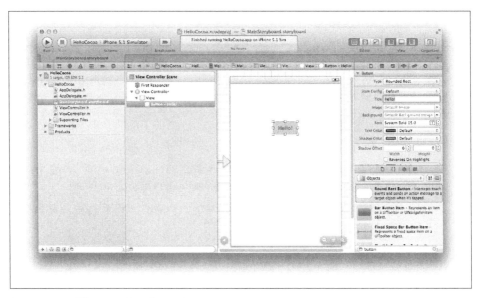

Figure 1-10. The completed interface

Connecting the Code

Applications aren't just interfaces—as a developer, you also need to write code. To work with the interface you've designed, you need to create connections between your code and your interface.

There are two kinds of connections that you can make:

- *Outlets* are variables that refer to objects in the interface. Using outlets, you can instruct a button to change color or size, or hide itself. There are also *outlet collections*, which allow you to create an array of outlets and choose which objects it contains in the Interface Builder.

- *Actions* are methods in your code that are run in response to the user interacting with an object. These interactions include the user touching a finger to an object, dragging a finger, and so on.

To make the application behave as we've described above—tapping the button displays a label and changes the button's text—we'll need to use both an outlet and an action. The action will run when the button is tapped, and will use the outlet connection to the button to modify its label.

To create actions and outlets, you need to have both the interface editor and its corresponding code open. Then hold down the Control key and drag from an object in the interface editor to your code (or to another object in the interface editor, if you want to make a connection between two objects in your interface).

The word *interface* has a double meaning in Cocoa programming. It refers to both the GUI that you design and to the publicly exposed methods and properties made available by Objective-C classes. For more information on this second meaning, see "Interfaces and Implementations" (page 23).

We'll now create the necessary connections:

1. *Open the assistant.* To do this, select the second tab in the editor selector in the toolbar.

   The assistant should show the corresponding code for interface *ViewController.h*. If it doesn't, click the small tuxedo icon (which represents the assistant) and navigate to Automatic→ViewController.h.

2. *Create the button's outlet.* Hold down the Control key and drag from the button into the space between the @interface and @end lines in the code.

   A pop-up window will appear. Leave everything as the default, but change the Name to **helloButton**. Click Connect.

   A new line of code will appear: Xcode has created the connection for you, which appears in your code as a property in your class.

3. *Create the button's action.* Hold down the Control key, and again drag from the button into the space between the @interface and @end lines. A pop-up window will again appear.

   This time, change the Connection from Outlet to **Action**. Change the Name to **showAlert**. Click Connect.

   A second new line of code will appear: Xcode has created the connection, which is a method inside the ViewController class.

4. *Open ViewController.m by selecting it in the project navigator.* You might want to close the assistant by selecting the leftmost tab in the editor selector in the toolbar.

5. *Scroll down to the showAlert: method.* You'll find it at the bottom of the file.

6. *Add in the new code.* Select the entire method and delete it. Replace it with the following code:

```
- (IBAction)showAlert:(id)sender {
    UIAlertView* alert = [[UIAlertView alloc] initWithTitle:@"Hello!"
                                             message:@"Hello, world!"
                                             delegate:nil
                                  cancelButtonTitle:@"Close"
                                  otherButtonTitles:nil];
    [alert show];

    [helloButton setTitle:@"I was clicked!" forState:UIControlStateNormal];
}
```

This code creates a `UIAlertView`, which displays a message to the user in a pop-up window. It prepares it by setting its title to Hello and the text inside the window to "Hello, world!" The alert is then shown to the user. Finally, the button has its title text changed to "I was clicked!"

The application is now ready to run. Click the Run button at the top-left corner. The application will launch in the iPhone simulator.

 If you happen to have an iPhone or iPad connected to your computer, Xcode will by default try to launch the application on the device rather than in the simulator. To make Xcode use the simulator, go to the Scheme menu at the top-left corner of the window and change the currently selected scheme to the simulator.

When the app finishes launching in the simulator, tap the button. An alert will appear; when you close it, you'll also notice that the button's text has changed.

Using the iOS Simulator

The iOS Simulator (Figure 1-11) allows you to test out iOS applications without having to mess around with devices. It's a useful tool, but keep in mind that the simulator and a real device behave very differently.

Figure 1-11. The iOS Simulator

For one thing, the simulator is a lot faster than a real device, and has a lot more memory. That's because the simulator makes use of your computer's resources. If you're building a processor-intensive application, it will run much more smoothly on the simulator.

The iOS Simulator is able to simulate four different kinds of devices: Retina-display iPhone-sized devices (which includes all iPhones and iPod touches sold in and after 2012); non-Retina iPhone-sized devices (all iPhones and iPod touches prior to the release of the iPhone 4 in 2010); and the iPad and iPad mini (starting with the third-generation iPad, released in 2012).

To change the device, open the Hardware menu, choose Device, and select the device you want to simulate.

You can also simulate hardware events, such as the home button being pressed or the iPhone being locked. To simulate pressing the home button, you can either click the virtual button underneath the screen, choose Hardware→Home, or press ⌘-Shift-H. To lock the device, press ⌘-L or choose Hardware→Lock.

 If there's no room on the screen, the simulator won't show the virtual hardware buttons. So if you want to simulate the home button being pressed, you need to use the keyboard shortcut ⌘-Shift-H.

There are a number of additional features in the simulator, which we'll examine more closely as they become relevant to the various parts of iOS we'll be discussing.

CHAPTER 2

Object-Oriented Programming with Objective-C

Objective-C is an object-oriented programming language. In this chapter, you'll learn what this means, how the Objective-C language works, and how your objects exist in the context of Objective-C applications.

Object-oriented programming is by no means a new thing, having shot to popularity in the 1980s. It's remained the most commonly used programming paradigm and is particularly useful for applications that present some sort of interface to the user, since humans are used to thinking in terms of objects they can see and interact with.

Objective-C takes a fairly idiosyncratic approach to how it implements object-orientation. This provides a number of benefits to you as a programmer, at the slight expense of having to understand a few more details about how it works and what Cocoa expects from your code.

Object-Oriented Programming

When developing any application for any platform, your code should be divided into different parts, where each part is responsible for a different area in your program. This means that the logic for each task that your program performs should avoid interfering with other tasks.

For example, code that talks to a database over the Internet should not be mixed with the code that displays the results to the user. Instead, you should have one section of code that does the database work and another that does the display. When these two sections need to communicate, they should do so over clearly defined interfaces.

This means that your code becomes easier to write, maintain, and debug. It also allows for easier modularity, since it becomes more straightforward to drop in new code (or replace code) without it affecting the rest of the program too much.

In addition to separating your logic based on its purpose, data in your program should also be separated. To continue our example, data relevant to the display of information (such as the font, color, and position on screen) should never be modified by the code responsible for communicating with the database, and vice versa. In addition, your logic should be able to work under the assumption that the data it's working with will not be modified by other parts of the program.

Object-oriented programming embraces and enforces these separations by introducing the concept of an *object*.

 Object-oriented programming has a lingo of its own, as most specialized fields do. Stand by for some important words that you'll see repeated quite often throughout this book.

Objects

Objects are chunks of data that come paired with code that operates on that data. Only the object's code is allowed to modify the data, but objects can communicate with each other to share data.

This hiding of data from other objects is called *encapsulation*, and guarantees that an object's data can only be changed by that object's functions.

Multiple copies of an object are allowed to exist at the same time. Each copy of an object is known as an *instance*. The template from which every instance is created is called the *class*. When writing object-oriented code, you write the classes, and your code creates one or more instances of each class.

Data that belongs to an object is called an *instance variable*. A function that belongs to an object is called a *method*.

In most object-oriented languages, it's also possible for a method to belong to a class, not just to an instance of the class. Objective-C calls these *class methods*, and they're most commonly used as methods that create instances of classes. For example, the class method dataWithContentsOfFile: in the NSData class loads a file and returns an NS Data object.

Inheritance

Object-oriented languages allow you to define one class as a *subclass* of another. Subclasses are identical to their superclass, but add additional methods and instance variables.

Subclassing allows you to create more specific versions of a class. For example, you could define a Server class, which handles tasks like accepting network connections, and then create separate FTPServer and HTTPServer subclasses of the Server class, which are more specialized.

In Objective-C, a class has only one superclass (unlike C++, which supports multiple superclasses).

Subclasses can also *override* methods from their superclasses. This means that you can write a class that replaces one or more methods of its superclass—and indeed, the majority of your useful work when coding using Cocoa involves replacing certain methods.

Interfaces and Implementations

There are two sides to every object: a private side, and a public one.

The public side of a class is known as its *interface*. The interface lists all of the methods that other classes can get at. (In Objective-C, there are no public instance variables. Instead, you use *properties*, which are similar, but you have more control over how other objects get at your object's data.)

The private side of a class is known as its *implementation*. The implementation contains the code for the class, as well as any private variables that belong to the class.

When you work with an object, you deal exclusively with its interface. This means that each object has a strict separation between what other objects can do with its data and what the object's functions can do.

In Objective-C, you declare a class's interface and implementation separately, and in two different files. The file that contains a class's interface is known as its *header file* (for historical reasons), and the file that contains the implementation is known as its *implementation file*. Header files have a .*h* extension; implementation files have a .*m* extension.

Here's what a class interface looks like in Objective-C:

```
@interface MyObject : NSObject {
[instance variables]
}

[method declarations]

@end
```

The `@interface` line defines the name of the class, as well as that of its superclass. Between the curly braces, you can include a list of instance variables that belong to the class—however, this is optional, and you can choose to place the instance variables in the implementation; see "Class Extensions" (page 30).

Its corresponding implementation looks like this:

```
@implementation MyObject

[method implementations]

@end
```

Methods

Methods are functions that belong to a class. Just like any other functions, they can take parameters and return a value.

As mentioned above, methods can be either instance methods or class methods. Instance methods belong to individual instances of a class, and have access to that instance's variables. Class methods don't have access to instance variables, because they don't belong to an instance.

Method declarations in Objective-C look like this:

```
- (void) launchPlane;
```

This is a method declaration for a method named `launchPlane` that takes no parameters and returns no value. The - at the start of the method name indicates that this is an instance method; class methods are declared with a + at the start.

One interesting thing that is rather unique to Objective-C is the fact that method parameters are mixed in with the method name. The easiest way to explain this is to demonstrate it.

Here, for example, is a method that takes a single parameter:

```
- (void) launchPlane:(NSString*)planeName;
```

This method takes a parameter that is a pointer to an `NSString` object named `planeName`.

Now compare this to a method that takes two parameters:

```
- (void) launchPlane:(NSString*)planeName fuelCapacity:(int)litresOfFuel;
```

This method takes an `NSString` pointer named `planeName` and an `int` named `litresOfFuel`. The parameters are embedded in the method name itself.

The full name (also known as the *selector*) for this method is launch
Plane:fuelCapacity: (note that the colons are included). When the
method is called, the parameters get inserted into the method name
after each colon. In Objective-C, the number of colons indicates how
many parameters a method accepts.

Objective-C's syntax for calling the methods of an object is also rather different from
other languages. The syntax for calling a method on a hypothetical object named
planeLauncher looks like this:

```
[planeLauncher launchPlane];
```

In this syntax, the object that the method is being called on is on the lefthand side of
the square brackets, and the name of the method is on the right. For method calls with
parameters, the syntax is similar, and embeds the parameters in much the same way as
in the method's declaration:

```
[planeLauncher launchPlane:@"Boeing 747-300" fuelCapacity:183380];
```

Objective-C is designed to allow code to be read out loud, from left to right, and make
sense. For example, try reading that example in the previous paragraph out loud (omit-
ting the punctuation). You could almost imagine it as an instruction being given. *"Plane
launcher, launch plane Boeing 747-300, fuel capacity 183,380."*

The method declarations for a class are kept in its interface. Here's an example of what
the interface for a class that defines some methods looks like:

```
@interface SomeObject : NSObject

- (void) launchPlane:(NSString*)planeName;
- (int) numberOfPlanesInTheAir;

@end
```

Messages

Objective-C is a message-passing language, much like Ruby. This is one of the key features that distinguishes it from early-bound method-calling languages like C++.

This means that when an object receives a method call, it does a runtime lookup to
determine what code to run. By contrast, C++ and many other compiled languages
perform this lookup at compile time.

When a method call is received by an Objective-C object, the Objective-C runtime
searches the list of methods that the object's class implements. If it finds a method with
the same *selector* (Objective-C's term for a method name) as that of the message that
the class received, it runs the code. If it does not find an appropriately named method,

it begins recursively searching the class's superclasses until it either finds a method with the right name, or runs out of places to look. At that point, the Objective-C runtime throws an exception, which usually results in the application terminating. It does not have to—you can catch this exception and deal with it yourself. Xcode is an example of a Cocoa application that does this: if there's an exception, Xcode displays an error message, and allows the user to ignore it or terminate the program.

This means that your objects are able to do some interesting tricks with the messages they receive. You can, for example, take a method call and bundle it up into an object, which you can keep around in memory and call later (this is known as an *invocation*). You can also write your own logic for dealing with cases where your object receives a message that it does not have a method for (this is often used in database code).

 One useful feature of Objective-C is that sending a message to nil results in no action being taken at all—the message is simply ignored, and zero is returned. This means that you do not have to do any null-checking before sending messages, since sending messages to nil does not raise any exceptions. However, this can lead to some frustrating bugs, such as features not working because a variable you assumed was a valid reference to an object was in fact nil.

Because Objective-C has this separation between method names and method code, it's a much more dynamic language than most other compiled ones. Much of Cocoa's power comes from this dynamic approach to programming. In your general day-to-day work, this distinction between methods and messages isn't hugely important. However, the more you know about how Objective-C works and how Cocoa exploits it, the better.

Properties

In object-oriented programming, it's considered bad practice for one object to directly access another object's data. Doing so breaks encapsulation, because it means that one object's code is now dependent on the data stored in another.

In order to access and change another object's variables, you use a pair of instance methods known as a *setter* and *getter*. The getter method returns the current value of the variable, and the setter method changes the value.

In Objective-C, setter and getter method names must follow an established pattern. For example, given an instance variable named planeName, the setter method would be named setPlaneName: and the getter method would be named planeName.

These naming conventions are used by the Objective-C runtime, and are therefore semi-enforced. If you try to set a property named *plane*, for example, the Objective-C compiler will generate code that calls a `setPlane:` method; if this method doesn't exist, your application will throw an exception.

There are some cases where this rule varies slightly, such as boolean instance variables, which may have a getter prefixed with `is` (so an instance variable named `active` could have a getter method named `isActive`).

Because instance variables aren't allowed to be accessed directly by other objects, any instance variable that an object wants to make available to other objects means that the object's class includes the getter and setter methods. Historically, this mean writing lots of setter and getter methods by hand. However, since the release of Objective-C 2.0 in 2007, the language contains some features that simultaneously remove the need to write these methods by hand and also make it easier to control how instance variables are exposed to other classes.

When you declare a property, you are telling other objects that getter and setter methods for accessing and changing one of the class's instance variables exist.

Declaring a property in an Objective-C class looks like this:

```
@interface SomeClass : NSObject

@property (strong, nonatomic) NSObject* myProperty;

@end
```

Properties are declared in the interface of a class and begin with the keyword `@property`. After this keyword, a list of property attributes appears in parentheses, followed by the property's type and finally its name.

Property attributes describe to other objects (and to the compiler) how the property behaves. Here's a list of the possible access specifiers that you can use.

strong
> This property is a strong (owning) reference to an object; see "Object Graphs in Objective-C" (page 32). Using `strong` and `weak` properties controls whether the object referred to by the property stays in memory or not.

weak
> This property is a weak (nonowning) reference to an object. When the object referred to by this property is deallocated, this property is automatically set to `nil`.

assign

This property's setter method simply assigns the property's variable to whatever is passed in, and performs no memory management.

copy

This property's setter copies any object passed to it, creating a duplicate object.

readwrite

This property generates both getter and setter methods. (This attribute is set by default—you need to explicitly use it only when overriding a superclass's property.)

readonly

This property does not generate a setter method, rendering the property read-only by other classes. (Your class's implementation code can still modify the property's variable, however.)

nonatomic

This property's setter and getter do not attempt to get a lock before making changes to the variable, rendering it thread-safe.

When you declare a property, the compiler will *synthesize* it for you. This means that it will create the instance variable that will store the property's value, as well as the getter and setter methods. The instance variable that the compiler creates will, by default, use the same name as the property; if you'd prefer the instance variable to be called something different, you can manually synthesize the property by using the @synthesize directive:

```
@implementation MyClass

@synthesize myProperty = _myCustomVariableName;

// the rest of the class code goes here

@end
```

You can also tell the compiler to *not* synthesize the property and methods, by using the @dynamic directive.

If you do choose to mark a property as @dynamic, you need to implement the getter and setter methods yourself:

```
@implementation MyClass

@dynamic myProperty;

- (int) myProperty {
        // this is the getter method for this property
        return 123;
}
```

```
- (void) setMyProperty:(int)newValue {
        // this is the setter method for this property
}

@end
```

Protocols

A *protocol* is a list of methods that your class promises to implement. Protocols are used to mark classes as having certain capabilities, like the ability to be copied, to be serialized and deserialized, or to act as a data source for some other class.

To declare a protocol, you use this syntax:

```
@protocol SomeProtocol

[ method declarations ]

@end
```

You can mark a class as *conforming* to a protocol by declaring so in the class's interface:

```
@interface SomeObject : NSObject <SomeProtocol>

@end
```

Doing this marks the SomeObject class as conforming to the SomeProtocol protocol. This is not the same as subclassing a class, where your class inherits a number of methods and can choose to override some or all of them. Rather, conforming to a protocol means that you must implement all of the required methods that the protocol specifies.

This means that other objects can rely on the fact that your class knows how to act in certain roles. Protocols are used quite heavily by Cocoa to allow it to work with classes that it has never seen before; if a class conforms to a protocol, it's guaranteed to implement necessary methods for whatever task Cocoa needs it for.

When working with an object, you generally explicitly refer to its type:

```
NSString* aString;
```

However, in some cases, you may end up writing code that you don't know the type of. To make sure that the objects you are working with conform to a protocol, use the following syntax:

```
id <SomeProtocol> someObjectConformingToAProtocol;
```

 In Objective-C, the type id means "an object of any type." You can use id to refer to objects that you don't know the type of.

In this example, the someObjectConformingToAProtocol object could be any class at runtime, but you are guaranteed that it implements the methods listed in the protocol.

Class Extensions

Classes in Objective-C can have additional instance variables and methods appended to them. This applies both to classes you write, and to system classes.

It's possible, therefore, to add extra methods and instance variables to system classes like NSString. Adding extra methods to a class means that *all* instances of that class have those methods.

Class extensions can be declared and implemented anywhere in your code.

There are two reasons for extending a class:

1. *You want to add extra behavior and logic to an existing class.*

   This is somewhat rare, but is used in some cases where you want to add some functionality to Cocoa. For example, if you wanted to add a method to the NSString class that inverts each letter's case ("lIKE tHIS"), you could do so by adding that method to a class extension.

2. *You want to break up one of your own classes into separate components.*

   This is becoming increasingly common among developers, since it allows you to put only your public methods and properties in your header file, and declare your more private items elsewhere.

This is what a class extension looks like in Objective-C:

```
@interface SomeClass() {
    [ additional instance variables ]
}

[ additional instance or class method declarations ]

@end
```

This should look pretty familiar—it's almost entirely identical to a class's interface. The only change is that instead of a superclass declaration, there is a pair of parentheses. (The superclass declaration is missing because a class extension isn't allowed to change the class's superclass.)

You can add as many class extensions as you like. As long as every method you add is implemented in an @implementation block somewhere in your project, you can just keep adding on to your classes.

To help you organize multiple extensions, you can name them in your code. Named class extensions are called *categories*, and their first line looks like this:

```
@interface SomeClass (SomeCategory)
```

The rest is all the same—the only extra thing is the extension's name.

Class extensions allow you to minimize the number of things you expose to other classes in your class's .h file. Consider the following example. Here is a class's .h file:

```
@interface SomeClass

- (void) doSomethingInteresting; // public, other classes can call this method

@end
```

And here is the class's corresponding .m file:

```
#import "SomeClass.h"

@interface SomeClass() {
    NSString* privateInstanceVariable; // Only visible to this class
}

// No other class can see this method because it's not in the header
// file, and therefore private
- (void) doSomethingPrivate;

@end

@implementation SomeClass

[ method implementation for both doSomethingInteresting and doSomethingPrivate ]

@end
```

In this way, you can keep your header files tidy, while still declaring everything that your class needs to have.

Memory Management

One problem that has faced programmers since computers were invented is the issue of storage. Simply put, it's impossible to keep every single piece of data around forever, which means that you need to remember to return memory back to the system when you're done using it. If you didn't return this memory, the machine would simply run out, and your computer wouldn't work.

So now that we've moved past "Computers 101," let's talk about how Objective-C handles memory management. Objective-C manages its memory through a system called *reference counting.*

Reference Counting

Reference counting involves having each object store a reference count as one of its variables. This reference count starts at 1 when the object is created, and can be incremented and decremented. When the reference count reaches zero, the object is deallocated, returning the memory back to the system.

When one object wants another object to stay around, it sends that object the `retain` message, which increments the reference count. When the first object doesn't want the second around anymore (or simply doesn't care—perhaps its usefulness to the first has expired), it sends the `release` message, decrementing the reference count.

The advantage to this is that memory management is rather easily understood, doesn't suffer the random slowdowns of garbage collection, and is safer to do—instead of carefully keeping track of when a block of memory is freed, an object will remove itself from memory when there are no more references to it.

The disadvantage is that everything must be done manually by the programmer, who's only human. You can run into trouble if you forget to release an object that you have retained (causing memory leaks, where memory is abandoned and never freed), or if you release an object more times than it has been retained. (Sending a message to an object that has been freed causes a crash, or worse, sometimes doesn't—leading to all sorts of tricky-to-diagnose behavior.)

Automatic Reference Counting

With the release of OS X Lion (10.7) and iOS 5, Apple introduced a new system based on reference counting that aims to have all of the advantages and none of the disadvantages of both. This system is called *automatic reference counting*, often abbreviated as ARC.

Automatic reference counting is identical to manual reference counting except that the programmer does not call `retain` and `release` on objects—the compiler does. The compiler is equipped with a source code analyzer, which is able to determine when and where an object starts using another object, and when it stops. Based on this information, the compiler inserts `retain` and `release` method calls at the appropriate times.

This means that the programmer can work with memory without worrying about memory leaks—effectively treating it as a garbage-collected environment without having to deal with the random pauses of garbage collection.

Object Graphs in Objective-C

One problem that exists in any memory management system is the issue of *retain cycles*. To understand this problem, it's worth considering under what circumstances ARC will free memory.

The reference counting system will only free an object's memory if that object's retain count is zero. ARC manages the retain count by watching when other objects make references to that object and when those references go away.

The problem occurs when you have two or more objects that refer to each other, but are not referred to anywhere else in the application. These objects can't be reached by the app, but because they each have an object referring to them, they cannot be freed.

To solve this problem, Objective-C has two different kinds of references: strong references and weak references.

- A *strong reference* (also called an *owning reference*) causes the referred object to stay in memory.

- A *weak reference* still points to that memory, but does not count as a strong reference, which means that ARC will not increment its reference count.

- Weak references have the additional benefit of automatically being set to nil when the referred object is deallocated. This means that weak references are always safe, since they are either a valid object or nil, and never refer to unallocated memory. Because Objective-C allows sending messages to nil (which causes nothing to happen), your program will continue functioning.

To declare a strong reference to an object, use the strong property attribute when declaring a property. To declare a weak reference to an object, use the weak property attribute.

Weak references are unavailable on OS X Snow Leopard (10.6) and iOS 4, as well as any earlier versions. If you're writing software that runs on those platforms, use the assign property attribute, which works identically to weak but does *not* cause the reference to be set to nil when the object is deallocated. (So be careful!)

The NSObject Lifecycle

Every object in Cocoa follows the same pattern, regardless of its type or purpose. To wrap up this chapter, here are the life and times of an Objective-C object in Cocoa.

These methods are defined in the NSObject class, which is the root class for all objects used in Cocoa (with some very rare exceptions).

Allocation and Initialization

Objects are created when the application allocates memory for them to exist in. This is done by sending the alloc message to the class.

The alloc method simply reserves memory for the object, but does not render it ready for use. To prepare an object for actual work, you must call its *designated initializer* method. The designated initializer is the method that the class designer has indicated must be called before the class is used.

The designated initializer for NSObject is init, which means that the majority of all classes use init as their designated initializer. So, the majority of your objects are created with this pattern:

```
SomeClass* anObject = [[SomeClass alloc] init];
```

Some classes use a different designated initializer, or have multiple initializers you can use. For example, the NSString class has several—here are a few:

```
NSString* myString      = [[NSString alloc]
        initWithFormat:@"here's a number: %i", 123];

NSString* anotherString = [[NSString alloc]
        initWithData:anNSDataObject encoding:NSUTF8Encoding];

NSString* oneMoreString = [[NSString alloc]
        initWithContentsOfFile:@"path to a file" encoding:NSUTF8Encoding
        error:someErrorPointer];
```

These all initialize an NSString object, but do it in different ways.

In addition to using the alloc and init methods, several classes provide class methods that return initialized objects for you. These are known as *factory methods*, since you can think of them as factories that generate objects for you. Here's an example of re-writing the myString statement above using a factory method:

```
NSString* myString = [NSString stringWithFormat:@"here's a number: %i", 123];
```

Retain and Release

Objects running in a reference-counting environment receive the retain and re lease messages. These methods are implemented in the NSObject superclass and man-age the object's reference count.

You as a programmer never call these methods. Indeed, under ARC, calling the re tain or release methods will result in an error.

Finalization and Deallocation

Eventually (well, hopefully) all objects are removed from memory when they're no longer needed. However, objects have one last opportunity to run code immediately before they're removed from memory. This allows them to remove any references to other objects, close any open files, and perform any other wrapping-up work.

When the object's retain count drops to zero, the object is sent the `dealloc` method. This is the last message an object receives, and is your opportunity to tidy up any remaining work before the object is deallocated.

After `dealloc` has been called, the object's memory is returned to the system.

CHAPTER 3

Foundation

Foundation is the underlying library that supports all Objective-C development. It provides basic support data structures such as strings, arrays, dictionaries, and other generic objects, as well as methods for working with them.

Foundation operates at a lower level of abstraction in your application than the higher-level Cocoa libraries. While Cocoa and UIKit are concerned with applications, views, and user input, Foundation is concerned with the lower-level task of organizing data. In this chapter, you'll work with several of the key classes that Foundation provides, and learn about the design patterns that Cocoa and Cocoa Touch are based on.

Mutable and Immutable Objects

Almost every data storage class in Foundation comes in two flavors: *mutable* and *immutable*. Mutable objects are objects that you can modify after creating them; immutable objects can't be changed after they're created.

As an example, let's look at the NSArray class, which we'll discuss in more detail later in this chapter. NSArray stores objects as a list, but you can't add, remove, or replace objects in an existing NSArray because it's immutable. If you want to be able to change the contents, you need to work with the NSMutableArray class, which *does* allow you to modify it.

Why do we have both immutable and mutable versions of an object? Two main reasons:

1. If an object is immutable, it knows that it will never have to change the way it's laid out in memory, and therefore is more efficient.

2. If you pass an immutable object to another object, you know for certain that its contents will never be changed by that object.

It's possible to create a mutable version of an existing object (and vice versa—you can create an immutable version of a mutable object). For example, here's how you can create an NSMutableArray from an NSArray (both of which we'll cover in more detail in this chapter):

```
// here, 'someArray' is an NSArray
NSMutableArray* mutableArray = [NSMutableArray arrayWithArray:someArray];
```

Both mutable and immutable objects have their use. For the most part, you'll work with immutable objects when writing Mac and iOS applications; objects are passed around a lot in Cocoa, and it helps to be sure that if you pass an NSArray to another method, that method cannot change the contents of the array. If you come from a development environment where objects are usually mutable, such as Java, this language-level distinction between mutable and immutable objects might seem a little foreign. Over time, though, you'll likely find that it's useful to differentiate between the two.

 The mutable versions of classes are always subclasses of the immutable versions. That is, NSMutableArray and NSMutableString are subclasses of NSArray and NSString, respectively. This means that if a method takes an NSArray as a parameter, you can provide your NSMutable Array and it will work identically.

For the same reason, mutable objects have the exact same methods as their immutable ancestors, as well as whatever methods are needed to modify their contents. For example, both NSArray and NSMutable Array have the objectAtIndex: method, but only NSMutableArray has the addObject: method.

Strings

A *string* is a chunk of text. This is a simple definition, but strings are actually extremely sophisticated things. In addition to simply storing text in strings, you can generate text from a template, change the capitalization, work with file paths, and much more. Whenever your application deals with text, you'll work with an NSString, and because almost all interaction with an application involves looking at some text on the screen, NSString will become extremely familiar to you.

Because strings store text, they're often used for storing written human language. This means that strings store text written as Unicode, which is an encoding standard that's capable of representing (as best as we can tell) every single written character and glyph ever invented and more. Foundation strings can handle right-to-left languages, Asian languages, and more.

The actual array of bytes that the NSString stores the text in isn't directly accessible by your code. If you need to get the raw bytes out of the NSString, you can use the dataUsingEncoding: method, which returns an NSData object that contains the bytes. When you call this method, you provide information about what encoding you would like the bytes to be returned in; examples include NSUTF8StringEncoding for UTF-8, which is the 8-bit version of Unicode, and NSWindowsCP1252StringEncoding, which is the Windows *Latin-1* encoding.

Creating Strings

Strings are stored in the NSString class, which makes them Objective-C objects just like everything else. You can create an empty string with this code:

```
NSString* aString = [[NSString alloc] init];
```

Doing this isn't terribly useful, because the NSString class is immutable [see "Mutable and Immutable Objects" (page 37)], so the above code creates a blank string that could never be changed. It's more useful to create a string in other ways, such as providing it in code or loading it from a file.

Strings are so commonplace when working in Objective-C that there's a shorthand technique for creating them in your code. The following code creates an NSString object that contains the text "Hello, world!":

```
NSString* aString = @"Hello, world!";
```

Note the @ in front of the quotes. This tells the compiler to create an NSString object instead of a standard C string, which is *not* an Objective-C object. Because this new string is a full-fledged Objective-C object, it can receive messages and generally interact with other objects in the application. For example, you can ask the new string how many letters it has:

```
NSInteger sizeOfString = [@"Hello, world!" length];
```

NSString objects defined with this syntax are known as NSString *literals*.

Working with Strings

Strings are very flexible objects and support a wide variety of methods. For the most part, strings are used for two purposes: human language and file paths. This means that NSString has a large number of methods that you can use to work with these kinds of data.

NSString objects are usually created in one of three ways:

- Using string literals like @"this example"
- Loading strings from other data, like files
- Generating strings from existing strings

To use a string literal, you use this syntax:

```
NSString* constantString = @"Text of the string";
```

 String literals don't get memory-managed, since their data is stored in your compiled binary and they're never modified.

Because string literals are objects they can be added to arrays and dictionaries, which are discussed later in this chapter.

Capitalization and working with paths

Because they contain text, strings are ideal for representing human languages. The NSString class recognizes this, and provides a number of utility methods that transform the text of the string.

To change the case (capitalization) of a string, you can send it one of several methods. For example:

```
NSString* originalString    = @"This is An EXAMPLE";

// "THIS IS AN EXAMPLE"
NSString* uppercaseString   = [originalString uppercaseString];

// "this is an example"
NSString* lowerCaseString   = [originalString lowercaseString];

// "This Is An Example"
NSString* capitalizedString = [originalString capitalizedString];
```

Note that calling these methods does not modify the original string, because strings are immutable; instead, these methods return a new string. This applies to all methods that work with the contents of a string—in all cases, because the string cannot be modified, a new string object is returned.

Finding substrings

When using strings, it's possible to extract substrings from them (for example, the string "Hello world" contains the substring "Hello").

To extract a substring, you can either specify that you want it to start at a point in the string and continue to the end of the string; to start from the beginning of the string and continue to a specific point; or to consist of a certain range of characters in the string.

To get the first five characters in a string, you do this:

```
NSString* startSubstring = [originalString substringToIndex:5]; // "This "
```

To get everything past the first five characters:

```
NSString* endSubstring = [originalString substringFromIndex:5]; // "is An EXAMPLE"
```

To get a substring of a range of characters, you first create an NSRange structure, which defines the start point and length of the range. For example, to create an NSRange that starts at the third character and is five characters long, you do this:

```
NSRange theRange = NSMakeRange(2, 5);
```

 Note the lack of asterisk after NSRange. NSRange is not an Objective-C class, but rather a plain old C structure.

Structures and Objects

There are two ways that data can be packaged in Objective-C: in *structures* and in *objects*. We've covered objects already: they're chunks of code and data that store information and can receive messages. Structures are similar, but contain only data—they don't have methods and can't receive messages.

One example of a commonly used structure is CGPoint, which represents a point inside a view. It's defined as follows:

```
struct CGPoint {
    float x;
    float y;
};
```

To access the information inside a structure you use dot notation, much the same way you use it to access a property in an Objective-C object:

```
CGPoint somePoint;
somePoint.x = 123;
somePoint.y = 456;
```

When referring to variables that contain structures, the variable contains the entire structure, and not just a pointer to where that structure is in memory. For this reason, you don't use an asterisk when defining the type of the variable:

```
// This is a variable that contains a pointer to an NSString
NSString* someString;

// This is a variable that contains a CGPoint
CGPoint somePoint;
```

Structures do not need to be initialized before they can be used.

Ranges have two variables: a location and a length. Locations start at 0, so a range with a location of 2 and a length of 5 would start at the third character and continue for five characters.

Once you have an NSRange, you can ask the NSString to return a substring:

```
NSRange theRange = NSMakeRange(2,5);
NSString* substring = [originalString substringWithRange:theRange]; // "is is"
```

Comparing Strings

It's often useful to check whether two string objects are the same. However, the following code does not accomplish this:

```
// firstString contains "one" and secondString is another object, also
// containing "one"

if (firstString == secondString) {
    // Do something
}
```

That's because the == operator only compares the pointer values of the two variables. Effectively, it's checking to see if those two variables are at the same place in memory, which they most likely are not.

To compare two strings, use the isEqualToString: method, like so:

```
if ([firstString isEqualToString:secondString]) {
    // Do something
}
```

The isEqualToString method returns TRUE when two strings are exactly the same, and FALSE when they're not. isEqualToString is case sensitive (that is, "Hello" and "helLo" are not the same because of differences in capitalization).

 Many other Foundation classes provide similar isEqualTo methods. For example, NSArray has isEqualToArray:, which checks to see if two arrays contain the same set of objects.

Searching Strings

In addition to determining if two strings are identical, you can get more specific information about what they contain. In Cocoa, you can search a string to see if it contains a specific substring, or compare two strings to see how they would be ordered.

To determine whether a string contains a substring, you can use the `rangeOfString` family of methods. These methods search a string for a substring, and return the `NSRange` that the substring exists at. If the string does not contain the substring, the method returns an `NSRange` whose location is the special value `NSNotFound`, which is a constant. For example:

```
NSString* sourceString = @"Four score and seven years ago";
NSRange range = [sourceString rangeOfString:@"seven"];

if (range.location == NSNotFound) {
    // the string was not found
} else {
    // the string was found; 'range' variable contains info on where it is
}
```

You can also search for substrings while restricting the search to a specific range, or by providing additional options for the search to take place under. For example, you can choose to search for the substring while ignoring capitalization by using the `rangeOf String:options:` method:

```
NSString* sourceString = @"Four score and seven years ago";
NSRange range = [sourceString rangeOfString:@"SEVEN"
                 options:NSCaseInsensitiveSearch];
```

Arrays

An *array* is simply a list of objects. Arrays store a collection of objects in order, and allow you to refer to a specific item in the collection or all of them at once.

Arrays are one of the fundamental container classes in Cocoa, since they can contain anything from one object to as many as will fit in memory. Whenever a method wants to work with one or more items, an `NSArray` object is almost always what's used to store them.

`NSArray`, like `NSString`, is immutable—once the array is created, objects cannot be added to the array or removed from it. This means that when working with an `NS Array`, you must provide the array's contents when the object is created. This can be done in a number of ways: you can create an array with specific objects with elements from another array.

Mutable versions of NSArray exist; see "Mutable Arrays" (page 46) for more information.

Arrays can contain objects of any type as long as they're Objective-C objects. These objects don't have to be all the same type, either—you can store NSStrings in the same array as an NSView. Arrays can also contain other arrays, because NSArray is itself an Objective-C object.

Much like with NSString objects, you can create NSArray objects with special, built-in syntax:

```
NSArray* myArray = @[@"one", @"two", @"three"];
```

Doing this creates a new, immutable NSArray that contains the NSString objects one, two, and three.

Array objects can't contain nil. If you want to include a value that represents nil, use [NSNull null], which is the standard "null" placeholder object.

This rule applies to all Foundation container classes.

You can also retrieve objects from an array, using syntax like this:

```
NSString* oneString = myArray[0];
NSString* twoString = myArray[1];
```

Some things to know about arrays:

- Don't forget that NSArrays start counting at zero, so index 0 is the first object, index 1 is the second, and so on.
- If you ask an array for an invalid index, it will throw an exception and crash. For example, if an array has three objects, and you ask for the object at index 3, the array will throw an exception. (Recall that index 3 refers to the fourth object.)
- The syntax for accessing elements in an NSArray doesn't work on iOS 5 and below. Instead, you need to use the slightly wordier method objectAtIndex:, like so:

  ```
  NSString* oneString = [myArray objectAtIndex:0];
  ```

  This method also works on iOS 6, so if you're writing code that needs to work on both platforms, it's best to go with this wordier syntax.

You can also ask an array how large it is by using the count property:

```
int count = myArray.count;
// count now equals 3
```

Since NSArray objects are Objective-C objects, they can therefore be sent messages just like any other object. For example, you can ask an NSArray object to tell you at what index an object exists by using the indexOfObject: method. If the object is not in the array, the method will return a special value of NSNotFound:

```
NSArray* myArray = @[@"one", @"two", @"three"];
int index = [myArray indexOfObject:@"two"];  // should be equal to 1

if (index == NSNotFound) {
        NSLog(@"Couldn't find the object!");
}
```

The indexOfObject: method only works if the object that you pass to it is the exact same object that exists in the array. If you want to look for an object that is *equal* to that object (for example, two string objects that are different instances but contain the same text), then you should use the indexOfObjectEqualTo: method.

To create an array that contains elements from another array, use the subArray WithRange: method. This method takes an NSRange and returns a new array that contains objects within that range. No objects are copied when you create this new array—an object that exists in two arrays doesn't have two copies of it in memory. This means that if an object is in two arrays and you modify one of its properties, those changes will be present whether you get the object from one array or the other.

If you *do* want to make a copy of an object, you can send it the copy method, which returns a duplicate of the original. Not all objects support being copied; those that do conform to the NSCopying protocol, which defines how an object should copy itself.

Here's an example of creating a subarray from an existing array:

```
NSArray* myArray = @[@"one", @"two", @"three"];
NSRange subArrayRange = NSMakeRange(1,2);
NSArray* subArray = [myArray subArrayWithRange:subArrayRange];

// subArray now contains "two", "three"
```

The NSRange you provide must fit within the size of the array—for instance, in the above example, trying to get a subarray with the range {2,42} would not work because there are only three items in the array. If you attempt to get an invalid subarray, the array will throw an exception and your application will crash.

Fast Enumeration

With any collection, it's often the case that you want to do some work with every object that is contained in it. Objective-C includes a feature called *fast enumeration*, which all container classes support. Fast enumeration allows you to very quickly and efficiently loop over the collection, performing work on each object.

To loop over an array, you do this:

```
NSArray* myArray = @[@"one", @"two", @"three"];

for (NSString* string in myArray) {
    // this code is repeated 3 times, one for each item in the array
}
```

In the background, the compiler is generating low-overhead code that loops over each item in the collection.

 If you're looping over an array of objects, the compiler won't check to see if the array contains objects of all the same type, or even of the type you specify. Use caution!

Mutable Arrays

As discussed above, all NSArray objects are immutable—they cannot be changed once they have been created. However, it's often convenient to be able to add, remove, and replace items in the array. When you want to do this, use the NSMutableArray class.

NSMutableArray is a subclass of NSArray, which means that everything that NSArray can do, NSMutableArray can do as well. You can also pass in an NSMutableArray object to any method that asks for an NSArray.

NSMutableArray allows you to add new objects to the array by using the addObject: and insertObject:atIndex: methods. The first method simply adds a new object to the end of the array, while the second inserts the object at a specific point:

```
NSMutableArray* myArray = [NSMutableArray arrayWithArray:@[@"One", @"Two"]];

// Add "Three" to the end
[myArray addObject:@"Three"];

// Add "Zero" to the start
[myArray insertObject:@"Zero" atIndex:0];

// The array now contains "Zero", "One", "Two", "Three".
```

You can also remove objects from the array in much the same manner. The two main methods for removing an object from an array are `removeObject:` and `removeObject AtIndex:`. The first method removes the provided object from wherever it is in the array, while the second removes whatever object is at that point in the array:

```
NSMutableArray* myArray = [NSMutableArray arrayWithArray:
        @[@"One", @"Two", @"Three"]];

[myArray removeObject:@"One"];   // removes "One"
[myArray removeObjectAtIndex:1]; // removes "Three", the second
                                 // item in the array at this point

// The array now contains just "Two"
```

 Note that `removeObject:` removes *all* instances of an object from an array. If the string @"One" were present twice in the array in the above example, `removeObject:` would remove both instances.

You can also replace an object in a mutable array by using the `replaceObjectAt Index:withObject:` method. This method takes the position of an object in the array, removes it, and replaces it with the object that is passed in.

```
NSMutableArray* myArray = [NSMutableArray arrayWithArray:@[@"One", @"Two",
                                                           @"Three"]];
[myArray replaceObjectAtIndex:1 withObject:@"Bananas"];
// myArray is now "One", "Bananas", "Three"
```

You can also ask the mutable array to set an object at a given index:

```
myArray[0] = @"Null";
```

 You can only modify mutable arrays in this way; because a regular array is immutable, using this syntax will cause an error at runtime.

You also can't use this syntax to add new objects or remove objects from the array—it's only for replacing existing objects. If you want to add objects, use `addObject:` or `insertObject:atIndex:`; if you want to remove objects, use `removeObject:` or `removeObjectAtIndex:`.

Dictionaries

While arrays simply store a list of objects, *dictionaries* are more complex. Dictionaries store objects that are mapped to *keys*, which are objects (usually strings, but they can be any object that supports being copied) used to identify other objects.

Dictionaries can be thought of as tables. Suppose you want to store information about a contact. You could represent this in a dictionary, as shown in (Table 3-1):

Table 3-1. Contact information

Key	Value
Name	Cave Johnson
Company	Aperture Science
Likes	Science
Dislikes	Lemons

When you wanted to work out what the person's company is, you would look up the Company key and note that the corresponding value is Aperture Science.

NSDictionary works the same way. Much like NSArray, NSDictionary stores any Objective-C object, and then maps it to a key. Keys can also be any Objective-C object.

When you create an NSDictionary, you provide both the keys and objects to it. An object can't exist without a key, so you must provide both.

The syntax for creating NSDictionary objects is similar to that for creating NSArrays:

```
NSDictionary* translationDictionary = @{
    @"greeting": @"Hello",
    @"farewell": @"Goodbye"
};
```

You can retrieve a value from the dictionary in a similar way to how you get objects out of an NSArray:

```
NSDictionary* translationDictionary = @{@"greeting": @"Hello"};
NSString* greeting = translationDictionary[@"greeting"];
```

If a dictionary does not have an object for a given key, the dictionary returns nil.

You can also use fast enumeration on dictionaries. Doing so loops over every key in the dictionary; for each key, you can use the dictionary's objectForKey: method to get the corresponding value, as seen in the following code:

```
// Here, aDictionary is an NSDictionary

for (NSString* key in aDictionary) {
    NSObject* theValue = aDictionary[key];
    // do something with theValue
}
```

Like NSArrays, NSDictionary objects are immutable. If you want to create a dictionary that you can add and remove items from, use the NSMutableDictionary class. This is a subclass of NSDictionary in the same way that NSMutableArray is a subclass of NS Array. It simply adds some methods that allow you to add and remove items from the dictionary.

To set an object for a key in a mutable dictionary, you can use the same syntax as for setting values in arrays. This inserts the object into the dictionary and maps it to the provided key; if an object already exists for the given key, it is replaced.

```
NSMutableDictionary* aDictionary = @{};
aDictionary[@"greeting"] = @"Hello";
aDictionary[@"farewell"] = @"Goodbye";
```

NSValue and NSNumber

Container classes such as NSArray and NSDictionary can only contain Objective-C objects. However, not everything that you work with in Objective-C is an object—numbers, such as integers and boolean values, and structures, such as the previously discussed NSRange, are not objects, and thus cannot be stored in arrays or dictionaries.

To solve this problem, Cocoa includes classes whose purpose is to store non-object values in objects. These objects can then be stored in container classes.

The NSValue class allows you to store a wide variety of non-object types. NSNumber, which is a subclass of NSValue, is specifically designed to store numbers.

To create an NSNumber from a number, simply put an @ in front of it. The compiler will work out what kind of number it is (double, float, character, boolean, and so on) and create an NSNumber for you:

```
NSNumber* theNumber = @123;
```

To retrieve the stored value, you simply query the object:

```
int myValue = [theNumber intValue];
```

This NSNumber instance can be included in any collection object:

```
// 'numbers' is an NSMutableArray
[numbers addObject:theNumber];
```

You can also set NSNumbers to the result of an expression. For example:

```
int a = 100;
NSNumber* number = @(a+1);
// 'number' contains 101
```

Data

When developing applications, you will often need to deal with chunks of arbitrary data. In most cases, this is data that you've loaded from disk and are about to process into Objective-C objects that you can work with, or it's data that you're about to write to disk. For example, if you load an image file into memory, that data is just bytes—you must convert it to a UIImage object before you can use it as an image.

The NSData class is designed to be a container for arbitrary data. It contains bytes, and doesn't make any assumptions about what kind of bytes they are. Whenever you deal with file operations or operations that load information from the network (including from the Internet), the information that you retrieve arrives in an NSData object, which can be processed into useful objects.

NSData, like the other classes discussed in this chapter, is an immutable class—once created, an NSData object cannot be modified. Likewise, there is also a mutable version: NSMutableData. The NSMutableData class is useful for situations where you may be progressively loading data where all of the bytes may not arrive at once, such as downloading a file.

Loading Data from Files and URLs

While it's possible to create an empty NSData object, it's immutable so there is not much purpose. In the vast majority of cases, you create NSData objects from other locations —either by loading files from disk or via URLs, or by converting an Objective-C object into an NSData object. This can then be written to disk, as discussed in more detail in "Serialization and Deserialization" (page 52).

To load a file from disk, you must first have the file's path, which specifies where the file is on the disk. You can also load a file given a URL, which allows you to load a file from disk or from a network location.

To load a text file into an NSData object, you can do the following:

```
// Assuming that there is a text file at /Examples/Test.txt:

NSString* filePath = @"/Examples/Test.txt";
NSData* loadedData = [NSData dataWithContentsOfFile:filePath];
```

Because an NSData object on its own is not very useful—such objects can do nothing but store the data, retrieve specific bytes, and write the data out to disk—many classes have methods designed to work with NSData objects.

For example, to convert an NSData object to an NSString, you can use the NSString class's initWithData:encoding: method, which takes an NSData object and an NSStringEncoding value (which indicates to the class how it should interpret the bytes).

```
NSString* loadedString = [[NSString alloc] initWithData:loadedData
                                               encoding:NSUTF8StringEncoding];
```

This method of loading a string (loading a file into data, then converting that data into a string) is not the most efficient way to load strings, but we show it as an example of how to use the NSData class. A more direct way to load strings from disk is NSString's stringWithContentsOf File:encoding:error: method, which loads the string from disk in one step.

You can write an NSData object to disk in a similar way, by using the writeToFile: atomically: method. This method takes a string that contains a path, as well as a BOOL value that indicates whether the writing should be done *atomically*—that is, whether it should either succeed completely or fail completely. If this flag is set to YES, NSData writes the bytes out to a temporary file, and then moves that file into position when done. If it's set to NO, the file is written out directly to the destination file. Writing files atomically is very slightly slower, because the filesystem has the additional work of moving the file at the end, but it avoids the problem of a program quitting or crashing halfway through a long write and leaving a partially written file.

```
// Here, loadedData is an NSData object
NSString* filePath = @"/Examples/Test.txt";
[loadedData writeToFile:filePath atomically:YES];
```

Serialization and Deserialization

When working with objects whose classes you have designed, it is often extremely useful to be able to store those objects on disk and load them back into memory. This is called *serialization*, and is the process by which you can convert any object into an NSData object and back again. Once you have an NSData, you can read and write it to disk, as we have seen. Converting an NSData object back into an instance of one of your classes is called *deserialization*.

Making your classes serializable is not something that you get for free. In order to be converted to and from NSData objects, your classes must conform to the NSCoding protocol. *Coding* is Apple's term for serialization, whereby a *coder* object (usually an instance of the NSKeyedArchiver class) encodes the relevant parts of your object into writable bytes. *Decoding* is Apple's term for deserialization, in which a *decoder* object reads in the bytes and reconstructs that object.

The NSCoding protocol contains two key methods, which your class must implement in order to be serializable:

- encodeWithCoder:
- initWithCoder:

The encodeWithCoder: method is called whenever the class is asked to encode itself. The method takes an NSKeyedArchiver object, which your class's implementation of the method uses to encode the variables that you as the developer consider necessary to be stored on disk.

The initWithCoder: method is called when an object is loaded from disk, and is your object's opportunity to re-create itself based on what was stored in the encode Coder: method. initWithCoder: takes an NSKeyedUnarchiver object, which you can query to recover the stored data.

The initWithCoder: method is called instead of the init method when loading an object, which means that any setup that is done in the init method implementation must also be done in the initWithCoder: method.

 While there's technically nothing stopping Cocoa from storing *all* of a class's variables on disk (which would obviate the need to implement these methods yourself), doing so would be terribly wasteful—in most cases, an object only needs to store a few key variables to disk, and can re-create the rest of the variables based on those stored. The more data is stored on disk, the more space is consumed, and the more time is taken when reading and writing. Only store what you need!

The NSKeyedArchiver object works very much like a mutable dictionary—you provide keys and objects to it, using the encodeObject:forKey: method (along with related methods like encodeInteger:forKey: and encodeFloat:forKey:). When the encode WithCoder: method returns, anything stored inside the coder is serialized and can be stored on disk.

Here is an example of an implementation of the encodeWithCoder: method:

```
- (void) encodeWithCoder:(NSKeyedArchiver*)aCoder {
    // Store a string (or any other Objective-C object that supports coding)
    [aCoder encodeObject:myStringVariable forKey:@"myString"];

    // Store a number
    [aCoder encodeInteger:myIntegerVariable forKey:@"anInteger"];
}
```

Here is the corresponding `initWithCoder:` method, which sets up the object and loads the encoded data:

```
- (id) initWithCoder:(NSKeyedUnarchiver*)aDecoder {
    self = [super init];

    myStringVariable = [aDecoder decodeObjectForKey:@"myString"];
    myIntegerVariable = [aDecoder decodeIntegerForKey:@"anInteger"];

    return self;
}
```

 If you attempt to decode a value for a key that was not encoded in `encodeWithCoder:`, the decoder will throw an exception and your app will crash.

Many Cocoa objects support coding and decoding—for example, you can encode `NSArray`, `NSData`, and `NSDictionary` objects in your `encodeWithCoder:` methods. Not all objects provided by Cocoa do, however, so check the documentation for the class that you're working with to see if it conforms to the `NSCoding` protocol. If it does, you can send it to the coder and load it back out of the decoder.

To actually convert an object to a usable `NSData`, you can do this:

```
// myObject is an object that
//conforms to NSCoding
NSData* object storedData = [NSKeyedArchiver archivedDataWithRootObject:myObject];

// storedData can now be written to a file
```

To load it back, you can do this:

```
// loadedData is an NSData loaded from somewhere, and SomeObject is
//a class that conforms to NSCoding
SomeObject* myObject = [NSKeyedUnarchiver unarchiveObjectWithData:loadedData];
```

Design Patterns in Cocoa

Cocoa is built around a number of design patterns, whose purpose is to make your life as a developer more consistent and (one hopes) more productive. Three key patterns are the *model-view-controller* (MVC) pattern, upon which most of Cocoa and Cocoa

Touch is built; the *delegation* pattern, which allows both your code and Cocoa to be highly flexible in determining what code gets run by whom; and *key-value observing*, which allows your code to watch for changes made by other objects without having to check in on them.

Model-View-Controller

The model-view-controller design pattern is one of the fundamental design patterns in Cocoa. It divides all objects into three categories: models, views, and controllers (hence the name).

- *Models* are objects that contain data or otherwise coordinate the storing, management, and delivery of data to other objects. Models can be as simple as an NSString or as complicated as an entire database—their purpose is to store data and provide it to other objects. They don't care what happens to the data once they give it to someone else; their only concern is managing how the data is stored.

- *Views* are objects that work directly with the user, providing information to them and receiving input back. Views do not manage the data that they display—they only show it to the user. Views are also responsible for informing other objects when the user interacts with them. Likewise with data and models, views do not care what happens next—their responsibility ends with informing the rest of the application.

- *Controllers* are objects that mediate between models and views, and contain the bulk of what some call the "business logic" of an application—the actual logic that defines what the application *is* and how it responds to user input. At a minimum, the controller is responsible for retrieving information from the model and providing it to the view; it is also responsible for providing information to the model when it is informed by the view that the user has interacted with it.

For an illustration of the model-view-controller design pattern in action, imagine a simple text editor. In this example, the application loads a text file from disk and presents its contents to the user in a text field. The user makes changes in the text field and saves those changes back to disk.

We can break this application down into model, view, and controller objects:

- The model is an object that is responsible for loading the text file from disk and writing it back out to disk. It is also responsible for providing the text as an NSString to any object that asks for it.

- The view is the text field, which asks another object for an NSString to display, and then displays the text. It also accepts keyboard input from the user; whenever the user types, it informs another object that the text has changed. It is also able to tell another object when the user has told it to save changes.

- The controller is the object responsible for instructing the model object to load a file from disk, and passes the text to the view. It receives updates from the view object when the text has changed, and passes those changes to the model. Finally, it is able to be told by the view that the user has asked to save the changes; when that happens, it instructs the model to do the work of actually writing the file out to disk.

By breaking the application into these areas of responsibility, it becomes easier to make changes to the application.

For example, if the developer decides that the next version of the application should add the ability to upload the text file to the Internet whenever the file is saved, the only thing that must be changed is the model class—the controller can stay the same, and the view never changes.

Likewise, by clearly defining which objects are responsible for which features, it's easier to make changes to an application while maintaining a clear structure in the project. If the developer decides to add a spellchecking feature to the application, that code should clearly be added to the controller, since it has nothing to do with how the text is presented to the user or stored on disk. (You could, of course, add some features to the view that would allow it to indicate which words are misspelled, but the bulk of the code would need to be added in the controller.)

The majority of the classes described in this chapter, such as NSData, NSArray, and NSDictionary, are model classes, since all they do is store and present information to other classes. NSKeyedArchiver is a controller class, since it takes information and performs logical operations on it. NSButton and UITextField are examples of view objects, since they present information to the user and do not care about how the data is managed.

The model-view-controller paradigm becomes very important when you start looking at the more advanced features in Cocoa, like the document architecture (Chapter 12) and bindings (Chapter 10).

Delegation

Delegation is Cocoa's term for passing off some responsibilities of an object to another. An example of this in action is the UIApplication object, which represents an application on iOS. This application needs to know what should happen when the application moves to the background. Many other languages handle this problem by subclassing— for example, in C++, the UIApplication class would define an empty placeholder method for applicationDidEnterBackground, and then you as a developer would subclass UIApplication and override the applicationDidEnterBackground method.

However, this is a particularly heavy-handed solution and causes additional problems —it increases the complexity of your code, and also means that if you want to override the behavior of two classes, you need two separate subclasses for each one. Objective-C's answer to this problem is built around the fact that an object is able to determine, at runtime, whether another object is capable of responding to a message.

An object that wants to let another object know that something is going to happen, or has happened, stores a reference to that object as an instance variable. This object is known as the *delegate*. When the event happens, it checks to see if the delegate object implements a method that suits the event—for delegates of the UIApplication class, for example, the application delegate is asked if it implements the applicationDid EnterBackground method. If it does, that method is called. An object can also be the delegate for multiple objects.

Because of this loose coupling, it's possible for an object to be the delegate for multiple objects. For example, an object could become the delegate of both an audio playback object and an image picker, and be notified both when audio playback completes and when an image has been captured by the camera.

Because the model-view-controller pattern is built around a very loose coupling of objects, it helps to have a more rigidly defined interface between objects so that your application can know with more certainty about how one object expects others to behave.

The specific messages used by delegates are often listed in protocols. For example, if your object wants to be the delegate of an AVAudioPlayer object, it should conform to the AVAudioPlayerDelegate protocol.

Key-Value Observing

Much of the model-view-controller paradigm relies on the controller providing timely updates from the model to the view and vice versa. One way to do this is to periodically check the model and ask it if anything has changed, and if it has, to provide the information to the view. However, this method (known as *polling*) is inefficient if the model does not change frequently, and in the case of most OS X and iOS applications, the model does not change very frequently at all. In order to be highly responsive, therefore, Cocoa implements a design pattern called *key-value observing*.

In this pattern, objects may register to be *observers* of properties on other objects. When those other objects change the observed properties, those observers are notified.

Key-value observing becomes important when you want to separate views and model objects, and we'll discuss it in much more detail in "Key-Value Coding" (page 146).

CHAPTER 4

Applications on OS X and iOS

As far as users are concerned, applications are the only thing on their computers besides their files. After all, a computer is defined by what it can do for the user, and what it can do is defined by the applications that are installed.

As a developer, it's easy to get drawn into the details of how an app is put together—the individual classes, methods, and structures. However, the application as a whole is what's sold to the user, and that's all users care about.

In this chapter, you'll learn how applications are structured on OS X and iOS, how they differ from other distributable code, what they can do on the system, and what they're prevented from doing by the built-in security measures provided by the OS.

What Is an Application?

Applications on iOS and OS X are packaged differently from applications on other platforms, most notably Windows. On other platforms, the end result of compiling your project is a binary file that contains the compiled code. It's then up to you as a developer to package that binary file up with the resources it needs. On Linux, you generate a package file (which can vary depending on the distribution you're using), and on Windows, it's traditional to create an "installer," which is an *additional* application that unpacks the binary and resources.

OS X and iOS take a different approach to applications. This approach stems from the concept of a "package"—a folder that contains a number of items but is presented to the user as a single file. Many document formats use packages as a convenient way to store and organize their data, since storing different chunks of data as separate files means that the program doesn't have to implement logic that unpacks a single file.

If you're coming from a Linux background, note that "package," in this context, means something different. A package file is just a folder that's presented as a single file, while on Linux "package" means a redistributable file used to install software. OS X also uses the word "package" in this way—you can generate .pkg files that contain software, which when opened install the software onto your machine. When you upload an app to the Mac App Store, for example, you upload a package.

And just to add to the confusion, Cocoa doesn't call these files packages, but rather calls them "bundles."

Applications, therefore, are actually folders that contain the compiled binary, plus any resources they may need. The structure of applications differs slightly between OS X and iOS, but the fundamental philosophy of how an application is packaged remains the same. You can take a look inside an application by right-clicking one in the Finder and choosing Show Package Contents.

When you compile a project in Xcode and generate an application, Xcode creates the application package, and copies in any resources needed. If you're creating a Mac application, you can then just zip it up and send it to anyone for them to run it. On iOS it's a little different, because apps must be code-signed and provisioned before being run on the device.

One advantage to this is that applications are entirely self-contained and can be moved anywhere on a Mac.

Because applications can be moved, it used to be commonplace to add code to an application that detected if the app was not in the Applications folder and offered to move itself there to keep the user's Downloads folder tidy.

This is less common in the days of the App Store, which installs all applications directly into the Applications folder. However, if your application is being distributed by means other than the Mac App Store, it's worthwhile to include this logic anyway.

Applications, Frameworks, Utilities, and More

Applications aren't the only products that you can produce from Xcode. You can also generate *frameworks*, which are loadable bundles of code and resources that other applications (including your own) can use. Frameworks are actually very similar to applications in structure—they contain a binary and any resources—but they're not standalone and are designed to be used by other apps.

One prime example of a framework is `AppKit.framework`, which is used by every Mac application. On iOS, the equivalent framework is `UIKit.framework`.

 "Cocoa" is the term used by Apple to refer to the collection of libraries used by applications on OS X. On iOS, the equivalent term is "Cocoa Touch," as it's adapted for touch-screen devices.

What Are Apps Composed Of?

In order to function as an application on iOS or OS X, an application must have two things at a minimum:

- The compiled binary
- An information file describing the app to the system

The compiled binary is simply the end result of Xcode compiling all of your Objective-C source code and linking it together.

Information describing the app to the system is saved in a file called *Info.plist*. Among other things, *Info.plist* contains:

- The name of the application's icon file
- What kinds of documents the application can open
- The name of the compiled binary
- The name of the interface file to load when the application starts up
- What languages the application supports (such as French, English, and so on)
- Whether the application supports multitasking (for iOS apps)
- The Mac App Store category the application is in (for OS X apps)
- And more.

Info.plist is really important—in fact, if you remove it from the application bundle, the app can't launch.

Applications also contain every resource that was compiled in—all the images, files, sounds, and other items that were added to the project via Xcode. The application is able to refer to these resources at runtime.

You can take a look at the structure of an OS X application by following these steps:

1. *Open Xcode, and create a new OS X application.* Don't bother changing any settings when Xcode asks—just name the app whatever you like and save it somewhere.

2. *Build the application.* Press ⌘-B, or choose Product→Build.

3. *Open the Products group in the project navigator.* It will now contain the .app, which is the end result of the build process. Right-click it and choose Show in Finder. The Finder will open, revealing where Xcode put the app.

4. *Right-click the application and choose Show Package Contents.* The Finder will show the contents of the bundle.

The structures of OS X and iOS application bundles are different. On iOS, everything is contained at the root of the package's folder; on OS X, the structure is more rigorous.

The structure of a Mac application named MyApp looks like this:

MyApp.app
    The top level of the package.

Contents
    A folder that contains the application itself.

Info.plist
    The file that describes the application to the system.

MacOS
    A folder that contains the app's compiled binary.

MyApp
    The app's compiled binary.

PkgInfo
    A file included for legacy reasons that describes the app's maker and what the app is.

Resources
    A folder that contains all of the compiled-in resources.

The structure of an iOS application named MyApp looks like this:

MyApp
    The app's compiled binary.

Info.plist
    The file that describes the application to the system.

Default.png
    The image that is shown while the app is launching.

Default@2x.png
> The high-resolution version of *Default.png*.

embedded.mobileprovision
> The provisioning profile that identifies the app as able to run on a device.

Entitlements.plist
> A file that describes what the application may or may not do.

Because your application could be anywhere on the system, your code can't use absolute paths to determine the location of resources. Thankfully, Cocoa already knows all about packages and how to work with them.

Using NSBundle to Find Resources in Applications

As far as your code goes, your application works the same regardless of which platform it's running on, thanks to a useful class called NSBundle. This class allows your code to know where it is on the disk and how to get at the compiled-in resources.

This is especially important for iOS applications, since these apps are placed in arbitrary folders by the OS when they're installed. This means that your code cannot depend upon being in a single place, and you can't hardcode paths. Of course, doing that is a bad idea anyway, but on iOS, it's guaranteed to cause failures.

You can use NSBundle to determine the location of the application's package on disk, but most of the time you only need to know about the location of the individual resources.

NSBundle allows you to determine both URLs and plain file paths for resources on the disk. All you need to know is the name and type of the resource.

For example, the following code returns an NSString that contains the absolute path for a resource called *SomeImage.png*:

```
NSString* resourcePath = [[NSBundle mainBundle] pathForResource:@"SomeImage"
    ofType:@"png"];
// resourcePath is now a string containing the
// absolute path reference to SomeImage.png
```

Note that call to [NSBundle mainBundle]—it's possible to have more than one bundle around. (Remember, Cocoa refers to packages—that is, folders containing app resources —as *bundles*.)

You can also get URLs to resources as well:

```
NSURL* resourceURL = [[NSBundle mainBundle] URLForResource:@"SomeImage"
                                           ofType:@"png"];
```

This method looks inside the Resources folder in the application bundle for the named file. (On iOS, it looks inside the root folder of the application bundle.)

Absolute paths and URLs are functionally the same when referring to files stored on disk, but using URLs is preferred—a string could theoretically contain anything, whereas a URL always points to a location. This includes file URLs, which look like this: `file:///Applications/Xcode.app/`. You can therefore use URLs in any case where you'd normally use a file path.

If you add an image or other resource to your project, it is copied into the application bundle when the project is built. For Mac apps, the resources are copied into the `Re sources` folder, and for iOS apps, the resources are copied into the root folder of the application.

The Application Lifecycle

Every program starts, runs, and quits. What's interesting is what it does in between. For the most part, applications on OS X and iOS behave similarly, with the exception that iOS handles multitasking in a different way from standard desktop applications.

In this section, we'll walk through the lifecycle of both kinds of applications, and discuss what happens at various stages of an app's life.

OS X Applications

When an application is launched, the first thing the system does is open the application's *Info.plist*. From this file, the system determines where the compiled binary is located, and launches it. From this point on, the code that you write is in control.

In addition to the compiled code, applications almost always have a collection of objects that were prepared at design time and are bundled with the application. These are usually interface objects—prepared windows, controls, and screens—which are stored inside a *nib file* when the application is built. When the application runs, these nib files are opened, and the premade objects are loaded into memory.

 For more information on nib files and how they're built, see "Constructing an Interface" (page 80).

The first thing an application does is open the nib file and deserialize its contents. This means that the application unpacks the windows, controls, and anything else stored in it, and links them together. The main nib also contains the application delegate object, which is unpacked with all the rest.

When an object is unpacked from a nib, it is sent the `awakeFromNib` message. This is the moment at which that object can begin to run code.

Objects that are unpacked from a nib are *not* sent an init message, because they were already initialized when the developer dragged and dropped them into the interface. When working with nib files, it's important to understand that when you add an object to a nib file, that object is created at that moment, and "freeze-dried" when the nib file is saved. When the nib file is opened, the object is "rehydrated" and gets back to work. After the object is rehydrated, it is sent the awakeFrom Nib message to let it know that it's awake.

To summarize: objects that are loaded from a nib receive the awakeFromNib message. Objects that are created by your code receive the init method.

At this point, the application is ready to start running properly. The first thing it does is to send the application delegate the applicationDidFinishLaunching: method. After that method completes, the application enters the run loop.

The *run loop* is an infinite loop, managed by Cocoa that continues looping until the application quits. The purpose of the run loop is to listen for events—keyboard input, mouse movement and clicks, timers going off, etc.—and send those events to the relevant destinations. For example, say you have a button hooked up to a method that should be run when the button is clicked. When the user clicks the button, the mouse-click event is sent to the button, which then causes its target method to get run.

On OS X, applications continue to run when the user selects another app. When the user changes applications, the application delegate receives the applicationWillRe signActive: message, indicating that the application is about to stop being the active one. Soon after, the app delegate receives the applicationDidResignActive: method.

The reason these two methods are separate is to let your code manage what happens to the screen's contents when the home button is tapped on iOS, or when the user switches to another app on OS X. When applicationWillResignActive: is called, your application is still present on the screen. When the application is no longer visible, the application delegate receives applicationDidResignActive:.

When the user comes back to the app, the application delegate receives a pair of similar methods: applicationWillBecomeActive: and applicationDidBecomeActive:. These are sent immediately before and after the application returns to being the active one.

The event loop is terminated when the application quits. When this happens, the application delegate receives the applicationWillTerminate: message, which is sent immediately before the app quits. This is the last opportunity an app has to save files before quitting.

iOS Applications

iOS applications behave in a broadly similar manner to OS X applications, with a few differences. The main one is that iOS applications are presented differently from desktop apps, and the tighter memory constraints on an iOS device mean that there are more stringent rules about multitasking.

On iOS, only one application is on the screen at any one time—any other applications are completely hidden. The visible application is known as the *foreground application*, and any apps also running are *background applications*. There are strict limits on how long an application may run in the background, which we'll discuss shortly.

When using an application on iOS, a user may be interrupted by something else—an incoming phone call, for example, which replaces the app with which the user was interacting. The application is still technically considered to be in the foreground, but it is now *inactive*. If the user accepts the phone call, the phone application becomes the foreground application, and the previous app moves to the background.

There are other methods by which an application can become inactive, such as when the user pulls down the notifications tray (by swiping down from the top of the screen), opens the task switcher (by double-tapping on the home button), or performs some other action. When an application becomes inactive, it's a signal that it may be exited, so your app should make sure to save any work.

The iOS application lifecycle is almost identical to that of an OS X application. When the app is launched, the *Info.plist* file is checked, the compiled binary is found and loaded, and the application begins running code, starting by unpacking the contents of the main nib.

When the application completes loading, the application delegate receives the `applica tionDidFinishLaunching:withOptions:` method. This is similar to the OS X counterpart, but adds an additional parameter—a dictionary, which contains information about why and how the application was launched.

Applications are most commonly launched directly by the user, by tapping on the icon. They can also be launched by other applications, such as when an app passes a file to another. The `options` dictionary contains information that describes the circumstances under which the application launched.

Just as with OS X applications, iOS applications also receive `applicationWillResign Active:` and `applicationDidBecomeActive:` methods (with one difference—on OS X, the parameter to these methods is an `NSNotification` object, whereas on iOS the parameter is a `UIApplication`).

When an application is quit by the user on OS X, we have seen that the application delegate receives the `applicationWillTerminate:` method. This was also the case for iOS applications, until iOS 4. At this point, multitasking was introduced, and the lifecycle of iOS applications changed.

Multitasking on iOS

Applications on iOS are permitted to run in the background, but only under certain very limited conditions. That's because iOS devices are much more constrained than OS X devices in the areas of CPU power, memory space, and battery capacity. A MacBook Pro is expected to run for around 7 hours on battery, with a full set of applications loaded and running—word processor, web browser, and so on. An iPhone 4S, by contrast, is expected to last for 8 hours on WiFi while browsing the Internet—on a battery with a fraction of the capacity of a full-size laptop battery. Additionally, a MacBook Pro (at the time of writing) ships with 8 GB of memory, while an iPhone 4S has only 512 MB.

There's simply no room to fit all the applications at once, so iOS is forced to make some decisions about what applications can run in the background and for how long.

When an application exits (for example, when the user hits the home button or another application launches), the application is *suspended*—it hasn't quit, but it stops executing code and its memory is locked. When the application resumes, it simply picks up where it left off.

This means that the application remains in memory, but stops consuming the system's power-draining resources such as the CPU and location hardware. However, memory is still tight on the iPhone, so if another app needs more memory, the application is simply terminated without notice.

Note that an application that is suspended doesn't get to run any code, and therefore can't get notified that it's being terminated while suspended. This means that any critical data must be saved when the application delegate is told that the application is being moved to the background.

Applications are not told when they are suspended or when they are woken up. They *are* told when they move into and out of the background, however, through the following delegate methods:

```
- (void)applicationDidEnterBackground:(UIApplication *)application;
- (void)applicationWillEnterForeground:(UIApplication *)application;
```

`applicationDidEnterBackground:` is called immediately after the application has moved to the background state. The application will be suspended after the method has run, which means that the app needs to save any data it's working on because it may be terminated while suspended.

`applicationWillEnterForeground:` is called just before the application comes back on screen, and is your application's opportunity to get set up to work again.

As mentioned above, applications that are suspended are candidates for termination if the new foreground app needs more memory. As an application developer, you can reduce the chances of this happening by reducing the amount of memory your application is using—by freeing large objects, unloading images, and so on.

 If you are able, try to reduce the amount of memory being used to under 16 MB. When the application is suspended and the memory usage is under 16 MB, the system will store the application's memory on the flash chips and remove it from memory entirely. When the application is resumed, the application's memory state is reloaded from the stored memory on the flash chips—meaning that the application won't be evicted from memory due to another application's memory demands. We'll look at how to measure memory usage in Chapter 16.

An application can request to run in the background for a short period of time. This background period can be no longer than 10 minutes, and it exists to allow your application to complete a long-running process—writing large files to disk, completing a download, or some other lengthy process. At the end of the 10 minutes, your application must indicate to the OS that it is done or it will be terminated (not suspended, but terminated—gone from memory completely).

To run tasks in the background, you need to add code that looks like this to your application delegate:

```
- (void)applicationDidEnterBackground:(UIApplication *)application
{
    backgroundTask = [application beginBackgroundTaskWithExpirationHandler:^{
        // Stop performing the task in the background (cancel downloads, stop
        // calculations, etc)
        // This expiration handler block is optional, but recommended!

        // Then, tell the system that the task is complete.
        [app endBackgroundTask:backgroundTask];
        backgroundTask = UIBackgroundTaskInvalid;
    }];

    // Start running a block in the background to do the work.
    dispatch_async(dispatch_get_global_queue(DISPATCH_QUEUE_PRIORITY_DEFAULT, 0),
                   ^{
        // Start doing the background work: download, write, calculate, etc.

        // Once the work is done, tell the system
        // that the task is complete.
```

```
        [application endBackgroundTask:backgroundTask];
        backgroundTask = UIBackgroundTaskInvalid;
    });
}
```

There are other cases in which an application can run in the background for longer periods of time, all of which are geared toward more specialized applications:

- Applications that play audio in the background can remain active for as long as they like, until the user starts playing audio from another app. For example, the Pandora Internet radio app can run in the background until the user starts playing music from the Music application.
- Applications that track the user's location can run for as long as they like.
- Voice over IP (VoIP) applications like Skype are allowed to run periodically to check in with their server, but aren't allowed to run indefinitely except when a call is active.

In summary, if you're writing an application for iOS, you can only expect to be running on the device when the user is directly accessing your app. When the user can't see your application, it quite literally becomes a case of "out of sight, out of mind."

The Application Sandbox

OS X and iOS implement a number of features to improve the overall level of security for the user. One of these features is the *application sandbox*, a tool that restricts what an application is allowed to do. The application exists inside the sandbox, and may not try to access any system resources (hardware, user data, and so on) that is outside the sandbox.

Sandboxes are somewhat optional for Mac applications, and mandatory for iOS applications.

A sandbox improves the security of the system by preventing an app from doing something that either Apple or the user does not want it to do. This is specifically useful for improving the security of apps, because the majority of hacks take the form of exploiting a bug in an existing application. Adobe's Acrobat Reader and Microsoft's Internet Explorer 6 are two applications through which malicious people have been able to compromise other users' systems (and install extra software, retrieve private data, and so on). These exploits take the form of modifying the compromised application to make it perform the intruder's bidding.

Sandboxes solve this problem by preventing (at a kernel level) an application from accessing user data, communicating with the network, accessing hardware like the camera and microphone, and so on. Even if the software has an exploitable bug, the intruder cannot access user data because the application is not permitted to reach outside of its sandbox.

Applications that are downloaded from the iOS App Store are automatically placed in a sandbox; we will discuss this in more detail in "Application Restrictions" (page 70). Applications that are distributed via the Mac App Store require being sandboxed as well; however, apps that you distribute yourself do not.

For more information on how the sandbox affects you as a developer, see "Working with the Sandbox" (page 159) in Chapter 9.

Application Restrictions

As mentioned above, a sandbox restricts what an application can do. The restrictions vary significantly between iOS and OS X, because applications on OS X have traditionally been less restricted in terms of what they're allowed to do.

For example, a Mac application can request read/write access to any of the user's files. An iOS application can only work with its own documents, and can't open any files outside of it.

iOS application restrictions

When an iOS app is installed on the device, it's placed in a folder that has a structure like that shown in Figure 4-1.

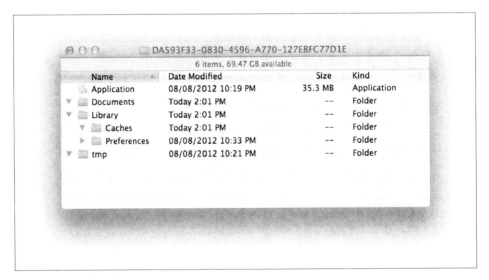

Figure 4-1. iOS application structure

This folder contains the following items:

Documents
    Stores all documents belonging to the application.

Library
>Stores all settings and configuration info.

Caches
>Contains data that is useful to have on disk, but could be regenerated. Items in this folder are deleted by the system if it needs to free some space.

Preferences
>Stores settings and preferences.

tmp
>Stores temporarily files. Items in this folder are periodically deleted by the system.

Application.app
>The application package.

An iOS application is not allowed to work with any file outside of its folder. This prevents the bundle from reading private information (like phone call logs) or modifying any system files.

This restriction on accessing files outside the folder is the only significant restriction imposed upon iOS apps. Mac applications have a much more fine-grained set of restrictions.

Mac application restrictions

The idea of putting restrictions on what Mac apps can do only arrived with the release of the Mac App Store, which means that Apple had quite a bit of time to decide how to implement it.

When you decide to make your application sandboxed, Xcode presents you with a number of options that determine what your application is allowed to do. These options are called *entitlements*.

The available entitlements that your Mac application can request are:

Filesystem
>You can determine whether the application has read/write, read-only, or no access to the filesystem. You can also control whether the application can work with the Downloads folder.

Network
>You can determine whether the application is allowed to make outgoing connections and accept incoming connections.

Hardware
>You can determine whether the application is allowed to access the built-in camera and microphone, communicate with devices via USB, and print.

App communication
> You can determine whether the application is allowed to work with the data managed by the Address Book or Calendar, and whether it is allowed to work with the user's location information.

Music, movies, and pictures folder access
> You can determine whether the application can work with the user's music, photos, and movies by controlling whether the app has read/write, read-only, or no access to these folders. You can set each folder's access permissions separately.

Private APIs

One of the rules that Apple imposes upon applications that are sold via the iTunes App Store or the Mac App Store is that apps are only allowed to communicate with the system via the classes and methods that Apple has documented and indicated are for developer use.

There are many "private" classes and methods that Apple uses behind the scenes. For example, the code that determines whether an iOS device is locked with a passcode is undocumented; Apple uses it (such as in the Find My Friends app), but developers like us may not.

Apple scans all submitted applications as part of the App Store review process. This happens automatically, before a human being sits down to review your application. If your application is rejected for using a private API, you must remove the private API usage and re-submit. If Apple notices that your app uses private APIs *after* the app has gone live in the App Store, they'll simply take down the app.

The point is clear: Apple does *not* like developers using undocumented APIs. The reason is that documented APIs are known by Apple to be safe and (mostly) bug-free. Documented APIs are also features that Apple has committed to, and won't change underneath you. Undocumented APIs, on the other hand, are often still under active development, or may provide access to parts of the OS that Apple considers out-of-bounds for app developers.

CHAPTER 5

Graphical User Interfaces

The graphical user interface is one of the defining features of modern computers. No personal computer sold to consumers these days lacks a GUI, and the only time people work with a machine that doesn't present information graphically is when they're working with a server, supercomputer, or other specialized tool. Displaying a graphical interface to your user is fundamental to developing with Cocoa, and understanding both how to design an appealing and usable GUI and how to implement that GUI are critical skills for Cocoa developers.

This chapter covers the user interface system available in Cocoa and Cocoa Touch, in addition to implementing a UI. Designing a usable and pleasant UI is a huge topic that wouldn't fit in this chapter (let alone in this book!), so if you're interested in learning about what makes a user interface great, take a look at *Tapworthy* by Josh Clark (O'Reilly). You'll also learn about Core Animation, the animation system on both OS X and iOS.

Interfaces in OS X and iOS

While both iOS devices and OS X present their interfaces via a screen, the differences in how they accept user input mean that these interfaces are quite different.

On OS X, the top-level object is the *window*. Windows contain controls, such as buttons, labels, and text fields, and can be moved around the screen to suit the user. More than one window is displayed on the screen at a time. Some windows can be resized, which means that windows need to know how to present their layout when the window grows larger or smaller. Finally, some windows can take up the entire screen; this feature has become increasingly common in OS X since the introduction of OS X 10.7 (Lion), which adds a standard way for windows to become full-screen and for more than one window to be full-screen at once.

iOS also deals with windows, but presents them in a rather different way. In iOS, the user only deals with one screenful of content at a time. Each screen is managed by an object called a *view controller*, which manages the presentation of screen-sized views. View controllers are embedded into the application's window, and there is only one window displayed on the screen at any one time. Almost every application on iOS only ever has one window. Some exceptions include applications that display content on multiple screens (such as when the device is connected to a television); in these cases, each screen has a window.

As mentioned in "OS X Applications" (page 64), applications load their user interfaces from files called *nib files*. Nib files take their name from an acronym that dates back to the days when Cocoa was being designed by NeXT, the company that Steve Jobs founded after leaving Apple in the late 1980s. NIB stands for "NeXT Interface Builder," the name of the program that designed the interfaces.

Interface Builder continued to be distributed as a separate application as part of the developer tools until the release of Xcode 4, at which point it was embedded in Xcode.

MVC and Application Design

In Chapter 4, we discussed how the model-view-controller paradigm shapes a lot of the design decisions in Cocoa. To recap, the MVC design pattern divides the responsibilities of an app into three categories: the model, which handles data storage; the view, which presents the user interface and accepts input such as mouse movement or touches on the screen; and the controller, which mediates between the view and the model and provides the main operating logic for the application.

The Interface Builder in Xcode deals exclusively with views. The rest of Xcode handles the model and controller parts of your application, allowing you to concentrate on building the interface in relative isolation.

However, because views and controllers are designed to communicate with each other, the interface builder in Xcode allows you to determine where instances of classes that you code go in your interface. This code is always invisible, but because the views (which only exist in the interface) need to communicate with these other objects, you can work with them in the interface builder.

Nib Files

At the broadest level, nib files are files that contain objects. In almost all cases, nib files contain only interfaces (see Figure 5-1), but it's possible to (mis)use nib files as a generic container for objects.

Nib files have the extension *.nib* or *.xib*. A *.xib* file is a nib file that's stored in an XML-based format.

Figure 5-1. Nib files contain user interfaces

Nib files work by "freeze-drying" (Apple's terminology) objects and storing them in a serialized form inside the file. All of the properties of the objects (e.g., in the case of a button, its position, label text, and other information) are stored in the nib file. When an application needs to display a window, it loads the nib file, "rehydrates" the stored objects, and presents them to the user.

This means that, for all practical purposes, the views and screens that are assembled in Xcode's interface builder are the exact same objects that appear on screen.

Because nib files simply contain objects, they can also contain objects that are instances of your own class. You can therefore create an instance of a class that is created when a nib is loaded, and connect it to your views.

On their own, views aren't terribly useful, unless you want to create an application that does nothing more than present some buttons that can be clicked on or a text field that does nothing with the text that is entered. If you want to create an application that actually responds to user input, you must connect the views to your controllers—that is, your application code.

The interface builder provides two ways for connecting views to code: *outlets* and *actions*. We will discuss both in more detail later in this chapter.

Structure of a Nib File

Nib files contain a tree structure of objects. This tree can have many roots—for example, a nib file could contain two windows, each with its own collection of buttons and controls. These objects at the top level of the tree are known as "top-level objects."

Top-level objects are usually the visible things that are presented to users—windows on OS X and view controllers on iOS. However, any object can be a top-level object in a nib.

On OS X, anything that's shown on screen is placed in a window. There are many different kinds of windows available in the Interface Builder.

Standard windows

> The common, garden-variety windows shown on the screen. They have a full-size title bar, and are usually the primary window for an application.

Panel windows

> These have a reduced-height title bar and are usually hidden when the application is not active. "Inspector" windows and other accessory windows usually use panels.

Textured windows

> Identical to standard windows, but have a different background color. These have changed quite a bit over the years; they've been pin-striped, brushed-metal, and now a plain gradient (as of OS X 10.7).

HUD (heads-up display)

> These windows are dark grey, translucent, and designed to show information about something that's currently selected or to contain auxiliary controls for your applications. These are most often seen in media applications like QuickTime, Logic, and Final Cut.

Windows can contain any view at all. For more information on views, see Chapter 7.

On iOS, as previously mentioned, there is only one window on the screen at any one time. In contrast to OS X, this window stays on the screen for as long as the app is in the foreground, and replaces its contents when the user moves from one screen of content to the next.

In order to manage the various screens of content, iOS uses a category of object called a *view controller*. View controllers are classes that manage a single view as well as its subviews. View controllers are discussed in more detail later in this chapter, but for practical purposes you can think of them as screens.

 View controllers also exist on OS X but their role is less important, as multiple windows can be shown on the screen at once.

Much like OS X's windows, view controllers on iOS come in a variety of different flavors. These variations are more functionally different that the styles of windows on OS X, which are primarily cosmetic; on iOS, the different categories of view controllers define the structure and behavior of the application.

Standard view controllers

> Present a view, and nothing more. It is most often subclassed to add logic to the screen—in fact, being subclassed is the primary purpose of this view controller.

Navigation controllers

> Present a stack of view controllers, which the application can push additional view controllers onto. When a new view controller is pushed onto the stack, the navigation controller animates the view controller's view into being visible with a sideways scrolling motion. When the navigation controller is instructed to pop a view controller from the stack, the view animates off with a reverse sliding motion. A good example of this view controller is the Settings application.

Tab bar controllers

> Present a set of view controllers, selectable through a tab bar at the bottom of the screen. When a button on the tab bar is tapped by the user, the tab bar controller hides the currently shown view controller and displays another. An example of this style of interface is the iPod application.

Page controllers

> Present view controllers in a "page-turning" interface, similar to the iBooks application on the iPad and iPhone. Each "page" in the book is a view controller, and the user can drag a finger across the screen to turn the page.

GLKit controllers

> Allow you to present 3D graphics to the user using OpenGL. These are a particularly specialized kind of view controller and we won't be discussing them here—the topic of 3D graphics is *way* outside the scope of a book about Cocoa.

Each kind of view controller is designed for a different style of presenting information to the user:

- Navigation controllers are great for presenting information that's hierarchical, where the user drills down into more specific information. For example, your application could have a main menu at the top level, with several view controllers for each available option in the menu that are pushed into the navigation controller's stack when they are selected.

- Tab bar controllers are best for presenting multiple ways of viewing the application's interface. For example, the App Store app is all about finding applications and purchasing them, and the tabs presented to the user are simply different angles on the same thing. Other applications may have more specific angles of presenting the key info that the app is designed around. For example, a chat application could use a tab bar that shows three different tabs: one that shows the list of contacts, one that shows the list of active chats, and an one that shows information about the user's profile.

- Page controllers are best for showing sequential information, as in a book or magazine.

Windows and view controllers are simply containers that present controls to the user. Controls are the visible items on the screen that the user interacts with: buttons, text fields, sliders, and so forth. To build an interface in Xcode, you drag and drop the controls you want from the Object Library in the Utilities panel onto the window or view controller. You can then reposition or resize the control.

 View controllers can contain other view controllers on iOS. For example, a navigation controller is a view controller that manages the appearance of the navigation bar at the top of the screen, as well as one or more additional view controllers.

View controller containment can be a complex topic. For more information, see "View Controller Basics" in the *View Controller Programming Guide for iOS* in the Xcode developer documentation.

Window Sizes

Windows can vary in size. On OS X, they can be any size at all, though you can limit their dimensions using constraints [see "Guidelines and Constraints" (page 80)]. On iOS, windows always fill the entire screen.

The size of an iOS device's screen can vary. On every model of the iPad, the screen is 1024 by 768 screen points (see "Pixels and Screen Points" (page 107) for an explanation of screen points). On the iPhone and iPod touch, it's a little more complicated: all devices up to the iPhone 5 and iPod touch (5th generation) have a screen that's 320 by 480. The iPhone 5 and iPod touch have a screen that's 320 by 568 screen points—88 screen points taller.

Because of this change, iPhone and iPod touch applications have to deliberately opt in to using the new screen size. If they don't, the OS pretends to have the older, smaller screen and displays the application's window in the center of the screen.

To opt in to the taller display, your application simply needs to have a PNG image called "Default-568h@2x.png" included in the application. This is the image that shows while the application is launching; its presence also indicates to the system that it should be drawn on a full-screen window, not letterboxed.

Outlets and Actions

Objects can exist in isolation, but this means that they don't participate in the application as a whole. A button can look very pretty, but unless it knows what should happen when it is clicked, it won't do anything *but* look pretty.

In most cases, an object in an application needs to work with other objects in order to do something useful. For example, a table view, which displays information in a list or grid, needs to be able to contact another object in order to ask it what information should be displayed. The table view does not store the information itself—to do so would violate the model-view-controller pattern. (Views should not know anything about the data they are presenting; they should ask their controller about it.)

Another kind of relationship is the one between a button and the application—when a button is pressed or tapped, the application should be informed of it and then run code as a response. If there are multiple buttons on the screen, which is rather common, the application should know which code to run when a particular button is tapped.

In Cocoa, this kind of relationship is known as a *target-action* relationship. When you add a button to a window or view controller, you can specify two things: what object should be contacted when the button is clicked or tapped, and what message the object should receive when this happens. The object that is contacted is known as the *target*, and the message that is sent is called the *action*. This is shown in Figure 5-2.

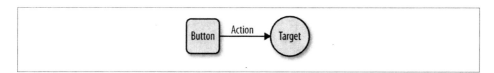

Figure 5-2. The target-action pattern

To allow these relationships between objects to be set up, Xcode allows you to make *connections* between objects in the interface. There are two kinds of connections: outlets and actions.

- *Outlets* are relationships in which one object "plugs in" to another to communicate. An example is the table view that needs to contact another object to know what data to display.

- *Actions* are relationships that describe what method another object should run when an event occurs.

These connections are defined in the nib file, and are used when reconstructing the objects as the nib file loads.

How Nib Files Are Loaded

When a nib file is loaded, usually as part of application startup, every object it contains is re-created based on information stored in the nib: its class, position, label, size, and all its other relevant properties.

Once all objects exist in memory, every outlet defined in the nib file is connected. A nib file effectively describes a source object, a destination object, and the name of a property on the destination object. To connect the objects together, then, the nib file loading process sets the value of the destination object's property to the source object.

After all outlets are connected, every single object that was loaded receives the `awake FromNib:` message. By the time this method is called, every outlet has been connected, and all relationships between the objects have been reestablished.

Actions are a slightly different matter. An action is represented as a *target* object and an *action* message that is sent to that object. When a button is clicked, for example, it sends the action message to the target object.

Outlets and actions are independent of each other. Having an outlet connection doesn't imply that an action is sent, and vice versa. If you want to receive a message from a button *and* also have a variable that points to that button, you'll need both an outlet and an action.

Constructing an Interface

All interfaces in the interface builder are built by dragging components out of the Object Library and into a container. For windows, which have no container, you just drag them out into the canvas.

The Objects Library is at the bottom-right corner of the Xcode window. It lists every single object that can be dragged into an interface file—windows, controls, and hidden objects like view controllers are all available. If you are building an OS X interface, Mac controls appear; if you are building an iOS interface, iOS controls appear.

You can filter the list by typing in the text field at the bottom of the list. This filter searches for the name of the object as well as its class name, so you can search for "NSButton" as well as just "button". If you know exactly what you're searching for, searching by class name is often faster—over time, you'll come to recognize objects by class name and start thinking in those terms.

Guidelines and Constraints

Cocoa tries to keep your views and windows laid out nicely. When you drag a button into a view, for example, Cocoa will attempt to constrain its position to within some standard of the window. If you drag in a button and place it next to another button, Cocoa will help you line them up and place the right amount of space between them. The same applies to resizing views—the interface builder will try to dissuade you from creating a layout that doesn't match up to Cocoa's standard sizes and margins.

The relationships between a view, its container view, and the other views around it are preserved in the form of *constraints*. You can view the constraints on an object by clicking on it and noting the blue lines that extend from it to other views or to the container view's edges.

 Constraints are a new system of laying out a user interface, available from OS X 10.7 Lion and iOS 6 onwards. They replace an earlier model called *springs and struts*, sometimes referred to as *autosizing masks*. For more information on this older system, see "Repositioning and Resizing Views" in the *View Programming Guide*, included in the Xcode developer documentation.

A constraint defines a relationship between a *property* of a view, like its height or the position of its left edge, and a property of another view. This means that you can define constraints like this:

The left position of the Add button is equal to the left position of the table view above it.

You can also create constraints that are based on constant values:

The width of the Delete button is equal to 50 screen points.

Constraints can work together. If you have multiple constraints on a view, or constraints that affect multiple views, the layout system will attempt to resolve them simultaneously:

*The width of the Delete button is equal to 50 screen points, **and** its left edge is equal to 10 screen points from the right edge of the Add button.*

Constraints allow you to create simple rules that define the position and size of all the views on your screen. When the window that those views are contained in resizes, the layout system will update to satisfy all of the constraints.

When you add a view to an interface, the layout system will create *implicit constraints* that define its position and size. The specific constraints that the layout system will add for you depend upon where you place the view; for example, if you place a button in the top-left corner of a window, the layout system will assume that you want the button to have a fixed distance from the left and top edges of the window.

You can also add your own constraints, or promote implicit constraints to *user constraints*. User constraints are customizable and are created via the *constraints menu* at the bottom-right of the interface builder (Figure 5-3).

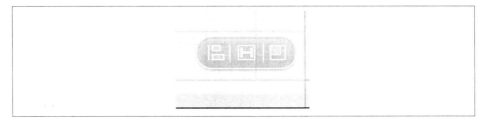

Figure 5-3. The constraints menu

The Constraints menu has three parts:

- *Alignment* defines how different views should line up relative to each other
- *Pinning* defines width, height, and spacing
- How constraints should be applied when resizing the window

Building an App with Nibs and Constraints

To demonstrate how to work with nibs and constraints, let's build a simple interface that makes use of different kinds of constraints. This application won't have any code—we'll only be looking at the constraint system.

This interface will be for an application that lists a bunch of text documents and provides a text field for editing that text. We'll also include some buttons to add, remove, and publish these documents. Let's jump right in.

1. *Create a new Cocoa application.*

   Create a new Cocoa application and name it Constraints.

2. *Open the interface file.*

   Open *MainMenu.xib* and select the window in the Outline pane to make it appear.

3. *Add the UI elements.*

   Start by dragging an NSTableView into the window and placing it in the top-left corner. You'll notice that blue guide lines appear, showing which implicit constraints the layout system will add for you.

   Drag in two gradient buttons, and place them underneath the table view.

   Drag in a wrapping text field, and place it to the right of the table view.

Finally, drag in another button, and place it underneath the text field at its left edge.

4. *Customize the UI elements.*

Select the button at the bottom-left, and open the Attributes inspector (the fourth button from the left in the Utilities pane). Set the button's Title to nothing—that is, select all of the text and delete it. Then change the Image of the button to NSAdd Template. This will make the button contain a plus button image.

Do the same thing for the button immediately to the right, but set the image to NSRemoveTemplate.

Finally, select the button at the bottom-right of the window, and set its Title to **Publish**.

When you're done, the window should look like Figure 5-4.

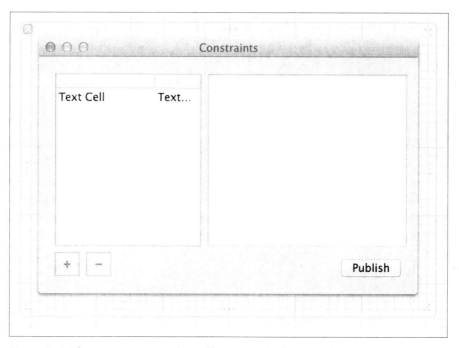

Figure 5-4. The constraints window, all set up with the controls

If you resize the window, however, the screen's carefully constructed layout breaks, and it looks ugly. So we're going to add constraints that make the layout look good at any size.

1. *Add constraints to the table view.*

   First, we'll make the table view resize properly when the window is resized. The table view should grow vertically, but not horizontally. At the same time, it should maintain the same distance from its bottom edge to the window's bottom edge. We can achieve this by pinning its width, and pinning the space between its bottom edge and the window's bottom edge.

   Select the table view and click the Pin menu, which is the middle button inside the Constraints menu. Choose Pin Width. A new constraint will appear and will be selected. Click on the table view again, because we're going to add a new constraint.

2. *Add constraints to the Publish button.*

   We want the Publish button to be aligned with the left edge of the text field.

   Select both the Publish button and the text field, and open the Align menu, which is at the left of the Constraints menu. Choose Left Edges.

3. *Add constraints to the text field.*

   The text field should expand to fill any available space, while still having enough spacing around its edges. We'll pin the height and width, and then configure these constraints to allow them to grow.

   Select the text field. A "pin width" constraint already exists on it, because one was added when we pinned the width of the table view. You can see this constraint as a blue line underneath the text field; click it to select it.

   With this constraint selected, open the Attributes inspector and change its Relation from Equal to Greater Than or Equal. This will allow the constraint to grow but maintain a minimum size.

The window will now resize correctly while preserving the layout.

Core Animation

At its most basic level, a view is a picture drawn in a rectangle, which is then displayed to the user alongside other views. Prior to modern computing hardware's ubiquitous graphics acceleration hardware, this involved carefully calculating how views overlapped and making sure that they didn't overlap or intersect other views. This made creating smooth animations for interfaces a challenge.

To address this, Apple developed *Core Animation*, which is a compositing and animation system for interfaces. Originally devised for iOS, it was ported to OS X in version 10.5.

Core Animation, like many frameworks developed on iOS and later brought to OS X, has an almost identical API on both platforms. This makes it straightforward to port interface code that uses Core Animation between the platforms.

Despite its name, Core Animation is not simply an animation tool, though it is tremendously good at that. Core Animation also provides the rendering architecture for displaying views, which allows for very fast transparency and effects.

 Core Animation is optional, though recommended, on OS X. On iOS, it's integral, and therefore required—but you rarely need to deal with it unless you want to.

Layers

Core Animation works with *layers*, which are rectangular regions of space rendered by the graphics card. Layers are what the user actually sees; when a view needs to show something, it renders it onto a layer.

Core Animation layers are instances of the CALayer class, and work like NSViews and UIViews in that you can add a layer as a sublayer of another layer. Unlike the view classes, however, a layer object does nothing more than display content.

View objects handle layers differently in OS X and iOS.

- On OS X, NSView objects *manage* a CALayer, which they keep separate from themselves. This is because on OS X, views are optionally allowed to have layers.

- On iOS, UIView objects are actually just thin wrappers around CALayers. When you set the position of a view on the screen, you're actually moving its CALayer.

 In the background, CALayers are actually just OpenGL quadrangles and textures. The reason for Core Animation's performance improvements is that OpenGL is very good at quickly drawing such quadrangles.

To access a view's layer, use the layer property (on both UIView and NSView):

```
// myView is an NSView or UIView
CALayer* layer = [myView layer];
```

Animations

As its name suggests, Core Animation is useful for animating visual content. For the most part, your animations will involve moving views around, or animating changes in parameters like background color or opacity.

Animations work differently on iOS and OS X.

Animations on OS X

On OS X, if you want to animate a view, you first access the view's layer and then change a property on the layer. This is called an *implicit animation*—Core Animation will notice that you're modifying a property that can be animated, and implicitly create an animation for you.

To change a layer's position on the screen, therefore, you would do this:

```
aLayer.position = CGPointMake(20,20);
```

To configure the duration of this implied animation, you can create a *transaction* and configure it. A transaction is a collection of state changes that are grouped together and executed as part of an animation. Transactions are represented by the CATransaction class.

To work with transactions, create one by calling [CATransaction begin], and end it by calling [CATransaction commit]. When you call commit, the state changes that were recorded when you changed the properties of the layer are grouped together as an animation, and that animation begins. If you don't create a CATransaction, one is created for you in the background.

You must always commit transactions that you begin. If you don't, Core Animation will throw exceptions or otherwise behave incorrectly.

The following code demonstrates how to create a CATransaction that animates over 10 seconds:

```
[CATransaction begin];
[CATransaction setValue:[NSNumber numberWithFloat:10.0f]
    forKey:kCATransactionAnimationDuration];

aLayer.position = CGPointMake(20,20);

[CATransaction commit];
```

Working with any of the CA classes requires that you import the Quartz-Core framework, and #import the QuartzCore/QuartzCore.h header file in your code.

Animations on iOS

The animation API on iOS is based on blocks, which are discussed in more detail in Chapter 6. To animate a view, call [`UIView animateWithDuration:animations:`], and provide the duration of the animation and a block that contains the actual state changes you want to have animated.

For example, to animate a change in position that lasts 0.25 seconds, you do this:

```
[UIView animateWithDuration:0.25 animations:^{
    aView.center = CGPointMake(20,20);
}];
```

When you call this code, an animation will be created for you that transitions from the view's current state to the state you specified.

Animation is another of those topics that's large and complex, and as always the Apple documentation on the subject is vast and comprehensive. To learn more about using Core Animation, a great place to start is *Core Animation Programming Guide*, included in the Xcode documentation.

CHAPTER 6

Blocks and Operation Quotes

Over the years, OS X and iOS have provided increasingly simple ways for developers to manage their code. Two of these features are *blocks*, which allow you to store chunks of code in variables and call them later, and *operation queues*, which dramatically simplify how you write applications that do multiple things at once.

These two features are closely tied together, and, once mastered, quickly become indispensable in developing applications.

In this chapter, you'll learn how to code with blocks, what they're good for, and how to use them in conjunction with operation queues, a powerful tool for performing tasks in the background.

Blocks

It's often useful to be able to store code in variables. Consider the following code sample:

```
int i = 53;
void (^someCode)() = ^{
    NSLog(@"The value of i is %i", i);
};
```

In Objective-C, this is called a *block*. Blocks store code, and can be assigned to variables, passed to functions, and generally treated like any other value. The big feature is that blocks can be called like functions, and they capture the state of things as they were when the block was created.

Calling a block is identical to calling a function:

```
someCode(); // prints out "The value of i is 53".
```

Note that the block remembered that the variable i was 53—because it captured the state of that variable when it was created. When a variable outside a block is referenced within that block, the value of that variable at the moment of the block's creation is captured and is available for the block's code to use.

This means that you can do some interesting things. For example, in iOS:

```
// Slide up a view controller, and then when the slide animation is
// finished, change its background color to yellow.
// The block captures the value of the "myViewController" variable,
// for use after the animation has completed (which will happen some
// time after this method finishes running)

SomeViewController* myViewController = [ code omitted ];
[self presentModalViewController:myViewController animated:YES completion:^{
    myViewController.view.backgroundColor = [UIColor yellowColor];
}];
```

Blocks allow you to defer the execution of something until you need it to actually happen. This makes them very useful in the context of animations ("when the animation's done, do this thing"), for networking ("when the download's done, do something else"), or in general user interface manipulation ("when I return from this new screen, do some work").

They also allow you to keep related pieces of code close together. For example, before the introduction of blocks, the only way that it was possible to filter an array was to create a function elsewhere in your code that was called for each element in the array. This made for a lot of scrolling around your source code. Now, you can do this:

```
// Filter an array of strings down to only strings that begin with the word
// "Apple"

NSPredicate* filterPredicate = [NSPredicate predicateWithBlock:^(id anObject) {
    NSString* theString = anObject;
    return [theString hasPrefix:@"Apple"];
}];

NSArray* filteredArray = [someArray filteredArrayWithPredicate:filterPredicate];
```

In this case, the code that actually performs the processing of the objects is very close to the line that instructs the array to be filtered. This means that your code isn't scattered in as many places, which makes it clearer and less confusing. The less confusing your code is, the less likely it is that bugs will be introduced.

Block Syntax

The syntax involved in declaring a block variable can look a little esoteric, particularly since it involves several characters that aren't often seen when writing C or Objective-C. To that end, let's take a closer look at how you define a variable that stores a block.

First, here is the definition of a block variable that takes no parameters and returns nothing:

```
void(^myBlockVariable)(void);
```

Breaking down the syntax, here's what each part means:

```
[Return Type] (^ [Variable Name]) ([Parameters]);
```

If a block has no parameters, you can omit the last void:

```
void(^myBlockVariable)();
```

If you want to define a block variable that takes some parameters, add them to the last set of parentheses:

```
void(^myBlockVariable)(BOOL booleanParameter, NSString* objectParameter);
```

Blocks, like standard functions, can take any Objective-C data type as a parameter.

Once a block variable has been declared, it must have a block assigned to it before it can be called.

When you define a block, you must again list the parameters that it accepts. For example, a block that returns nothing and takes a single BOOL parameter is defined like so:

```
void(^myBlockVariable)(BOOL parameter);

myBlockVariable = ^(BOOL parameter) {
    // Code goes here.
};
```

If a block doesn't have any parameters, you can omit the list of parameters between the ^ and opening brace ({):

```
void(^myBlockVariable)();

myBlockVariable = ^{
    // Code goes here.
};
```

You can also do the declaration and definition in a single line:

```
void(^myBlockVariable)() = ^{
    // Code goes here.
};
```

Once a block has been defined, you can call it in the same way you would with a function:

```
myBlockVariable();
```

Block Lifecycles

Blocks are Objective-C objects. This means that they can receive messages—they can be retained, released, and copied. You can also send them the invoke message, which causes them to be run.

However, blocks are stored in memory slightly differently from the way other objects are stored. To understand this difference, it's necessary to understand where objects can be placed in memory.

There are two main locations in memory where data can be stored: the *stack* and the *heap*. The stack is a chunk of memory designed for local working data. All local variables in a method are stored on the stack, and when the function ends, those variables are destroyed. The stack is a comparatively small, fast chunk of memory—because the memory for it has already been allocated by the system, there are no additional costs in creating a variable that is stored there.

Because the stack automatically wipes out a function's local memory when the function returns, there's no need for you to perform memory management on local variables. This is why, for example, when you declare a local integer variable, you don't need to indicate to the system that you're done with it before the function returns—it will be removed from memory when the program returns to where your function or method was called from.

By contrast, the heap is a much larger region of memory, which any part of the program may allocate memory from. Memory allocated from the heap stays allocated until it's explicitly returned to the system, which is why memory management is needed. Unlike stack memory, if you manually allocate memory from the heap and then throw away the variable that stored the pointer to that memory, the memory stays allocated and inaccessible. This is known as a *memory leak*, and is a very bad thing. All Objective-C objects are stored on the heap.

When you create a block, it is stored on the stack. However, if you were to create a block, store it in an instance variable, and then return from the current method, the block (which exists only on the stack) is removed from memory but the instance variable still points to where it was. If you were to then call the block variable, your program would crash—the block no longer exists.

To solve this problem, you must *copy* the block to the heap if you wish to keep it around for longer than until the function returns. To do this, send the block the copy message, in the same way you would send a message to any other Objective-C object. Once a block has been copied to the heap, it can be safely stored anywhere. Of course, it must later be deallocated to avoid a memory leak, but both the garbage collector and Automatic Reference Counting will handle this for you.

Here's an example of how to store a block as an instance variable, and how *not* to:

```
// myBlockProperty is a property of this class that can store the block.

void(^myBlockVariable)() = ^{
    // code goes here
};

self.myBlockProperty = myBlockVariable; // INCORRECT! The block
// won't exist after this function returns, and calling it will crash.

self.myBlockProperty = [myBlockVariable copy]; // SAFE. The
// block will be copied and stored on the heap, and stick around.
```

Methods with Block Parameters

Methods can accept blocks as parameters. This is actually one of the key features of blocks, since it allows callers of your methods to provide code at the moment they call the method. We have already seen how this can be used to filter an array, but it has other uses as well.

Blocks are useful for running code that will take place at a later time. This often occurs when dealing with networked code—a network request will go out, and the data from the network request will return at a later time. Because it is impractical to pause the application until the request is complete (doing so would freeze up the app, which is a very bad thing for the user), the program must be set up to run the code that handles the returned data at a later time.

Blocks make this easy. For example, here is some code that downloads a file and reports on when the download is complete—all without having to pause the application:

```
NSURL* location = [NSURL URLWithString:@"http://www.example.com/test.txt"];
NSURLRequest* request = [NSURLRequest requestWithURL:location];

[NSURLConnection sendAsynchronousRequest:request
                     queue:[NSOperationQueue mainQueue]
         completionHandler:^(NSURLResponse* response,
                             NSData* loadedData,
                             NSError* error) {
    // This code runs when the data has completed downloading.
    // The NSURLResponse contains information from the server
    // about the request, the NSData contains the raw downloaded
    //  bytes, and the NSError contains any error information, if
    // anything went wrong.
}];
```

To write a method that accepts a block as a parameter, you simply define the variable type as you would any other parameter. For example, here is the declaration for a method that takes a block as a parameter, which itself takes a single BOOL parameter:

```
- (void) someMethod:(void(^)(BOOL aParameter)) handler;
```

The implementation of this method would look something like this:

```
- (void) someMethod:(void(^)(BOOL aParameter)) handler {
    // Call the passed-in block:
    handler(YES);
}
```

You could then call this method like so:

```
[anObject someMethod:^(BOOL aParameter) {
    // The called method will call this method
}];
```

Because working with blocks leads to some rather thorny-looking syntax, it's often useful to create *block types*, and use them rather than list the entire block type definition over and over. To do this, you use the `typedef` keyword, which allows you to define a data type.

For example, here is code that defines a block data type, and then later creates a block variable of that type:

```
// somewhere in your source code, outside of a function or method:
typedef void(^ABlockType)(BOOL aParameter);

// and later, in a function:
ABlockType myBlock = ^(BOOL aParameter) {
    // do some work
};
```

Using this technique reduces the amount of typing you need to do, and makes sure that the blocks you are working with have the same type. You can also use these declared types in your method declarations:

```
- (void) someMethod:(ABlockType)handler; // much tidier!
```

Blocks and Memory Management

We discussed above how blocks capture the values of variables that they reference. However, Objective-C objects are too big to be copied in by value, and simply capturing the pointer to their memory is unsafe. To solve this problem, any time you refer to an Objective-C object in a block, it is retained by that block and released when the block is released. This causes the object to stay around for as long as the block exists and guarantees that the block can always be safely called, since the objects that it refers to are still in memory.

Modifying Local Variables from Inside Blocks with __block

When you use a variable in a block that was defined outside of that block, you can access that variable's data as much as you like. For objects, the variable is retained, and for non-objects, the data inside that variable is copied into the block at the moment the block is created.

Sometimes, however, it's useful for a block to be able to *modify* a variable that was defined outside of it. When you want to do this, mark the variable with the __block keyword. This lets you modify the variable inside the block.

For example, this code won't work as you expect:

```
int i = 0;

void(^myBlock)() = ^{
    i = 4;
};

myBlock();

NSLog(@"i is now %i", i); // will print "0"
```

To fix it, you need to do this:

```
__block int i = 0;

void(^myBlock)() = ^{
    i = 4;
};

myBlock();

NSLog(@"i is now %i", i); // will print "4"
```

Concurrency with Operation Queues

In many cases, your application will need to do more than one thing at the same time. At least one of those things is responding to the user and ensuring that the user interface is responsive; other things could include talking to the network, reading and writing large amounts of data, or processing a chunk of data.

The highest priority of your application is to be responsive at all times. Users are happy to wait a few more seconds for a task to complete rather than to feel that the application (and, by their logic, the expensive computer they bought) is slow.

The second priority of your application is to make sure that all of the resources available are being used so that the task completes quickly.

Operation queues allow you to achieve both goals. Operation queues are Objective-C objects; they are instances of the NSOperationQueue class. They manage a list, or queue, of operations, which are Objective-C objects that know how to perform a chunk of work.

More than one operation queue can exist at the same time, and there is always at least one operation queue, known as the *main queue*. So far, all the code in this book has been run on the main queue. All work that is done with the GUI is done on the main queue, and if your code takes up too much time in processing something, the main queue is slowed down and your GUI starts to lag or freeze up.

Operation queues are not quite the same thing as *threads*, but they share some similarities. The operation queue system manages a pool of threads, which are activated whenever work needs to be done. Because threads are a rather resource-intensive way of doing work concurrently (to say nothing of the development complexity involved in managing them properly), operation queues provide a much simpler and more efficient way of dealing with them.

Operation queues are also aware of the computing resources available on whatever hardware your application is running on. If you create an operation queue and add operations to it, the operation queue will attempt to balance those operations across as many CPU cores as are available on your computer. Almost every single device that Apple ships now has two or more CPU cores, which means that code that uses operation queues automatically gains an increase in speed when performing concurrent work.

Operation Queues and NSOperation

At its simplest, an operation queue runs operations in a first-in-first-out order. Operations are instances of the NSOperation class, which define exactly how the work will be done. NSOperations can be added to an NSOperationQueue; once they are added, they will perform whatever task they have been designed to do.

The simplest way to add an operation to an operation queue is to provide a block to the queue by sending the addOperationWithBlock: message to an NSOperationQueue object:

```
NSOperationQueue* mainQueue = [NSOperationQueue mainQueue];
[mainQueue addOperationWithBlock:^{
    // Add code here
}];
```

There are other kinds of operations, including *invocation operations* and concrete subclasses of the NSOperation base class, but they're very similar to block operations—they offer more flexibility and features at the cost of having to write more setup code.

If you don't deliberately choose to run code on another queue, it will run on the main queue. You can also explicitly instruct the main queue to perform an operation; when you do this, the work for this operation is scheduled to take place at some point in the future.

Performing Work on Operation Queues

To add things to an operation queue, you need an NSOperationQueue instance. You can either ask the system for the main queue, or you can create your own. If you create your own queue, it will run asynchronously. If you add multiple operations to a background queue, the operation queue will run as many as possible at the same time, depending on the available computing hardware.

```
// Getting the main queue (will run on the main thread)
NSOperationQueue* mainQueue = [NSOperationQueue mainQueue];

// Creating a new queue (will run on a background thread, probably)
NSOperationQueue* newQueue = [[NSOperationQueue alloc] init];
```

Queues aren't the same as threads, and creating a new queue doesn't guarantee that you'll create a new thread—the operating system will reuse an existing thread if it can, since creating threads is expensive. The only thing using multiple queues guarantees is that the operations running on them won't block each other from running at the same time.

Once you have a queue, you can put an operation on it:

```
[mainQueue addOperationWithBlock:^{
    NSLog(@"This operation ran on the main queue!");
}];

[newQueue addOperationWithBlock:^{
    NSLog(@"This operation ran on another queue!");
}];
```

If your code is running on a background queue and you want to update the GUI, you need to run the GUI updating code on the main queue. One way to do this is to add a block to the main queue:

```
[newQueue addOperationWithBlock:^{
    // Do some work in the background

    // Schedule a block on the main queue
    [mainQueue addOperationWithBlock:^{
        // GUI work can safely be done here.
    }];
}];
```

Any work involving the GUI can only be done from the main queue. If you access it from any other queue, your application will crash.

Putting It All Together

We'll now write an application that downloads the favicons from a number of websites asynchronously. It will also contact a server when the application exits. Follow the steps below to create the new app:

1. Create a new single-view application.

2. Add a table view to the view controller.

3. Change the table view's prototype cell style to Basic.

4. Select the prototype cell and change its identifier to **IconCell**.

5. Change the table's Selection style to No Selection.

6. Make the view controller the table view's data source and delegate.

7. Open *ViewController.h* in the Assistant. Make `ViewController` conform to the `UITableViewDataSource` and `UITableViewDelegate` protocols.

8. Control-drag from the table view into the `ViewController`'s interface. Make a new outlet, and call it **tableView**.

9. Add the following code to the start of *ViewController.m*:

    ```
    @interface ViewController () {
        NSArray* websites;
        NSMutableArray* websiteIcons;
    }
    @end
    ```

10. Add the following code to the end of `viewDidLoad`:

    ```
    - (void)viewDidLoad
    {
        [super viewDidLoad];

        // Set up the list of websites that we want to get icons for.
        websites = [NSArray arrayWithObjects:@"google.com", @"amazon.com",
                    @"microsoft.com", @"apple.com", @"meebo.com", nil];

        websiteIcons = [[NSMutableArray alloc] init];

        // For each website in the 'websites' array, insert an NSNull into the
        // website icons array.
        // These NSNulls will be replaced when the images are loaded from the
        // network.
    ```

```objc
    for (NSString* website in websites) {
        [websiteIcons addObject:[NSNull null]];
    }
}
```

11. Add the following methods to *ViewController.m*:

```objc
- (NSInteger)numberOfSectionsInTableView:(UITableView *)tableView {
    return 1;
}

- (NSInteger)tableView:(UITableView *)tableView
 numberOfRowsInSection:(NSInteger)section {
    // Number of cells = number of websites
    return [websiteIcons count];
}

- (UITableViewCell *)tableView:(UITableView *)tableView
    cellForRowAtIndexPath:(NSIndexPath *)indexPath {
    // Get a cell from the table view.
    UITableViewCell* cell = [tableView
        dequeueReusableCellWithIdentifier:@"IconCell"];

    // Take the website name and give that to the cell
    NSString* websiteName = [websites objectAtIndex:indexPath.row];
    cell.textLabel.text = websiteName;

    // If we have an image for this website, give it to the cell
    UIImage* websiteImage = [websiteIcons objectAtIndex:indexPath.row];
    if ((NSNull*)websiteImage != [NSNull null]) {
        cell.imageView.image = websiteImage;
    }

    return cell;
}
```

12. Run the application. The app will show a list of websites.

Now let's make it load the website icons in the background.

13. Add the following code to the end of `viewDidLoad`:

```objc
// Get a new operation queue.
NSOperationQueue* backgroundQueue = [[NSOperationQueue alloc] init];

int websiteNumber = 0; // for keeping track of which index to
                       // insert the new image into

for (NSString* website in websites) {
    [backgroundQueue addOperationWithBlock:^{

        // Construct a URL for the website's icon
        NSURL* iconURL = [NSURL URLWithString:
```

```
                [NSString stringWithFormat:@"http://%@/favicon.ico", website]];

        // Construct a URL request for this URL
        NSURLRequest* request = [NSURLRequest requestWithURL:iconURL];

        // Load the data
        NSData* loadedData = [NSURLConnection
            sendSynchronousRequest:request returningResponse:nil error:nil];

        if (loadedData != nil) {
            // We got image data! Convert it to an image.
            UIImage* loadedImage = [UIImage imageWithData:loadedData];

            // If the data wasn't able to be turned into an image, stop
            if (loadedImage == nil) {
                return;
            }

            // If it was, insert the image into the
            // table view on the main queue.
            [[NSOperationQueue mainQueue] addOperationWithBlock:^{
                [websiteIcons replaceObjectAtIndex:websiteNumber
                                        withObject:loadedImage];
                [self.tableView reloadData];
            }];
        }
    }];
    websiteNumber++;
}
```

14. Run the application. Website icons will be loaded in the background.

Finally, we'll make the application run some code in the background when the application quits.

15. Open *AppDelegate.m.*

16. Replace `applicationWillEnterBackground:` with the following method:

```
- (void)applicationDidEnterBackground:(UIApplication *)application
{
    // Register a background task. This keeps the app from being
    // terminated until we tell the system that the task is complete.

    UIBackgroundTaskIdentifier backgroundTask =
        [application beginBackgroundTaskWithExpirationHandler:nil];

    // Make a new background queue to run our background code on.
    NSOperationQueue* backgroundQueue = [[NSOperationQueue alloc] init];

    [backgroundQueue addOperationWithBlock:^{
        // Send a notification to the server.
```

```objc
    // Prepare the URL
    NSURL* notificationURL = [NSURL
        URLWithString:@"http://www.oreilly.com/"];

    // Prepare the URL request
    NSURLRequest* notificationURLRequest = [NSURLRequest
        requestWithURL:notificationURL];

    // Send the request, and log the reply
    NSData* loadedData = [NSURLConnection
        sendSynchronousRequest:notificationURLRequest
            returningResponse:nil
                        error:nil];

    // Convert the data to a string
    NSString* loadedString = [[NSString alloc] initWithData:loadedData
                                    encoding:NSUTF8StringEncoding];

    NSLog(@"Loaded: %@", loadedString);

    // Tell the system that the background task is done
    [application endBackgroundTask:backgroundTask];
    }];
}
```

CHAPTER 7

Drawing Graphics in Views

The fundamental class for showing any kind of graphical image to the user is the view. Graphical images are things like buttons, photos, text—anything that the user can see.

Cocoa and UIKit provide a wide variety of controls that suit almost all needs—you can display text, images, buttons, and so on. However, some data needs to be drawn in a specific way: you might want to draw a chart for data, or create a custom button class that displays exactly the way you want it to. If you're making a graphics app, you'll need to be able to display any kind of graphical content, which means that your code will need to know how to draw it.

In this chapter, you'll learn how to create custom view objects that display any kind of image to the user. You'll learn how to use the high-level Objective-C APIs for drawing, and create a custom view class that will scale up to any size at all without losing quality. Finally, you'll learn how the Retina display works on both iOS and OS X.

How Drawing Works

Before we start writing code that draws content for the user to see, it's helpful to review how graphics work in OS X and iOS. Note that the same terminology and techniques apply for both OS X and iOS, but the specific API is different.

When an application draws graphics, it does so by first creating a canvas for drawing in. Cocoa calls this the graphics *context*. The context defines, among other things, the size of the canvas and how color information is used (for example, you can have a black-and-white canvas, a grayscale canvas, a 16-bit color canvas, and more).

Once you have a graphics context to draw in, you start asking Cocoa to begin drawing content.

The fundamental drawing unit is the *path*. A path is just the name for any kind of shape: circles, squares, polygons, curves, and anything else you can imagine.

Paths can be stroked or filled. *Stroking* a path means drawing a line around its edge (Figure 7-1). *Filling* a path means filling the area that it contains with a color (Figure 7-2).

When you stroke or fill a path, you tell the drawing system which color you want to use. You can also use gradients to stroke and fill paths. The color that you use to stroke and fill can be partially transparent, which means that you can build up a complex graphic by combining different paths and colors (Figure 7-3).

Figure 7-1. A stroked path

Figure 7-2. A filled path

Figure 7-3. A stroked and filled path

The Pixel Grid

Every display system in iOS and OS X is based on the idea of a grid of pixels. The specific number of pixels on the display varies from device to device, as does the physical size of each pixel. The trend is toward larger numbers of smaller pixels, since the smaller the pixels get, the smoother the image looks.

When you create a graphics context, you indicate what size that context should be. So, for example, if you create a context that is 300 pixels wide by 400 pixels high, the canvas is set to that size. Any drawing that takes place outside the canvas is ignored, and doesn't appear on the canvas (Figure 7-4).

Creating a context defines a *coordinate space* where the drawing happens. This coordinate space puts the coordinate (0,0) in either the top-left corner (on iOS) or the bottom-left corner (on OS X). When you build a path, you specify the points that define it. So, for example, a line that goes from the top-left corner (on iOS) to 10 pixels below and to the right looks like Figure 7-5.

Retina Displays

The newest devices sold by Apple feature a *Retina display*. A Retina display, according to Apple, is a screen where the pixels are so small that you can't make out the individual dots. This means that curves and text appear much smoother, and the end result is a better visual experience for the user.

At the time of publishing, Retina displays are available on the MacBook Pro with Retina Display, iPod touch 4th generation and later, iPhone 4 and later, and iPad third-generation and later.

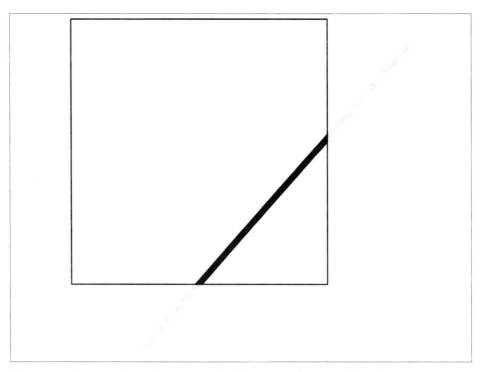

Figure 7-4. Content that is drawn outside of the context's canvas doesn't appear

Retina displays are so named because, according to Apple, a 300 dpi (dots per inch) display held at a distance of about 12 inches from the eye is the maximum amount of detail that the human retina can perceive.

Apple achieves this resolution by using displays that are the same physical size as more common displays, but double the resolution. For example, the screen on the iPhone 3GS (and all previous iPhone and iPod touch models) measures 3.5 inches diagonally and features a resolution of 320 pixels wide by 480 pixels high. When this resolution is doubled in the iPhone 4's Retina display, the resolution is 640 by 960.

This increase in resolution can potentially lead to additional complexities for application developers. In all other cases where the resolution of a display has increased, everything on the screen appears smaller (because the drawing code only cares about pixel distances, not physical display size). However, on a Retina display, everything remains the same size, because even though the pixels are twice as small, everything on the screen is drawn *twice as large*. The net result is that the graphics on the screen look the same size, but much smoother.

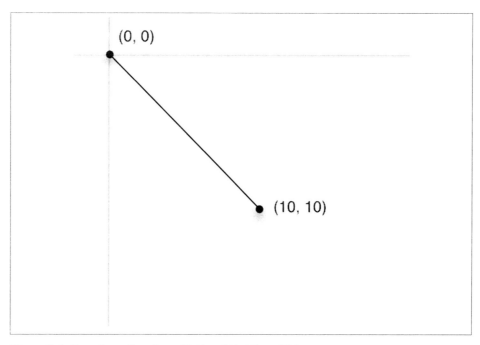

Figure 7-5. Drawing a line from (0,0) to (10,10) on iOS

Pixels and Screen Points

Of course, we application developers don't want to write code for both Retina and non-Retina displays. Writing a chunk of code twice for the two resolutions would lead to twice the potential bugs!

To solve this problem, don't think about pixels when you're writing your graphics code and thinking about the positions of the points your paths are constructed with. Instead, think in terms of *screen points*.

A pixel is likely to change between different devices, but a screen point does not. When you construct a path, you specify the position of each screen point that defines the path. On a non-Retina display, one screen point is equal to one pixel. On a Retina display, one screen point is equal to two pixels. This scaling is done for you automatically by the operating system.

The end result is that you end up with drawing code that doesn't need to be changed for different resolutions.

Drawing in Views

As discussed earlier, objects that display graphics to the user are called *views*. Before we talk about how to make your own view objects that display your pixels before the user's very eyes, let's take a closer look at how views work.

A view is defined by a rectangle inside its content window. If a view isn't inside a window, the user can't see it.

 Even though only one app is displayed at a time on iOS, all views shown on the screen are technically inside a window. The difference is that only one window is shown on the screen at a time, and it fills the screen.

Frame Rectangles

The rectangle that defines the view's size and position is called its *frame rectangle*.

Views can contain multiple *subviews*. When a view is inside another view (its *superview*), it moves when the superview moves. Its frame rectangle is defined relative to its superview (Figure 7-6).

On OS X, all views are instances of NSView (or one of NSView's subclasses). On iOS, they're instances of UIView. There are some minor differences in how they work, but nothing that affects what we're talking about here. For now, we'll talk about NSView, but everything applies equally to UIView.

When the system needs to display a view, it sends the -drawRect: message to the view. The drawRect method looks like the following:

```
- (void) drawRect:(NSRect)rect {

}
```

(This method is the same on iOS, but CGRect is used instead of NSRect.)

When this method is called, a graphics context has already been prepared by the OS, leaving the method ready to start drawing. When the method returns, the OS takes the contents of the graphics context and shows it in the view.

The single parameter that drawRect receives is the *dirty rectangle*. This eyebrow-raising term is actually a lot more tame than it sounds—"dirty" is simply the term for "something that needs updating." The dirty rectangle is the region of the view that actually needs updating. This concept becomes useful when you have cases where a view that was previously covered by up another view—there's no need to redraw content that was previously visible, and so the dirty rectangle that's passed to drawRect will be a reduced size.

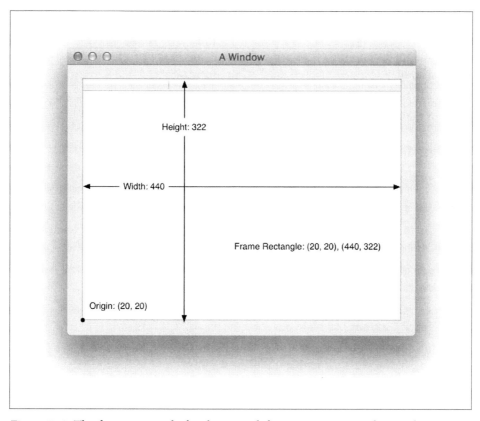

Figure 7-6. The frame rectangle for the view defines its position and size relative to its superview

Bounds Rectangles

The frame rectangle defines the size and position of its view, but it's also helpful for a view to know about its size and position relative to itself. To support this, view objects also provide a *bounds rectangle*. While the frame rectangle is the view's size and position relative to its superview's coordinate space, the bounds rectangle is the view's position and size relative to its own coordinate space. This means that the (0,0) coordinate always refers to the top-left corner on iOS (the bottom-left on OS X).

While the bounds rectangle is usually the same size as the frame rectangle, it doesn't have to be. For example, if the view is rotated, the frame rectangle will change size and position, but the bounds will remain the same.

Building a Custom View

We'll now create a custom view that displays a solid color inside its bounds. This will be a Mac application, so we'll be using NSView. Later in the chapter, we'll see how the same techniques apply to iOS and the UIView class.

When we create the application, we'll use the interface builder to include an NSView in the app's main window, and then make it use a custom NSView subclass that we'll code.

Creating the Project

First, create your project by following these steps:

1. Create a new Cocoa application and name it CustomViews.

2. Leave the class prefix as blank, leave Create Document-Based Application turned off, and make sure that Use Automatic Reference Counting is turned on.

3. Create a new Objective-C subclass. Make it a subclass of NSView and call it **Custom View**.

4. Open *MainWindow.xib*. We're going to add a custom view to the main window, which will use our newly created class.

5. Add a custom view. Locate Custom View in the Object Library, and drag it into the main window. Resize it so that it fills the window.

6. Make the custom view use the CustomView class. Select the newly added view, and go to the Identity inspector (the third button to the left at the top of the Inspector pane). Change the view's class from NSView to CustomView.

The application's window should look like Figure 7-7.

Filling with a Solid Color

Now, when the application displays the window's content, your view code will be used to draw the view. Let's start by making the view fill itself with the color green. Afterward, we'll start making the view show more complex stuff.

Open *CustomView.m*, and replace the drawRect: method with the following code:

```
- (void)drawRect:(NSRect)dirtyRect
{
    NSBezierPath* path = [NSBezierPath bezierPathWithRect:self.bounds];

    [[NSColor greenColor] setFill];
    [path fill];
}
```

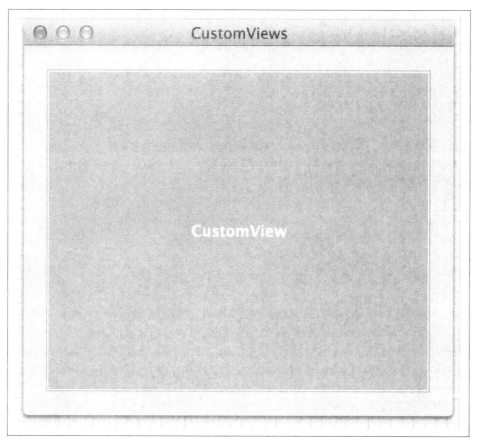

Figure 7-7. The layout of the application's window

This view code creates an `NSBezierPath` object, which represents the path that you'll be drawing. In this code, we create the Bézier path with the `bezierPathWithRect:` method, which creates a rectangular path. We use the view's bounds to create a rectangle that fills the entire view.

Once the path is created, we can fill it. Before we do that, however, we tell the graphics system to use green as the fill color. Colors in Cocoa are represented by the `NSColor` class, which is capable of representing any color you can think of. `NSColor` provides a number of convenience methods that return simple colors, like green, red, and blue, which we use here.

So, we create the path, set the color, and then fill the path. The end result is a giant green rectangle.

The exact same code works on iOS, with two changes: NSBezierPath becomes UIBezierPath, and NSColor becomes UIColor:

```
- (void)drawRect:(NSRect)dirtyRect
{
    UIBezierPath* path = [UIBezierPath bezierPathWithRect:self.bounds];

    [[UIColor greenColor] setFill];
    [path fill];
}
```

Now run the application. The view you added will display as green, as shown in Figure 7-8.

Figure 7-8. A green view

Working with Paths

We'll now update this code and create a slightly more complex path: a rounded rectangle. We'll also stroke the path, drawing an outline around it.

Replace the `drawRect` method with the following code:

```
Code:
- (void)drawRect:(NSRect)dirtyRect
{
    NSRect pathRect = NSInsetRect(self.bounds, 1, 1);

    NSBezierPath* path = [NSBezierPath bezierPathWithRoundedRect:pathRect
                                xRadius:10 yRadius:10];
    [[NSColor greenColor] setFill];
    [[NSColor blackColor] setStroke];
    [path fill];
    [path stroke];
}
```

The first change you'll notice is a call to the `NSInsetRect` function. This function takes an `NSRect` and shrinks it while preserving its center point. In this case, we're insetting the rectangle by one pixel on the X axis and one pixel on the Y axis. This causes the rectangle to be pushed in by one pixel from the left and one pixel from the right, as well as one pixel from the top and bottom.

We do this because when a path is stroked, the line is drawn around the outside—and because the bounds are the size of the view, some parts of the line are trimmed away. This can look ugly, so we shrink the rectangle a bit to prevent the problem.

We then create another `NSBezierPath`, this time using the newly shrunk rectangle. This path is created by calling the `bezierPathWithRoundedRect:xRadius:yRadius:` method, which lets you specify how the corners of the rounded rectangle are shaped.

The final change to the code is setting black as the stroke color, and then stroking the path after it's been filled.

Now run the application. You'll see a green rounded rectangle with a black line around it (Figure 7-9).

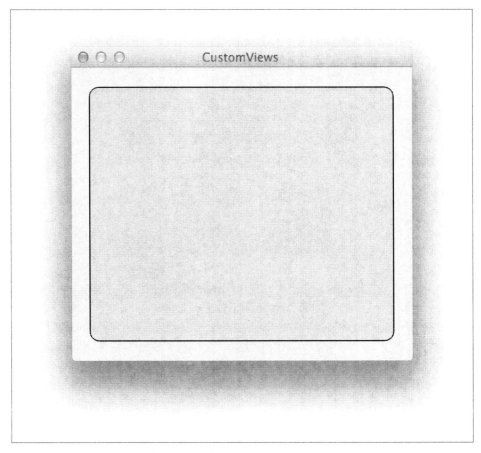

Figure 7-9. A stroked rounded rectangle

All drawing operations take place in the order in which you call them. In this code, we stroke the rectangle after filling it. If we instead swapped the order of the calls to [path fill] and [path stroke], we'd get a slightly different effect, with the green fill overlapping the black stroke slightly.

Creating Custom Paths

Creating paths using rectangles or rounded rectangles is useful, but you often want to create a shape that's entirely your own—a polygon, perhaps, or an outline of a character.

The NSBezierPath class is capable of representing any shape that can be defined using Bézier curves. You can create your own custom curves by creating a blank curve and then adding the control points that define the curve. Once you're done, you can use the finished NSBezierPath object to fill and stroke, just like any other path.

To create a custom path, you first create an empty path, and then start issuing commands to build it. As you build the path, you can imagine a virtual pen that you move around the canvas. You can:

- Move the pen to a point
- Draw a line from where the pen currently is to another point
- Draw a curve from where the pen currently is to another point, using two additional control points that define how the curve bends
- Close the path by drawing a line from where the pen currently is to the first point

We'll now updated our drawing code to draw a heart shape by replacing the drawRect method with the code below. Because this shape depends on specifying the locations of the various control points, there are quite a few numbers to type in here. Don't worry if you don't get them perfect—the shape should remain largely correct.

```
- (void)drawRect:(NSRect)dirtyRect
{
    NSBezierPath* bezierPath = [NSBezierPath bezierPath];
    [bezierPath moveToPoint: NSMakePoint(145.97, 241.04)];

    [bezierPath curveToPoint: NSMakePoint(248.61, 293.5)
        controlPoint1: NSMakePoint(145.97, 241.04)
        controlPoint2: NSMakePoint(155.7, 293.64)];

    [bezierPath curveToPoint: NSMakePoint(145.97, 11.51)
        controlPoint1: NSMakePoint(341.51, 293.36)
        controlPoint2: NSMakePoint(257.52, 13.23)];

    [bezierPath curveToPoint: NSMakePoint(47.48, 290.78)
        controlPoint1: NSMakePoint(34.42, 9.78)
        controlPoint2: NSMakePoint(-46.75, 290.73)];

    [bezierPath curveToPoint: NSMakePoint(145.97, 241.04)
        controlPoint1: NSMakePoint(141.72, 290.83)
        controlPoint2: NSMakePoint(145.97, 241.04)];

    [bezierPath closePath];

    [[NSColor redColor] setFill];
    [bezierPath fill];
```

```
    [[NSColor blackColor] setStroke];
    [bezierPath stroke];
}
```

Now run the application. The window will show a red heart shape (Figure 7-10).

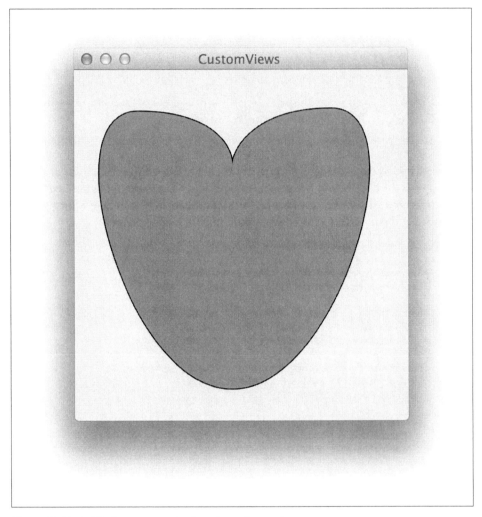

Figure 7-10. A filled custom path, showing a heart shape

Multiple Subpaths

So far, the paths that we've been drawing have contained only one *subpath*. A subpath is a connected series of points in a Bézier path. This means that you can have a path that contains two circles—every time you issued a stroke or fill command, you would be drawing those two circles.

Using subpaths is also a great way to create complex shapes. In this next example, we'll create a circle that contains a star-shaped hole in it. We'll do this by first creating a circular path, and then adding a star-shaped subpath. Replace the drawRect: method with the following code:

```
- (void)drawRect:(NSRect)dirtyRect
{
    //// Bezier Drawing
    NSBezierPath* bezierPath = [NSBezierPath bezierPath];

    // Draw the star.

    [bezierPath moveToPoint: NSMakePoint(42.5, 77.5)];
    [bezierPath lineToPoint: NSMakePoint(30.51, 60)];
    [bezierPath lineToPoint: NSMakePoint(10.16, 54.01)];
    [bezierPath lineToPoint: NSMakePoint(23.1, 37.2)];
    [bezierPath lineToPoint: NSMakePoint(22.52, 15.99)];
    [bezierPath lineToPoint: NSMakePoint(42.5, 23.1)];
    [bezierPath lineToPoint: NSMakePoint(62.48, 15.99)];
    [bezierPath lineToPoint: NSMakePoint(61.9, 37.2)];
    [bezierPath lineToPoint: NSMakePoint(74.84, 54.01)];
    [bezierPath lineToPoint: NSMakePoint(54, 60)];
    [bezierPath lineToPoint: NSMakePoint(42.5, 77.5)];
    [bezierPath closePath];

    // Draw the circle outside it.

    [bezierPath moveToPoint: NSMakePoint(70.64, 71.64)];

    [bezierPath curveToPoint: NSMakePoint(70.64, 14.36)
        controlPoint1: NSMakePoint(86.45, 55.82)
        controlPoint2: NSMakePoint(86.45, 30.18)];

    [bezierPath curveToPoint: NSMakePoint(13.36, 14.36)
        controlPoint1: NSMakePoint(54.82, -1.45)
        controlPoint2: NSMakePoint(29.18, -1.45)];

    [bezierPath curveToPoint: NSMakePoint(13.36, 71.64)
        controlPoint1: NSMakePoint(-2.45, 30.18)
        controlPoint2: NSMakePoint(-2.45, 55.82)];

    [bezierPath curveToPoint: NSMakePoint(70.64, 71.64)
        controlPoint1: NSMakePoint(29.18, 87.45)
        controlPoint2: NSMakePoint(54.82, 87.45)];
```

```
    [bezierPath closePath];

    // Fill the path.
    [[NSColor darkGrayColor] setFill];
    [bezierPath fill];
}
```

In this code, we're creating a new Bézier path and drawing a star by calling lineTo
Point: several times. We then close the subpath by sending the closePath message to
the path object, and begin constructing a circle around the star by moving to a new point
and issuing a bunch of curveToPoint: instructions. Once the circle is complete, the
subpath is closed again (Figure 7-11).

When two paths overlap, they cancel each other out. This means that you can create
negative shapes in a path rather easily, simply by overlapping several subpaths.

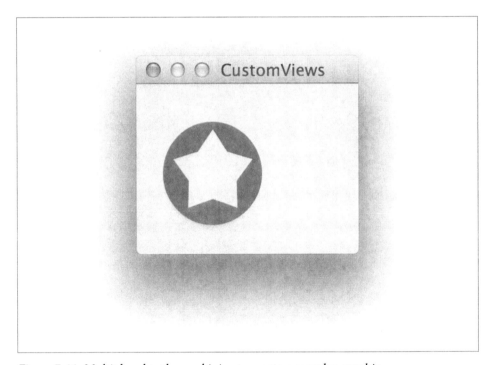

Figure 7-11. Multiple subpaths combining to create a complex graphic

Shadows

Shadows are a great way to imply depth in your graphics. If a shape casts a shadow, it
appears "closer" than one that does not.

On OS X, shadows are drawn using the `NSShadow` class. [On iOS, the technique is similar but not identical—see "Drawing shadows on iOS" (page 121).] An `NSShadow` object stores all of the information needed to draw a shadow. Three pieces of information are needed:

- The color to use for the shadow (an `NSColor`)
- How many pixels the shadow should be offset by (an `NSSize` struct)
- How blurry the shadow should be (a `CGFloat`)

To draw a shadow, you create an `NSShadow` object, provide it with the drawing settings you want to use, and then send it the `set` message:

```
NSShadow* shadow = [[NSShadow alloc] init]; // 1
[shadow setShadowColor: [NSColor blackColor]]; // 2
[shadow setShadowOffset: NSMakeSize(3, -3)]; // 3
[shadow setShadowBlurRadius: 5]; // 4

[shadow set]; // 5
```

This code does the following things:

1. Creates the shadow object.
2. Sets the color to black.
3. Sets the shadow offset to be drawn three pixels to the right, and three pixels down from what's drawn.
4. Sets the blur radius to be five pixels.
5. Sets the shadow. Anything drawn after this call will cast a shadow.

Saving and restoring graphics contexts

The `set` method causes the shadow to be applied to anything that you ask Cocoa to draw. This lasts until another shadow is set or the context is closed by the graphics system (which is what happens after the `drawRect:` call returns). This means that once you set a shadow, it could stay around forever.

However, you might want to draw an object with a shadow followed by an object that doesn't have one. To support this, and to help deal with similar cases where the graphics context itself is changed (such as when you set the stroke and fill color, or change the current transformation matrix or CTM—more on that in the section "Transforms" (page 126)), the drawing system allows you to save the state of the context and restore it later.

To save the graphics context, you send the `saveGraphicsState` message to the `NSGraphicsContext` class. This saves all of your drawing settings and pushes the context state onto a stack for you to retrieve later. It doesn't affect the pixels you've drawn, though.

```
[NSGraphicsContext saveGraphicsState];
```

When you're done, you retrieve the saved context state by sending the NSGraphicsCon text class the restoreGraphicsState message. This pops the most recently saved state from the stack, and restores its settings (such as the shadow and colors).

```
[NSGraphicsContext restoreGraphicsState];
```

 Always make sure to balance every call to saveGraphicsState with a call to restoreGraphicsState, or the usual behavior such as crashes may occur.

Drawing a shadow

We'll now update the drawing code to draw a circle with a shadow. Replace the drawRect: method with the following code:

```
- (void)drawRect:(NSRect)dirtyRect
{
    // Shadow Declarations
    NSShadow* shadow = [[NSShadow alloc] init];
    [shadow setShadowColor: [NSColor blackColor]];
    [shadow setShadowOffset: NSMakeSize(3, -3)];
    [shadow setShadowBlurRadius: 5];

    // Rectangle Drawing

    NSRect pathRect = NSInsetRect(self.bounds, 20, 20);

    NSBezierPath* rectanglePath = [NSBezierPath bezierPathWithRect: pathRect];
    [NSGraphicsContext saveGraphicsState];
    [shadow set];
    [[NSColor darkGrayColor] setFill];
    [rectanglePath fill];
    [NSGraphicsContext restoreGraphicsState];
}
```

This code starts by creating the NSShadow object and prepares it much like we saw above. A rectangular NSBezierPath object is also created. The code then saves the graphics state, sets the shadow, and fills the rectangle path. Once the drawing is done, the graphics state is restored. Any further drawing that's done won't include a shadow.

Now run the application. You'll see a box with a shadow (Figure 7-12).

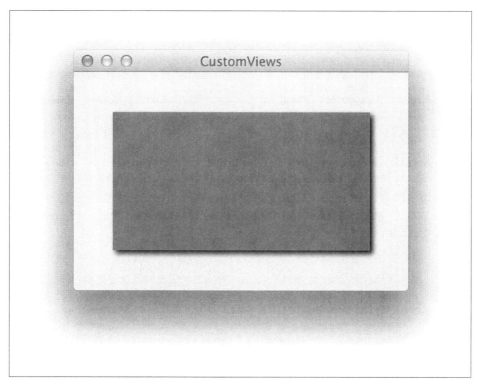

Figure 7-12. Drawing a shadow

Shadows are a tremendously useful tool for making your applications look great, but they are easy to make ugly. This isn't a design book, but we can't help but advise that you make your shadows look subtle. Please.

Drawing shadows on iOS

The NSShadow class exists only in OS X. The techniques for drawing shadows on iOS are similar, but instead of using Objective-C classes to draw the shadows, you use some C functions that belong to Core Graphics, the C-based drawing API that Cocoa wraps.

Here's the equivalent drawing code for drawing a shadow on iOS:

```
// General Declarations
CGContextRef context = UIGraphicsGetCurrentContext();

// Shadow Declarations
CGColorRef shadow = [UIColor blackColor].CGColor;
CGSize shadowOffset = CGSizeMake(3, 3);
CGFloat shadowBlurRadius = 5;
```

```
// Rectangle Drawing

CGRect pathRect = CGRectInset(self.bounds, 20, 20);

UIBezierPath* rectanglePath = [UIBezierPath bezierPathWithRect: pathRect];
CGContextSaveGState(context);
CGContextSetShadowWithColor(context, shadowOffset, shadowBlurRadius, shadow);
[[UIColor lightGrayColor] setFill];
[rectanglePath fill];
CGContextRestoreGState(context);
```

You'll note that instead of creating an Objective-C object, we instead store the settings in separate variables and then call the CGContextSetShadowWithColor function. Also, instead of calling saveGraphicsState and restoreGraphicsState like we do on OS X, we call CGContextSaveGState and CGContextRestoreGState. Otherwise, it's almost exactly the same.

 One other thing to note is that the shadow offset used on iOS is (3, 3) while on OS X it's (3, -3). That's because the coordinate system on iOS is flipped from that of OS X: on iOS, (0, 0) is the top-left corner and positive Y values advance down the screen, while on OS X, (0, 0) is the bottom-left corner and positive Y values advance up the screen.

Gradients

So far, we've worked entirely with solid colors when filling our shapes. However, the human eye quickly tires of seeing large blocks of solid color, and adding a gradient between two colors is a great way to add visual interest.

Drawing a gradient on OS X is much like drawing a shadow—you create an NSGradient object, and then set it up. However, instead of setting the gradient as a color, you instruct the gradient object to fill itself into a path object you provide. This is necessary because the gradient needs to know precisely where to start blending.

A gradient has at least two colors; when the gradient is drawn into an area, the area is filled with a smooth shade that blends between the gradient's colors. Each color also has a location, which controls how the blending is performed.

When you draw the gradient, you also specify the angle at which you want the gradient to be drawn. If you provide an angle of zero, the gradient draws from left to right, using each color you provide in sequence. If you provide an angle of 90 degrees, the gradient draws from bottom to top.

Drawing gradients on iOS is different, because you use Core Graphics C functions instead of using the NSGradient class. See "Drawing gradients on iOS" (page 124).

When constructing the gradient, the only information you need to provide is the list of colors and their positions. You do this with the initWithColorsAndLocations: method, which takes a comma-separated list of NSColor objects and their locations, terminated with nil.

```
NSColor* gradientStartColor = [NSColor whiteColor];
NSColor* gradientEndColor = [NSColor blackColor];

NSGradient* gradient = [[NSGradient alloc] initWithColorsAndLocations:
    [NSColor blackColor], 0.0,
    gradientStartColor, 0.0,
    gradientEndColor, 1.0, nil];
```

 Warning: Do not actually use these colors in a real app. Black-to-white gradients look *terrible*.

Then, when you want to draw the gradient, give it the shape you want it to fill. (You can also stroke shapes with gradients.)

```
[gradient drawInBezierPath: myPath angle: 90];
```

We'll now update the code to draw a gradient inside the custom view. Replace the drawRect: method with the following code:

```
- (void)drawRect:(NSRect)dirtyRect
{
    // Color Declarations
    NSColor* gradientStartColor = [NSColor colorWithCalibratedRed: 0.0
                                                            green: 0.2
                                                             blue: 0.7
                                                            alpha: 1];

    NSColor* gradientEndColor = [NSColor colorWithCalibratedRed: 0.3
                                                          green: 0.4
                                                           blue: 0.8
                                                          alpha: 1];

    // Gradient Declarations
    NSGradient* gradient = [[NSGradient alloc]
                initWithStartingColor: gradientStartColor
                          endingColor: gradientEndColor];

    // Rounded Rectangle Drawing

    NSRect pathRect = NSInsetRect(self.bounds, 20, 20);

    NSBezierPath* roundedRectanglePath = [NSBezierPath
```

```
                     bezierPathWithRoundedRect: pathRect xRadius: 4 yRadius: 4];

            [gradient drawInBezierPath: roundedRectanglePath angle: 90];
    }
```

Now run the application. You'll see a blue gradient (Figure 7-13).

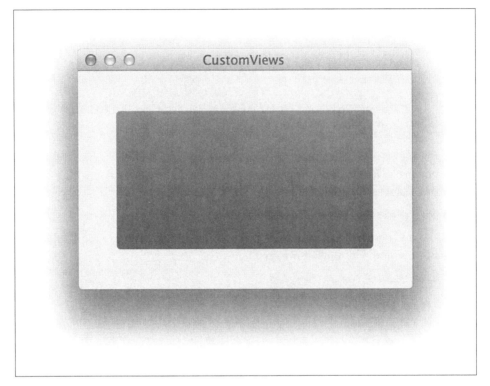

Figure 7-13. Drawing a gradient

Drawing gradients on iOS

On iOS, the process of drawing gradients is a little more verbose but conceptually the same. You still create an *object*, but it's done via the Core Graphics C function calls.

Instead of providing a path object to a gradient and asking the gradient to draw itself, you instead *clip* the current graphics context, and then draw the gradient from one point on the screen to another. Clipping means to restrict the drawing to a shape, which prevents the view from being completely filled with the gradient.

In addition, instead of providing an angle at which the gradient should be drawn, you pass in the coordinates converted into the coordinate space of the view that the gradient should be drawn from and to.

Here's the equivalent drawing code for iOS:

```
- (void) drawRect:(CGRect)dirtyRect {
    CGColorSpaceRef colorSpace = CGColorSpaceCreateDeviceRGB();
    CGContextRef context = UIGraphicsGetCurrentContext();

    //// Color Declarations
    UIColor* gradientStartColor = [UIColor colorWithRed: 0.0
                                                 green: 0.2
                                                  blue: 0.7
                                                 alpha: 1];

    UIColor* gradientEndColor = [UIColor colorWithRed: 0.3
                                               green: 0.4
                                                blue: 0.8
                                               alpha: 1];

    // Gradient Declarations
    NSArray* gradientColors = [NSArray arrayWithObjects:
        (id)gradientStartColor.CGColor,
        (id)gradientEndColor.CGColor, nil];
    CGFloat gradientLocations[] = {0, 1};
    CGGradientRef gradient = CGGradientCreateWithColors(colorSpace,
        (CFArrayRef)gradientColors, gradientLocations);


    // Rounded Rectangle Drawing

    CGRect pathRect = CGRectInset(self.bounds, 20, 20);

    CGPoint topPoint = CGPointMake(self.bounds.size.width / 2, 20);
    CGPoint bottomPoint = CGPointMake(self.bounds.size.width / 2,
        self.bounds.size.height - 20);

    UIBezierPath* roundedRectanglePath = [UIBezierPath
        bezierPathWithRoundedRect: pathRect cornerRadius: 4];
    CGContextSaveGState(context);
    [roundedRectanglePath addClip];
    CGContextDrawLinearGradient(context, gradient, bottomPoint, topPoint, 0);
    CGContextRestoreGState(context);

    // Cleanup
    CGGradientRelease(gradient);
    CGColorSpaceRelease(colorSpace);
}
```

Transforms

Drawing shapes is fine, but sometimes you want to be able to handle something slightly more complex, like rotating or stretching a shape. It's certainly possible to simply create a new path by providing a different set of coordinates, but it's often better to just ask the OS to do the rotation for you.

To do this, you use *transforms*, which are representations of transformation matrices. We won't go into the math of them in this book, but they're tools that can be used to translate, rotate, scale, skew, and generally perform any kind of distortion or manipulation of content.

All drawing that's done by your code is affected by the *current transform matrix* (CTM), which transforms every path and drawing operation that's performed. By default, the transform matrix is the *identity matrix*—that is, it doesn't do anything at all. However, the CTM can be modified to affect your drawing.

To modify the CTM, you first need a reference to the low-level drawing context. This context, which is set up for you by Cocoa before your `drawRect:` method is called, is a `CGContextRef` pointer, and not an Objective-C object. On OS X, you get the context with the following code:

```
CGContextRef context = [[NSGraphicsContext currentContext] graphicsPort];
```

On iOS, you get the context with this code:

```
CGContextRef context = UIGraphicsGetCurrentContext();
```

Once you have the context, you can change the CTM. In the following example, we'll change the CTM so that everything that gets drawn is rotated around the origin (the lower-left corner on OS X) by a few degrees.

 If you change the CTM, that change will stick around until the context's state is restored. If you only want to rotate part of your drawing, save the context's state before changing the CTM, and restore the state when you're done. See "Saving and restoring graphics contexts" (page 119).

Replace the `drawRect:` method with the following code:

```
- (void) drawRect:(NSRect)dirtyRect
    NSRect pathRect = NSInsetRect(self.bounds, 100, 100);

    // Create a transform that rotates the drawing by a
    // small amount around the origin point.
    CGAffineTransform rotationTransform =
        CGAffineTransformMakeRotation(M_PI / 8.0);

    CGContextRef context = [[NSGraphicsContext currentContext] graphicsPort];
```

```
NSBezierPath* path = [NSBezierPath bezierPathWithRoundedRect:pathRect
        xRadius:10 yRadius:10];

// Save the context before we start drawing
[NSGraphicsContext saveGraphicsState];

// Rotate
CGContextConcatCTM(context, rotationTransform);

[[NSColor greenColor] setFill];
[[NSColor blackColor] setStroke];
[path fill];
[path stroke];

// Restore the context.
[NSGraphicsContext restoreGraphicsState];

}
```

Now run the application. You'll see a green rectangle that's been rotated slightly (Figure 7-14).

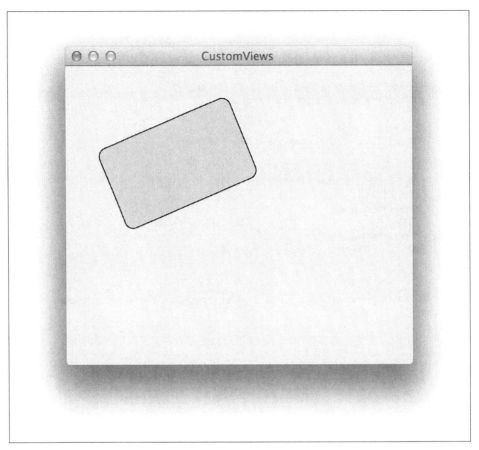

Figure 7-14. A rotated, stroked, filled rounded rectangle

CHAPTER 8

Audio and Video

As we've seen, Cocoa and Cocoa Touch have a lot of support for displaying still images and text. The APIs also have great support for displaying video and audio—either separately or at the same time.

OS X and iOS have historically had APIs for displaying audiovisual (AV) content, but it's only recently that Apple introduced a comprehensive API for loading, playing, and otherwise working with AV content. This API, *AV Foundation*, is identical on both OS X and iOS, and is the one-stop shop for both AV playback and editing.

In this chapter, you'll learn how to use AV Foundation to display video and audio. We'll demonstrate how to use the framework in OS X, but the same API applies to iOS as well.

You'll also learn how to access the user's photo library on iOS, as well as how to capture photos and videos using the built-in camera available on iOS and OS X.

 AV Foundation is a large, and powerful framework, capable of performing very complex operations with audio and video. Final Cut Pro, Apple's professional-level video editing tool, uses AV Foundation for all of the actual work involved in editing video. Covering all the features of this framework is beyond the scope of this book, so we address only audio and video playback in this chapter. If you want to learn about the more advanced features in AV Foundation, check out the *AV Foundation Programming Guide* in the Xcode documentation (*http://bit.ly/TQDmVg*).

AV Foundation

AV Foundation is designed to load and play back a large number of popular audiovisual formats. The formats supported by AV Foundation are:

- QuickTime
- MPEG4 audio (including .mp4, .m4a, and .m4v formats)
- 3GPP
- Wave, AIFF, and CAF audio
- MP3 and AAC audio

From a coding perspective, there's no distinction between these formats—you simply tell AV Foundation to load the resource, and start playing.

AV Foundation refers to media that can be played as an *asset*. Assets can be loaded from URLs—which can point to a resource on the Internet or a file stored locally—or they can be created from other assets (content creation apps, like iMovie, do this). In this chapter, we'll be looking at media loaded from URLs.

When you have a file you want to play—such as an H.264 movie or an MP3 file—you can create an AVPlayer to coordinate playback.

Playing Video with AVPlayer

The AVPlayer class is a high-level object that can play back any media that AV Foundation supports. AVPlayer is capable of playing both audio and video content, though if you only want to play back audio, AV Foundation provides an object dedicated to sound playback (AVAudioPlayer, discussed later). In this section, we talk about playing videos.

When you want to play back media, you create an AVPlayer and provide it with the URL of the video you want to play back:

```
NSURL* contentURL = /* an URL pointing to some video or audio */
AVPlayer* player = [AVPlayer playerWithURL:contentURL];
```

When you set up a player with a content URL, the player will take a moment to get ready to play back the content. The amount of time needed depends on the content and where it's being kept. If it's a video file, the decoder will take longer to get ready than for an audio file, and if the file is hosted on the Internet, it will take longer to transfer enough data to start playing.

AVPlayer acts as the controller for your media playback. At its simplest, you can tell the player to just start playing:

```
[player play];
```

In the background, the play method actually just sets the playback rate to 1.0, which means that it should play back at normal speed. You could also start playback at half-speed by saying [player setRate:0.5]. In the same vein, setting the rate to 0 pauses playback—which is exactly what the pause method does.

AVPlayerLayer

AVPlayer is only responsible for coordinating playback, not for displaying the video content to the user. If you want video playback to be visible, you need a Core Animation layer to display the content on.

AV Foundation provides a Core Animation layer called AVPlayerLayer that presents video content from the AVPlayer. Because it's a CALayer, you need to add it to an existing layer tree in order for it to be visible. We'll recap how to work with layers later in this chapter.

You create an AVPlayerLayer with the playerLayerWithPlayer: method:

```
AVPlayerLayer* playerLayer = [AVPlayerLayer playerLayerWithPlayer:player];
```

(Yes, we are now in tongue-twister territory.)

Once created, the player layer will display whatever image the AVPlayer you provided tells it to. It's up to you to actually size the layer appropriately and add it to the layer tree:

```
CALayer* parentLayer = /* a layer, usually one owned by a view in your window */
[parentLayer addSublayer:playerLayer];
playerLayer.frame = parentLayer.bounds; // make it fill its superlayer
```

Once the player layer is visible, you can forget about it—all of the actual work involved in controlling video playback is handled by the AVPlayer.

Putting It Together

To demonstrate how to use AVPlayer and AVPlayerLayer, we'll build a simple video player application for iOS.

 The same API applies to iOS and OS X.

Before you start building this project, download the sample video from here (*http://examples.oreilly.com/0636920023203/*).

1. *Create the application.*

   Create a new Cocoa application named **VideoPlayer**.

   Once the project has been created, you need to add the required frameworks. Select the VideoPlayer project at the top of the project navigator; the project information will open in the main editor.

   Click the + button underneath the list of frameworks in the Linked Frameworks and Libraries section.

   Add the AVFoundation, CoreMedia, and QuartzCore frameworks to the projects.

   Drag the sample video into the project navigator.

   The interface for this project will consist of an NSView, which will host the AVPlayer Layer, as well as buttons that make the video play back at normal speed, play back at one-quarter speed, and rewind.

In order to add the AVPlayerLayer into the view, that view must be backed by a CALayer. This requires checking a checkbox in the Interface Builder—once that's done, the view will have a layer, to which we can add the AVPlayerLayer as a sublayer.

2. *Create the interface.*

   Open *MainWindow.xib*.

   Drag a custom view into the main window. Make it fill the window, but leave some space at the bottom. This view will contain the video playback layer.

   Drag in three NSButtons and place them underneath the video playback view. Label them **Play**, **Play Slow Motion**, and **Rewind**.

To add an AVPlayerLayer to the window, the view that it's being inserted into must have its own CALayer. To make this happen, you tell either the video playback view or any of its superviews that it should use a CALayer. Once a view has a CALayer, it and all of its subviews use CALayers to display their content.

3. *Make the window use a CALayer.*

   Click inside the window and open the View Effects inspector, which is the last button at the top of the inspector.

   The Core Animation Layer section of the inspector will list the selected view. Check the checkbox to give it a layer (Figure 8-1).

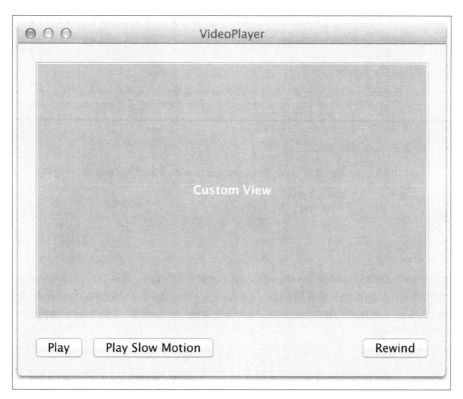

Figure 8-1. The completed interface for this application, as laid out in the interface builder.

4. *Connect the code to the interface.*

   Now that the interface is laid out correctly, we'll make the code aware of the view that the video should be displayed in, and create the actions that control playback.

   Open *AppDelegate.h* in the assistant.

   Control-drag from the video container view into `AppDelegate`'s interface. Create an outlet called **playerView**.

   Control-drag from each of the buttons underneath the video container view into `AppDelegate`'s interface, and create actions for each of them. Name these actions **play**, **playSlowMotion**, and **rewind**.

Now we'll write the code that loads and prepares the `AVPlayer` and `AVPlayerLayer`. Because we want to control the player, we'll keep a reference to it around by adding a class extension that contains an instance variable to store the `AVPlayer`. We don't need to keep the `AVPlayerLayer` around in the same way, because once we add it to the layer tree, we can forget about it—it will just display whatever the `AVPlayer` needs to show.

We'll also need to import the AV Foundation and Quartz Core framework headers in order to work with the necessary classes.

5. *Import the headers.*

   Add the following code to the import statements at the top of *AppDelegate.m*:

   ```
   #import <AVFoundation/AVFoundation.h>
   #import <QuartzCore/QuartzCore.h>
   ```

6. *Add the class extension.*

   Add the following code to *AppDelegate.m* above the `@implementation` line:

   ```
   @interface AppDelegate () {
       AVPlayer* player;
   }

   @end
   ```

Next, we'll create and set up the `AVPlayer` and `AVPlayerLayer`. To set up the `AVPlay` `er`, you need something to play. In this case, we'll make the application determine the location of the test video that was compiled into the application's folder, and give that to the `AVPlayer`.

Once the `AVPlayer` is ready, we can create the `AVPlayerLayer`. The `AVPlayerLayer` needs to be added to the video player view's layer and resized to fill the layer. Setting the `frame` property of the layer accomplishes this. As a final touch, we'll also make the layer automatically resize when its superlayer resizes.

Finally, we'll tell the `AVPlayer` that it should pause when it reaches the end of playback.

7. *Set up the AVPlayer.*

   Replace the `applicationDidFinishLaunching:` method in *AppDelegate.m* with the following code:

   ```
   - (void)applicationDidFinishLaunching:(NSNotification *)aNotification
   {
       NSURL* contentURL = [[NSBundle mainBundle] URLForResource:@"TestVideo"
           withExtension:@"m4v"];
       player = [AVPlayer playerWithURL:contentURL];

       AVPlayerLayer* playerLayer =
       [AVPlayerLayer playerLayerWithPlayer:player];
       [self.playerView.layer addSublayer:playerLayer];
       playerLayer.frame = self.playerView.layer.bounds;
       playerLayer.autoresizingMask = kCALayerWidthSizable |
           kCALayerHeightSizable;
   ```

```
        player.actionAtItemEnd = AVPlayerActionAtItemEndNone;
    }
```

The last step in coding the application is to create the control methods, which are run when the buttons are clicked. These controls—play, play in slow motion, and rewind—simply tell the `AVPlayer` to set the rate of playback. In the case of rewinding, it's a matter of telling the player to seek to the start.

8. *Add the control methods.*

    Replace the `play:`, `playSlowMotion:`, and `rewind:` methods in *AppDelegate.m* with the following code:

    ```
    - (IBAction)play:(id)sender {
        [player play];
    }

    - (IBAction)playSlowMotion:(id)sender {
        [player setRate:0.25];
    }

    - (IBAction)rewind:(id)sender {
        [player seekToTime:kCMTimeZero];
    }
    @end
    ```

It's time to test the app, so go ahead and launch it. Play around with the buttons and resize the window. Video should be visible in the window, as seen in Figure 8-2.

Playing Sound with AVAudioPlayer

`AVPlayer` is designed for playing back any kind of audio or video. AV Foundation also provides a class specifically designed for playing back sounds, called `AVAudioPlayer`.

`AVAudioPlayer` is a simpler choice than AVPlayer for playing audio. It's useful for playing back sound effects and music in apps that don't use video, and has a couple of advantages over `AVPlayer`:

- `AVAudioPlayer` allows you to set volumes on a per-player basis (`AVPlayer` uses the system volume)
- `AVAudioPlayer` is easier to loop
- You can query an `AVAudioPlayer` for its current output power, which you can use to show volume levels over time

Figure 8-2. Playing back video

AVAudioPlayer works in the same way as AVPlayer. Given an NSURL that points to a sound file that OS X or iOS supports, you create an AVAudioPlayer, set it up the way you want (by setting balance, volume, and looping), and then play it.

```
NSURL* soundFileURL = /* a local or remote URL */
NSError* error = nil;
AVAudioPlayer* player = [[AVAudioPlayer alloc] initWithContentURL:soundFileURL
    error:error];

// if there was a problem, 'player' is nil and
// 'error' contains additional info
```

 You need to keep a strong reference to AVAudioPlayer, or it will be removed from memory and stop playing. Therefore, you should keep an instance variable around that stores a reference to the player to keep it from falling out of memory.

Telling an `AVAudioPlayer` to play is a simple matter:

```
[player play];
```

You can also set the volume and indicate how many times the sound should loop. The volume is a number between 0 and 1. The number of loops defaults to 0 (play once); if you set it to 1, it will play twice. Set the number of loops to –1 to make the sound loop forever until stopped.

```
player.volume = 0.5; // half-volume
player.numberOfLoops = -1; // loop forever
```

To seek to a point in the sound, set the `currentTime` property. This property is measured in seconds, so to seek to the start of the sound, set `currentTime` to 0.

```
player.currentTime = 0; // seek to the start
```

Seeking to a point in the sound doesn't affect whether the sound is playing or not. If you seek while the sound is playing, the sound will jump.

Working with the Photo Library

In addition to playing back video and audio, iOS and OS X allow you to access the built-in camera system to capture video and audio. Similar hardware is available on both systems—in fact, Apple refers to the front-facing camera on the iPhone, iPad, and all Mac machines as the "FaceTime camera," suggesting that users are meant to treat the camera the same way across all devices. The camera can record still images as well as video.

The APIs for accessing the camera are different on OS X and iOS. The camera was introduced on the Mac well before iOS was released, and iOS's implementation is somewhat easier to use and cleaner, since the API benefited from several years of development experience.

 If you really need a consistent API for recording camera content across both iOS and OS X, AV Foundation provides a set of classes for capturing content, the key ones including `AVCaptureSession`, `AVCaptureInput` and `AVCaptureOutput`. However, this system is designed for much finer-grained control over data flows from the camera to consumers of that data, and isn't terribly convenient for simple uses like recording video and saving it to a file. In this chapter, therefore, we'll only be covering the iOS implementation. For OS X developers, please refer to the *QTKit Application Tutorial*, included in the Xcode documentation.

Capturing Photos and Video from the Camera

To capture video and photos from the camera on iOS, you use a view controller called `UIImagePickerController`.

 For more information on view controllers, see "Structure of a Nib File" (page 75).

At its simplest, `UIImagePickerController` allows you to present an interface almost identical to the built-in camera application on the iPhone and iPad. Using this interface, the user can take a photo that is delivered to your application as a `UIImage` object.

You can also configure the `UIImagePickerController` to capture video. In this case the user can record up to 30 minutes of video and deliver it to your application as an `NSString` that contains the path to where the captured video file is kept.

`UIImagePickerController` can be set up to control which camera is used (front-side or back-side camera), whether the LED flashlight is available (on devices that have them), and whether the user is allowed to crop or adjust the photo he took or trim the video he recorded.

`UIImagePickerController` works like this:

1. You create an instance of the class.
2. You optionally configure the picker to use the settings that you want.
3. You provide the picker with a delegate object that conforms to the `UIImagePicker ControllerDelegate` protocol.
4. You present the view controller, usually modally, by having the current view controller call `presentViewController:animated:completion:`.
5. The user takes a photo or records a video. When he's done, the delegate object receives the `imagePickerController:didFinishPickingMediaWithInfo:` message.

   This method receives a dictionary that contains information about the media that the user captured, which you can query to retrieve data like the original or edited photos, the location of the video file, and other useful information.

   In this method, your view controller must dismiss the image picker controller, by calling the `dismissViewControllerAnimated:completion:` method on the current view controller.

6. If the user chooses to cancel the image picker (by tapping the Cancel button that appears), the delegate object receives the `imagePickerControllerDidCancel:` message.

In this method, your view controller must also dismiss the image picker by calling `dismissViewControllerAnimated:completion:`. If this doesn't happen, the Cancel button won't appear to do anything when tapped, and the user will think that your application is buggy.

When using `UIImagePickerController`, it's important to remember that the hardware on the device your app is running on may vary. Not all devices have a front-facing camera, which was only introduced in the iPhone 4 and the iPad 2; on earlier devices, you can only use the rear-facing camera. Some devices don't have a camera at all, such as the early iPod touch models and the first iPad.

You can use `UIImagePickerController` to determine which features are available and adjust your app's behavior accordingly. For example, to determine if any kind of camera is available, you use the `isSourceTypeAvailable:` class method:

```
if ([UIImagePickerController
     isSourceTypeAvailable:UIImagePickerControllerSourceTypeCamera]) {
    // a camera exists on this device
} else {
    // we can't use the camera
}
```

You can further specify if a front- or rear-facing camera is available, using the class method `isCameraDeviceAvailable::`:

```
if ([UIImagePickerController
    isCameraDeviceAvailable:UIImagePickerControllerCameraDeviceFront]) {
    // a front facing camera is available
}

if ([UIImagePickerController
    isCameraDeviceAvailable:UIImagePickerControllerCameraDeviceRear) {
    // a rear facing camera is available
}
```

 The iOS simulator does not have a camera, and `UIImagePicker Controller` reports this. If you want to test out using the camera, you must test your app on a device that actually has a camera built-in. This doesn't stop you from using `UIImagePickerController` itself, since you can still access the user's saved photos library. We'll be talking about this in more detail in the next section.

Building a Photo Application

To demonstrate how to use `UIImagePickerController`, we'll build a simple application that allows the user to take a photo, which is then displayed on the screen. The image picker will be configured to take only photos, and will use the front-facing camera if it's available and the rear-facing camera if it's not.

1. *Create the application.* Create a single-view iPhone application and name it **Photos**.

    The interface for this application will be deliberately simple: a button that brings up the camera view, and an image view that displays the photo that the user took.

2. *Create the interface.* Open *MainStoryboard.storyboard*.

    Drag a `UIImageView` into the main screen. Resize it so that it takes up the top half of the screen.

    Drag a `UIButton` into the main screen and place it under the image view. Make the button's label read **Take Photo**.

3. *Connect the interface to the code.* Open *ViewController.h* in the assistant.

    Control-drag from the image view into `ViewController`'s interface. Create an outlet called **imageView**.

    Control-drag from the button into `ViewController`'s interface. Create an action called **takePhoto**.

4. *Make the view controller conform to* the `UIImagePickerControllerDelegate` *and* `UINavigationControllerDelegate` *protocols.*

    Update the `@interface` line in *ViewController.h* to look like the following code:

    ```
    @interface ViewController : UIViewController
        <UIImagePickerControllerDelegate, UINavigationController>
    ```

5. *Add the code that shows the image picker.*

    When the button is tapped, we need to create, configure, and present the image picker view. Replace the `takePhoto:` method with the following code:

    ```
    - (IBAction)takePhoto:(id)sender {

        UIImagePickerController* picker = [[UIImagePickerController alloc] init];

        if ([UIImagePickerController
            isSourceTypeAvailable:UIImagePickerControllerSourceTypeCamera]) {

            // We can use the camera.
            picker.sourceType = UIImagePickerControllerSourceTypeCamera;

            // Use the front-facing camera if available.
            if ([UIImagePickerController
                isCameraDeviceAvailable:
    ```

```
                UIImagePickerControllerCameraDeviceFront])
            picker.cameraDevice = UIImagePickerControllerCameraDeviceFront;
        else
            picker.cameraDevice = UIImagePickerControllerCameraDeviceFront;

        // Make this object be the delegate
        picker.delegate = self;

        [self presentViewController:picker animated:YES completion:nil];
    }
}
```

6. *Add the* `UIImagePickerControllerDelegate` *methods.*

   We now need to add the methods for `UIImagePickerControllerDelegate`—
   specifically, the one called when the user finishes taking a photo, and the one called
   when the user cancels taking a photo.

   Add the following methods to *ViewController.m*:

```
- (void)imagePickerController:(UIImagePickerController *)picker
    didFinishPickingMediaWithInfo:(NSDictionary *)info {


    UIImage* image = [info
    objectForKey:UIImagePickerControllerOriginalImage];
    self.imageView.image = image;

    [picker dismissViewControllerAnimated:YES completion:nil];

}

- (void)imagePickerControllerDidCancel:(UIImagePickerController *)picker {
    [picker dismissViewControllerAnimated:YES completion:nil];
}
```

Now run the application and test it out on an iPhone or iPad. Take a photo of yourself,
and see that it appears in the image view.

If you try to test out the application on the iOS simulator, the button won't appear to do
anything at all. That's because the `if` statement in the `takePhoto:` method keeps the
image picker from trying to work with hardware that isn't there.

 If you ask `UIImagePickerController` to work with a camera and there
isn't one present on the device, an exception will be thrown and your
application will crash.

The Photo Library

Capturing a photo with the camera is useful, but the user will likely also want to work with photos that he's previously taken or downloaded from the Internet. For example, a social networking application should include some method of sharing photos from the user's photo collection.

To let the user access his photo library from within your app, you use UIImagePicker Controller again. If you want to present the photo library instead of the camera, set the sourceType property of the image picker to UIImagePickerControllerSourceTy pePhotoLibrary or UIImagePickerControllerSourceTypeSavedPhotosAlbum.

 UIImagePickerControllerSourceTypePhotoLibrary makes the UIIm agePickerController display the entire photo library. UIImagePicker ControllerSourceTypeSavedPhotosAlbum makes the UIImagePicker Controller display only the Camera Roll album on devices that have a camera, or the Saved Photos album on devices that don't.

When you present an image picker controller that has been set up to use a noncamera source, the photo library interface used in the built-in Photos application appears. The user then browses for and selects a photo, at which point the image picker's delegate receives the imagePickerController:didFinishPickingMediaWithInfo: message, just like if the image picker had been set up to use the camera.

To demonstrate this, we'll update the application to include a button that displays the Saved Photos album.

1. *Update the interface.*

   Add a new button to the application's main screen and make its label read **Photo Library**.

2. *Connect the interface to the code.*

   Open *ViewController.h* in the assistant again. Control-drag from the new button into ViewController's interface, and create a new action called **loadFromLibrary**.

3. *Add the code.*

   Replace the loadFromLibrary: method in *ViewController.m* with the following code:

```
- (IBAction)loadFromLibrary:(id)sender {

    UIImagePickerController* picker = [[UIImagePickerController alloc] init];
    picker.sourceType = UIImagePickerControllerSourceTypeSavedPhotosAlbum;

    picker.delegate = self;
    [self presentViewController:picker animated:YES completion:nil];

}
```

Test the application by running the app and tapping the Photo Library button. Select a photo to make it appear on the screen.

Adding Photos to the Simulator

If you're testing this in the simulator, you'll want to add photos to its built-in photo library. However, there's no built-in tool for adding photos to the "device" like there is with a real device and iTunes. To add a photo to the simulator, you can use Safari:

1. Find the image file you want to use and drag it into the simulator's window. The image will open in Safari.
2. Tap and hold the image. A menu will appear; choose Save Image.
3. The image will be saved in the Saved Photos album, which you can then access in your application via a UIImagePickerController.

CHAPTER 9

Model Objects and Data Storage

Unless your application is a trivial one, it will need at some point to work with data. This data could be as simple as a list of high scores that the user has achieved, or as complex as a multimedia document like a presentation.

This information needs to be accessible to other parts of your application, such as the controller objects, so that work can be done on it. The information needs to be stored somewhere—either in memory, on disk, or on the network.

OS X and iOS provide tools for storing information on disk and on the network. One of the more recent additions to the APIs available to developers is *iCloud*, a network-based storage system that is designed to allow users to keep the same information on all their devices, without having to do any work to enable this.

Additionally, Cocoa is designed to make the connection between the model, the view and the controller as flexible as possible, while at the same time reducing the amount of code that you need to write. To this end, Cocoa uses features called *key-value coding*, which allows you to refer to properties of objects by name rather than by hardcoding method calls, and *key-value observing*, which allows you to have an object be notified when another object changes the value of one of its properties.

In this chapter, you will learn how key-value coding and key-value observing work, why they're useful, and how to use them in your code. You will also learn how to work with the filesystem to store your information on disk. You'll learn how to work with iCloud storage to store files in the cloud. Finally, you'll learn how the sandbox works on OS X, and how to use security-scoped bookmarks to allow your application to access data outside its sandbox across multiple launches.

While iCloud provides the means for storing files and folders in the cloud, you also need to know how to present documents to the user. This chapter only covers the mechanics of storing the data; to learn more about how to write a document-based application on OS X and iOS, head to Chapter 12.

Key-Value Coding

Key-value coding is a feature of Cocoa that allows you to set and get values of objects by name, rather than by explicitly calling the appropriate methods. As long as your classes follow a few simple rules for naming your properties and methods, you can refer to the data inside your classes using strings rather than by calling methods. This feature is used by several other parts of Cocoa, most notably Core Data.

Let's assume that you have an application that retrieves information about products from somewhere (such as the network). This application represents each product as the following class:

```
@interface Product : NSObject

@property (strong) NSString* productName;
@property (assign) float price;
@property (strong) NSString* stockCode;
@property (assign) int numberInStock;

@end
```

The application receives NSDictionaries, which it must then turn into instances of the Product class. One such method of doing so would be this:

```
- (Product*) productWithDictionary:(NSDictionary*)dictionary {
    Product* aProduct = [[Product alloc] init];

    aProduct.productName = [dictionary objectForKey:@"productName"];
    aProduct.price = [[dictionary objectForKey:@"price"] floatValue];
    aProduct.stockCode = [dictionary objectForKey:@"stockCode"];
    aProduct.numberInStock = [[dictionary
                            objectForKey:@"numberInStock"] intValue];

    return aProduct;
}
```

This method is quite repetitious, and if you wanted to add extra properties to the class, you would need to add more code. Additionally, if the dictionary passed to the product WithDictionary: method happened to not contain one of the values—perhaps the stockCode value was not set—the application would crash when objectFor Key:@"stockCode" is called.

Another way of doing the same thing is this:

```
+ (Product*) productWithDictionary:(NSDictionary*)dictionary {
    Product* aProduct = [[Product alloc] init];

    for (NSString* key in dictionary) {
        NSObject* theValue = [dictionary objectForKey:key];
        [aProduct setValue:theValue forKey:key];
    }

    return aProduct;
}
```

By calling setValue:forKey:, you can set the value of any property by name, given as a string. This is more flexible than directly calling the setter and getter methods, since strings can be constructed and modified at runtime.

Key-Value Coding Gotchas

Key-value coding has a few gotchas.

- If you try to set a value for a key that does not exist in your class, the key-value coding system will throw an exception because the runtime won't know where to store the value.

- There is no access protection in key-value coding, and your class doesn't even need to expose a protocol for it to work—it still works when used on private variables.

  It's possible for another object to reach inside your class and change data inside it. Note that doing so is a very bad idea for both objects involved, since it bypasses the usual compile-time checks. Use key-value coding with care!

To get the value of a property from an object, you can use the valueForKey: method:

```
// aProduct is a Product object
NSString* productName = [aProduct valueForKey:@"productName"];

// This is exactly the same as:
NSString* productName = aProduct.productName;

// Which is also the same as:
NSString* productName = [aProduct productName];
```

Key-value coding is not designed to replace accessor methods, but rather exists to provide a more flexible way to set and get values in objects.

Key-Value Observing

Consider the following common scenario. You have a view on the screen—a text field, say—that displays some information that is drawn from the model. In the model-view-controller design pattern, the controller is responsible for knowing when information in the model changes and instructing the view to update its display to reflect it. But how does the controller know when to update the view?

There are two options available: repeatedly checking the model to see if anything has changed, or waiting for the model to inform the controller of changes. The first option is the simplest to implement—create a timer that periodically gets the latest value from the model, and provide that to the view. The problem with this technique, though, is that it's wasteful—if the model does not change often, most of the updates will be redundant, which wastes time and CPU resources. On a battery-powered device, using the CPU more than you have to wastes the battery.

To solve this problem, Cocoa provides a feature called *key-value observing*. Key-value observing allows an object to register to be notified when another object changes the value of one of its properties. In the above scenario, the controller would ask the model object for notification when the data changes; when the controller receives the message from the model, the view is updated. This keeps the number of updates to the minimum.

Key-value observing helps to simplify the process of registering for notifications, and for notifying any objects that need to be told of changes. Any property on any object can be observed, as long as that property's name is key-value coding compliant.

Registering for Change Notifications

When you register to be notified of changes, you tell the object you wish to observe three things: the object that should be notified when the property changes, the name of the property that should be observed, and the information the observer should be told about when a change happens. Optionally, you can also include a pointer or object reference that should be passed to the method that is run when the property changes value.

Here's an example of how to register to be notified when a `Product` object changes its price:

```
// aProduct is a Product object

// Make this current object (self) be notified when the product
//   changes its price; we want to be notified of both the old
// value and the new value
[aProduct addObserver:self
          forKeyPath:@"productName"
             options:(NSKeyValueObservingOptionNew |
               NSKeyValueObservingOptionOld)
             context:nil];
```

When an object is registered as an observer of another object, that object receives the `observeValueForKeyPath:ofObject:change:context:` message. This message has as its parameters:

- The key path of the property that changed
- The object whose property changed
- An `NSDictionary` that contains information about the change
- The context variable that was passed in when `addObserver:forKeyPath:op tions:context:` was called

The `NSDictionary` contains different information depending on what options were passed in when the observer was added. If the options included `NSKeyValue ObservingOptionNew`, the dictionary contains a value with the `NSKeyValueChange NewKey` key, whose object is the value that the property has been set to. Conversely, if the `NSKeyValueObservingOptionOld` option was set when registering the observer, the dictionary contains a value with the `NSKeyValueChangeOldKey` key, which you can use to get the previous value of the property.

 These aren't the only keys that can exist in the change dictionary—for example, if the property that you are observing is an `NSArray` or other collection object, you can be notified when an object is added or removed from the collection. For more information, refer to the *Key-Value Observing Guide* in the Xcode documentation (*http://bit.ly/SGDWru*).

Here's an example of how an object can handle a `Product` object changing its `product Name` property:

```
- (void)observeValueForKeyPath:(NSString *)keyPath
                      ofObject:(id)object
                        change:(NSDictionary *)change
                       context:(void *)context
{
    if ([keyPath isEqualToString:@"productName"]) {

        NSString* newName = [change objectForKey:NSKeyValueChangeNewKey];

        // tell the appropriate view to update, based on the newName variable.
    }
}
```

Notifying Observers of Changes

In order for the key-value observation system to work, objects need to notify their observers when their properties change.

If you are using Objective-C properties (that is, you declare your properties with the @property syntax and have the compiler synthesize the accessor methods), Cocoa will automatically notify any registered observers when the setter methods are called.

If you aren't using Objective-C properties, or if you override the setter methods for a property, you need to manually notify the system of the changes that are being made. To do this, you call the willChangeValueForKey: and didChangeValueForKey: methods on the self object. This allows the key-value observing system to keep track of the previous and new values of a property.

For example, here's how to override the productName setter method while still allowing key-value observing to work:

```
- (void) setProductName:(NSString*)newProductName {
    [self willChangeValueForKey:@"productName"];
    productName = newProductName;
    [self didChangeValueForKey:@"productName"];
}
```

Notifications with NSNotification

In addition to having objects be notified of changes in properties, it's also often useful to broadcast notifications to any interested application when something of relevance happens.

For example, when the user presses the home button on an iOS device, the only object that receives a notification by default is the application delegate, which receives the applicationDidEnterBackground: message. However, objects in the application may wish to be notified of events like this, and while it's possible for the application delegate to do something like maintain an array of objects to send messages to when an app-wide event takes place, it can be cumbersome.

Enter the NSNotification class. NSNotification objects, or *notifications* for short, are broadcast messages sent by an object to any other object that has registered to be notified of such notifications. Notifications are managed by the NSNotificationCenter, which is a singleton object that manages the delivery of notifications.

Notifications are created by the object that wants to broadcast, or *post*, the notification. The NSNotification object is given to the notification center, which then delivers the notification to all objects that have registered for that notification type.

When an object wants to start receiving notifications, it first needs to know the name of the notification it wants to be told about. There are hundreds of different notification types; to carry on our earlier example, the specific notification posted when the application enters the background is `UIApplicationDidEnterBackgroundNotification`.

Therefore, to register for this notification, all an object needs to do is this:

```
[[NSNotificationCenter defaultCenter] addObserver:self
    selector:@selector(applicationEnteredBackground:)
    UIApplicationDidEnterBackgroundNotification object:nil];
```

Then, whenever a `UIApplicationDidEnterBackgroundNotification` is posted, the object that registered with the notification center will run its `applicationEnteredBack ground:` method. This method needs to be a part of that object—if it doesn't exist, the application will throw an exception.

Notification handler methods take one parameter: the `NSNotification` object that was posted. This is useful, since `NSNotification` objects can contain additional contextual information about why they were posted:

```
- (void) applicationEnteredBackground:(NSNotification*)notification {
    // Application entered background, so do something about it!
}
```

Finally, when an object no longer wishes to receive notifications, it can contact the notification center and remove itself:

```
[[NSNotificationCenter defaultCenter] removeObserver:self]
```

Preferences

Most applications need to store some information about the user's preferences. For example, if you open the Safari web browser and go to its preferences (by pressing ⌘-, [comma] or choosing Safari→Preferences), you'll see a rather large collection of settings that the user can modify. Because these settings need to remain set when the application exits, they need to be stored somewhere.

The `NSUserDefaults` class allows you to store settings information in a key-value based way. You don't need to handle the process of loading and reading in a settings file, and preferences are automatically saved.

To access preferences stored in `NSUserDefaults`, you need an instance of the `NSUser Defaults` class. To get one, you ask the `NSUserDefaults` class for the `standardUserDe faults`:

```
NSUserDefaults* defaults = [NSUserDefaults standardUserDefaults];
```

It's also possible to allocate and initialize a new NSUserDefaults object instead of using the standard user defaults. You only need to do this if you want more control over exactly whose preferences are being accessed. For example, if you are creating an application that manages multiple users on a Mac and accesses their preferences, you can create an NSUserDefaults object for each user's preferences.

Registering Default Preferences

When your application obtains a preferences object for the first time (that is, on the first launch of your application), that preferences object is empty. In order to create default values, you need to provide a dictionary containing the defaults to the defaults object.

 The word *default* gets tossed around quite a lot when talking about the defaults system. To clarify:

- A *defaults object* is an instance of the class NSUserDefaults.
- A *default* is a setting inside the defaults object.
- A *default value* is a setting used by the defaults object when no other value has been set. (This is the most common meaning of the word when talking about non-Cocoa environments.)

To register default values in the defaults object, you first need to create an NSDiction ary. The keys of this dictionary are the same as the names of the preferences, and the values associated with these keys are the default values of these settings.

You can create this dictionary using either the methods discussed in "Dictionaries" (page 47) in Chapter 3, or by loading a dictionary from a file. Once you have the dictionary, you provide it to the defaults object with the registerDefaults: method.

 All items in a defaults object must be NSObjects. This means that numbers and other non-object values need to be wrapped in NSNumber or NSValue objects.

```
// Create the default values dictionary
NSDictionary* defaultValues =
  [NSDictionary dictionaryWithObjectsAndKeys:
    @"hello", "greeting", [NSNumber numberWithInt: 1], @"numberOfItems"];

// Provide this dictionary to the defaults object
[[NSUserDefaults standardUserDefaults] registerDefaults:defaultValues];
```

Once this is done, you can ask the defaults object for values.

 The defaults that you register with the registerDefaults: method are not saved on disk, which means that you need to call this every time your application starts up. Defaults that you set in your application [see "Setting Preferences" (page 154)] are saved, however.

Accessing Preferences

Once created, an NSUserDefaults object can be treated much like a dictionary, with a few restrictions. You can retrieve a value from the defaults object by using the object ForKey: method:

```
// Retrieve a string with the key "greeting" from the defaults object
NSString* greeting = [[NSUserDefaults standardUserDefaults]
                    objectForKey:@"greeting"];
```

However, unlike an NSDictionary, only a few kinds of objects can be stored in a defaults object. The only objects that can be stored in a defaults object are *property list objects*, which are:

- NSString
- NSArray
- NSDictionary
- NSData
- NSNumber
- NSDate

If you need to store any other kind of object in a defaults object, you should first convert it to an NSData by archiving it (see "Serialization and Deserialization" (page 52) in Chapter 3).

Everything stored in an NSUserDefaults needs to be an NSObject. That means that if you want to get an integer from an NSUserDefaults, what you get back is an NSNum ber object that contains the number:

```
// Get the NSNumber from the settings database
NSNumber* integerSetting = [[NSUserDefaults standardUserDefaults]
        objectForKey:@"integerSetting"];

// Extract the number from the NSNumber
int theInteger = [integerSetting intValue];
```

Because values stored in an `NSUserDefaults` object are often things like numbers or Boolean values, `NSUserDefaults` provides a number of convenience methods for accessing non-object values directly:

```
int integerSetting = [[NSUserDefaults standardUserDefaults]
    integerForKey:@"integerSetting"];
float floatSetting = [[NSUserDefaults standardUserDefaults]
    floatForKey:@"floatSetting"];
BOOL booleanSetting = [[NSUserDefaults standardUserDefaults]
    boolForKey:@"booleanSetting"];
```

 Additional methods exist for retrieving values from an `NSUser Defaults` object. For more information, see the *Preferences and Settings Programming Guide*, available in the Xcode documentation (*http:// bit.ly/SQznt7*).

Setting Preferences

In addition to retrieving values from a defaults object, you can also set values. When you set a value in an `NSUserDefaults` object, that value is kept around forever (until the application is removed from the system).

To set an object in an `NSUserDefaults` object, you use the `setObject:forKey:` method, just as you would with an `NSMutableDictionary`:

```
NSString* greeting = @"hello"
[[NSUserDefaults standardUserDefaults] setObject:greeting forKey:@"greeting"];
```

As noted above, you can only set `NSObject` values in an `NSUserDefaults` object. However, `NSUserDefaults` provides a number of convenience methods for wrapping non-object values in `NSNumber`s:

```
// yam count, saved as an integer
[[NSUserDefaults standardUserDefaults] setInteger:32 forKey:@"numberOfYams"];

// yam appreciation index, saved as a floating-point number
[[NSUserDefaults standardUserDefaults] setFloat:0.98 forKey:@"yamQuality"];
```

Working with the Filesystem

Most applications work with data stored on disk, and data is most commonly organized into files and folders. With the introduction of iCloud, an increasing amount of data is also stored in the cloud.

All Macs and iOS devices have access to iCloud, Apple's data synchronization and storage service. The idea behind iCloud is that users can have the same information on all the devices and computers they own, and don't have to manually sync or update anything —all synchronization and updating work is done by the computer.

Because of iCloud, it's now more and more the case that working with the user's data means working with one of potentially many copies of that data. This means that the copy of the data that exists on the current machine may be out of date or may conflict with another version of the data. iCloud works to reduce the amount of effort required to solve these issues, but they're factors that your code needs to be aware of.

Cocoa provides a number of tools for working with the filesystem and with files stored in iCloud. iCloud is such a large topic that we've devoted an entire chapter to it, so for more information, see Chapter 20.

 This chapter deals with files in the filesystem, which is only half the story of making a document-based application. To learn how to create an application that deals with documents, turn to Chapter 12.

Files may be stored in one of two places: either inside the application's bundle or elsewhere on the disk.

Files that are stored in the application's bundle are kept inside the *.app* folder and distributed with the app. If the application is moved on disk (e.g., if you were to drag it to another location on your Mac), the resources move with the app.

When you add a file to a project in Xcode, it is added to the current target (though you can choose for this not to happen). Then, when the application is built, the file is copied into the relevant part of the application bundle, depending on the OS—on OS X, the file is copied into the bundle's `Resources` folder, while on iOS, it is copied into the root folder of the bundle.

Files copied into the bundle are mostly resources used by the application at runtime— sounds, images, and other things needed for the application to run. The user's documents aren't stored in this location.

 If a file is stored in the application bundle, it's part of the code-signing process—changing, removing, or adding a file to the bundle after it's been code-signed will cause the OS to refuse to launch the app. This means that files stored in the application bundle are read-only.

Retrieving a file from the application's bundle is quite straightforward, and is covered in more detail in "Using NSBundle to Find Resources in Applications" (page 63). This chapter covers how to work with files that are stored elsewhere.

Some files are processed when they're copied into the application bundle. For example, *.xib* files are compiled from their XML source into a more quickly readable binary format, and on iOS, PNG images are processed so that the device's limited GPU can load them more easily (though this renders them unopenable with apps like Preview). Don't assume that files are simply copied into the bundle!

Using NSFileManager

Applications can access files almost anywhere on the system. The "almost anywhere" depends on which OS your application is running on, and whether the application exists within a sandbox.

As discussed in "The Application Sandbox" (page 69), sandboxes restrict what your application is allowed to access. So even if your application is compromised by malicious code, for example, it cannot access files that the user does not want it to.

By default, the sandbox is limited to the application's private working space, and cannot access any user files. To gain access to these files, you make requests to the system, which handle the work of presenting the file-selection box to the user and open *holes* in the sandbox for working with the files the user wants to let your application access (and only those files).

Your interface to the filesystem is the NSFileManager object, which allows you to list the contents of folders; create, rename, and delete files; modify attributes of files and folders; and generally perform all the filesystem tasks that the Finder does.

To access the NSFileManager class, you use the shared manager object:

```
NSFileManager* fileManager = [NSFileManager defaultManager];
```

NSFileManager allows you to set a delegate on it, which receives messages when the file manager completes operations like copying or moving files. If you are using this feature, you should create your own instance of NSFileManager instead of using the shared object:

```
NSFileManager* newFileManager = [[NSFileManager alloc] init];
// we can now set a delegate on this new file manager to be
// notified when operations are complete
newFileManager.delegate = self;
```

You can use `NSFileManager` to get the contents of a folder, using the following method: `contentsOfDirectoryAtURL:includingPropertiesForKeys:options:error:`. This method can be used to simply return `NSURL`s for the contents of a folder, but also to fetch additional information about a file:

```
NSURL* folderURL = [NSURL fileURLWithPath:@"/Applications/"];
NSFileManager* fileManager = [NSFileManager defaultManager];
NSError* error = nil;
NSArray* folderContents = [fileManager contentsOfDirectoryAtURL:folderURL
                            includingPropertiesForKeys:nil
                            options:0
                            error:error];
```

After this call, the `NSArray` variable `folderContents` contains `NSURL`s that point to each item in the folder. If there was an error, the method returns `nil`, and the `error` variable contains an `NSError` object that describes exactly what went wrong.

You can also ask the individual `NSURL` objects for information about the file that they point to. You can do this via the `-resourceValuesForKeys:error:` method, which returns an `NSDictionary` that contains the attributes for the item pointed to by the URL:

```
// anURL is an NSURL object

// Pass in an NSArray containing the attributes you want to know about
NSArray* attributes = [NSArray arrayWithObjects:NSURLFileSizeKey,
    NSURLContentModificationDateKey, nil];

// In this case, we don't care about any potential errors, so we
// pass in 'nil' for the error parameter.
NSDictionary* attributesDictionary = [anURL resourceValuesForKeys:attributes
    error:nil];

// We can now get the file size out of the dictionary:
NSNumber* fileSizeInBytes = [attributesDictionary
    objectForKey:NSURLFileSizeKey];

// And the date it was last modified:
NSDate* lastModifiedDate = [attributesDictionary
                    objectForKey:NSURLContentModificationDateKey];
```

 Checking each attribute takes time, so if you need to get attributes for a large number of files, it makes more sense to instruct the `NSFileManager` to prefetch the attributes when listing the directory's contents:

```
NSArray* attributes = [NSArray arrayWithObjects:NSURLFileSizeKey,
    NSURLContentModificationDateKey, nil];
NSArray* folderContents = [fileManager contentsOfDirectoryAtURL:folderURL
                            includingPropertiesForKeys:attributes
                            options:0
                            error:error];
```

Creating directories

Using `NSFileManager`, you can create and remove items on the filesystem. To create a new directory, for example, use:

```
[fileManager createDirectoryAtURL:anURL
        withIntermediateDirectories:YES
                          attributes:nil
                               error:nil];
```

Note that you can pass in an `NSDictionary` containing the desired attributes for the new directory.

> If you set a `YES` value for the `withIntermediateDirectories` parameter, the system will create any additional folders that are necessary to create the folder. For example, if you have a folder named Foo, and want to have a folder named Foo/Bar/Bas, you would create an `NSURL` that points to the second folder and ask the `NSFileManager` to create it. The system would create the Bar folder, and then create the "Bas" folder inside that.

Creating files

Creating files works the same way. You provide a path in an `NSString`, the `NSData` that the file should contain, and an optional dictionary of attributes that the file should have:

```
[fileManager createFileAtPath:aPath contents:someData attributes:nil];
```

Removing files

Given a URL, `NSFileManager` is also able to delete files and directories. You can only delete items that your app has permission to delete, which limits your ability to write a program that accidentally erases the entire system.

To remove an item, you do this:

```
[fileManager removeItemAtURL:anURL error:nil];
```

> There's no undo for removing files or folders using `NSFileManager`. Items aren't moved to the Trash—they're immediately deleted.

Moving and copying files

To move a file, you need to provide both an original URL and a destination URL. You can also copy a file, which duplicates it and places the duplicate at the destination URL.

To move an item, you do this:

```
[file moveItemAtURL:sourceURL toURL:destinationURL error:nil];
```

To copy an item, you do this:

```
[file copyItemAtURL:sourceURL toURL:destinationURL error:nil];
```

Just like all the other file manipulation methods, these methods return YES on success, and NO if there was a problem.

File Storage Locations

There are a number of existing locations where the user can keep files. These include the Documents directory, the Desktop, and common directories that the user may not ever see, such as the Caches directory, which is used to store temporary files that the application would find useful to have around but could regenerate if needed (like downloaded images).

Your code can quickly determine the location of these common directories by asking the NSFileManager class. To do this, you use the URLsForDirectory:inDomains: class method in NSFileManager, which returns an array of NSURL objects that point to a directory that matches the kind of location you asked for. For example, to get an NSURL that points to the user's Documents directory, you do this:

```
NSArray* URLs = [[NSFileManager defaultManager]
    URLsForDirectory:NSDocumentDirectory inDomains:NSUserDomainMask];

NSURL* documentURL = [URLs lastObject];
```

You can then use this URL to create additional URLs. For example, to generate a URL that points to a file called *Example.txt* in your Documents directory, you can use -URLByAppendingPathComponent:

```
NSURL* fileURL = [documentURL URLByAppendingPathComponent:@"Example.txt"];
```

Working with the Sandbox

An application that runs in a sandbox may only access files that exist inside that sandbox, and is allowed to read and write without restriction inside its designated sandbox container. In addition, if the user has granted access to a specific file or folder, the sandbox will allow your application to read and/or write to that location as well.

 If you want to put your application in the Mac App Store, it must be sandboxed. Apple will reject your application if it isn't. All iOS apps are automatically sandboxed by the system.

Enabling Sandboxing

To turn on sandboxing, follow these steps.

1. Select your project at the top of the navigation pane.

2. In the Summary section, scroll down to Entitlements.

3. Turn on Enable Entitlements.

4. Turn on Enable App Sandboxing.

Your application will then launch in sandboxed mode, which means that it won't be able to access any resources that the system does not permit it to.

In the sandbox setup screen, you can specify what the application should have access to. For example, if you need to be able to read and write files in the user's Music folder, you can change the Music Folder Access setting from None (the default) to Read Access or Read/Write Access.

If you want to let the user choose which files and folders should be accessible, change User Selected File Access to something other than None.

Open and Save Panels

One way that you can let the user indicate that your app is allowed to access a file is to use an NSOpenPanel or NSSavePanel. These are the standard open and save windows that you've seen before; however, when your application is sandboxed, the panel being displayed is actually not being shown by your application, but rather by a built-in system component called *Powerbox*. When you display an open or save panel, Powerbox handles the process of selecting the files; when the user chooses a file or folder, it grants your application access to the specified location and then returns information about the user's selection to you.

Here's an example of how you can get access to a folder that the user asks for:

```
NSOpenPanel* panel           = [NSOpenPanel openPanel];
panel.canChooseFiles         = NO;
panel.canChooseDirectories = YES;
[panel beginWithCompletionHandler:^(NSInteger result) {
        NSURL* chosenDirectory = panel.URL;
        // the application may now do something with chosenDirectory
}];
```

Security-Scoped Bookmarks

One downside to this approach of asking for permission to access files is that the system will not remember that the user granted permission. It's a potential security hole to automatically retain permissions for every file the user has ever granted an app access to, so OS X instead provides the concept of *security-scoped bookmarks*. Security-scoped bookmarks are like the bookmarks in your web browser, but for files; once your application has access to a file, you can create a bookmark for it and save it. On application launch, your application can load the bookmark and have access to the file again.

There are two kinds of security-scoped bookmarks: *app-scoped bookmarks*, which allow your application to retain access to a file across launches, and *document-scoped bookmarks*, which allow your app to store the bookmark in a file that can be given to another user on another computer. In this book, we'll be covering app-scoped bookmarks.

To use security-scoped bookmarks, you need to explicitly indicate that your app uses them in its entitlements file. This is the file that's created when you turn on the Enable Entitlements option: it's the file with the extension *.entitlements* in your project. To enable app-scoped bookmarks, you open the Entitlements file and add the following entitlement: `com.apple.security.files.bookmarks.app-scope`. Set this entitlement to **YES**.

You can then create a bookmark file and save it somewhere that your application has access to. When your application later needs access to the file indicated by your user, you load the bookmark file and retrieve the URL from it; in doing this, your application will be granted access to the location that the bookmark points to.

To create and save bookmark data, you do this:

```
// Get the location in which to put the bookmark
NSURL* bookmarkStorageURL = [[[NSFileManager defaultManager]
    URLsForDirectory:NSApplicationSupportDirectory
    inDomains:NSUserDomainMask] lastObject];

bookmarkStorageURL = [bookmarkStorageURL
    URLByAppendingPathComponent:@"saved_bookmark.bookmark"];

// Create the bookmark data itself
NSError* error = nil;
NSData* bookmarkData = [panel.URL
    bookmarkDataWithOptions:NSURLBookmarkCreationWithSecurityScope
    includingResourceValuesForKeys:nil relativeToURL:nil error:&error];

// Save the bookmark data
[bookmarkData writeToURL:bookmarkStorageURL atomically:YES];
```

To retrieve a stored bookmark, you do this:

```
// Get the location for where the bookmark was created
NSURL* bookmarkStorageURL = [[[NSFileManager defaultManager]
    URLsForDirectory:NSApplicationSupportDirectory inDomains:NSUserDomainMask]
    lastObject];

bookmarkStorageURL = [bookmarkStorageURL
    URLByAppendingPathComponent:@"saved_bookmark.bookmark"];
```

```
// Load the bookmark data
NSData* bookmarkData = [NSData dataWithContentsOfURL:bookmarkStorageURL];
NSURL* bookmark = nil;

if (bookmarkData) {
        // Get the URL for the bookmark
        BOOL isStale = NO;
        NSError* error = nil;
        bookmark = [NSURL URLByResolvingBookmarkData:bookmarkData
            options:NSURLBookmarkResolutionWithSecurityScope
            relativeToURL:nil bookmarkDataIsStale:&isStale
            error:&error];

        [[NSUserDefaults standardUserDefaults] setURL:bookmark forKey:@"path"];
}
```

When you want to start accessing the file pointed to by the bookmarked URL, you need to call startAccessingSecurityScopedResource on that URL. When you're done, call stopAccessingSecurityScopedResource.

You can find a full working project that demonstrates this behavior in this book's source code.

CHAPTER 10

Cocoa Bindings

So far in this book, we've talked at length about how the model-view-controller paradigm works in Cocoa and Cocoa Touch, and how dividing up your application's code into these separate areas of responsibility leads to easier-to-manage codebases.

However, sometimes it may seem like overkill to write separate models, views, and controllers, especially when all the controller needs to do is pass information directly from the model to the view and vice versa. In many cases, the only behavior you want is for a label to display information stored in a model object.

To solve this problem, Apple introduced *bindings* in OS X. Bindings are connections between views and objects, where the contents of the object are used to directly drive what the view displays. Bindings mean you can write less code for the same excellent features.

In this chapter, you'll learn how to use bindings to connect your interface directly to data. You'll also learn how to use the built-in controller classes that Apple provides to manage collections of objects. By the end of the chapter, you'll have created a sophisticated note-taking application while writing minimal code.

 Bindings are only available on OS X. Sorry, iOS developers!

Binding Views to Models

A binding is simply an instruction that you give to a view about where its content comes from. Something like "OK, text field, the text that you should show comes from this object over here. If it ever changes, update yourself. Likewise, when you change, tell the object to update the text it's storing."

When a view is bound to an object, you indicate which property you wish to be bound. For example, imagine that the app delegate has a property called myString. If you bound a label to that object's property, the two would be linked—whatever the myString property contains, the label would display.

Bindings know about what data to display. More importantly, they also know about *when* that display should be updated. Bindings work through *key-value observing*, which we discussed in detail in Chapter 9. When the value of a property is changed, the bindings system informs every view bound to it that they should update themselves.

Bindings also work in reverse. If you have an editable view, such as a text field, the bindings system updates the object with updated content when the user makes changes.

You can bind many different properties of views to model object properties. The most common property you bind is the view's value, which in most cases is the text that the view displays (for label, text, views, and so on). You can also bind properties to things like whether the view should be enabled or hidden, what font or color the view should use, which image should be used, and so on. The specific view properties that can be bound vary from view to view.

Because bindings largely remove the work of mediating between your model code and your views, you can focus on simply building the user-facing features of your app. Simply put, using bindings means writing less code, which means that you get to make your end product faster and with less potential for bugs.

A Single Bindings App

To demonstrate how to bind views directly to model objects, let's build a simple application that connects a slider and a text field to a property that we'll add to the app delegate object.

1. *Create the application.*

   Create a new Cocoa application and call it **SimpleBindings**.

2. *Add the property to* AppDelegate.

   We'll start by adding the property to the AppDelegate object. This property will simply store a number. Open *AppDelegate.h* and add the following property to it:

   ```
   property (assign) NSInteger numberValue;
   ```

Once that's added, open *AppDelegate.m* and synthesize it by adding the following code to AppDelegate's `@implementation`:

```
@synthesize numberValue;
```

We're now ready to create the interface. This application will show both a text field and a horizontal slider.

3. *Open the interface and add the interface components.*

   Open *MainMenu.xib* and then open the main window.

   Drag in a text field and place it on the lefthand side of the window.

   Next, drag in a horizontal slider, and place it on the right of the text field.

4. *Make both controls continuous.*

   We want both views to update the application as the user works with them. This means that we want both controls to be *continuous*—that is, they'll send their information out to the application the moment the user moves the mouse or types a key. If a control isn't continuous, it waits until the user is done interacting with it before sending its new value (which can save work for the application).

   To make the controls continuous, select both the text field and the slider and then open the Attributes inspector, which is the fourth tab from the left in the Inspector pane. Turn the Continuous checkbox on.

Now that the interface has been set up, it's time to create bindings.

 Remember that the AppDelegate object now has a property, called value, which stores an integer. We're going to bind both of these controls to this property, which will cause the property's value to be displayed in the controls. Having both controls bound to the same thing also has the effect of making them control each other—by dragging the slider from left to right, the text field will update.

5. *Bind the text field to the app delegate.* Select the text field and then the Bindings inspector. (It's the second tab from the right, at the top of the Inspector pane—its icon looks like a little knot.)

   The Bindings inspector displays the list of all possible bindable properties in text field. In this case, we want to bind the text field's value, which is the text that is displayed, so open the Value property.

   When binding to an object, we need to provide two things: the object that we are binding to, and the *key* that we want to bind to. The key is simply the name of the property, method, or instance variable that has the content that we want to display.

In this case, the object that we want to bind to is the app delegate. The Bindings inspector lists all top-level objects in the nib as things that you can bind to, which means you can easily select it. The key that we want to bind to is `value`, because that's the name of the property in the app delegate object.

You'll notice that there are two "key" fields shown: the *controller key* and the *model key path*. The controller key refers to the property exposed by the object that you're binding to, while the model key path refers to the property inside the object that's returned by accessing the controller key from the bound object. Because we're not working with a controller object in this case, we provide a model key path that points directly to the property we want.

6. *Bind the text field's Value.*

   Select App Delegate in the Bind to drop-down list.

   Set the model key path to **numberValue**.

A little red alert icon will appear next to the word `numberValue`. This is because the text field usually expects an `NSString` to be provided, and the `numberValue` property is an `NSInteger`. This is fine, because the bindings system knows how to convert integers to strings. However, if you see the red alert icon appear, double-check to make sure that you're binding properties of the correct data types.

7. *Make the binding update continuously.* Just as the text field updates continuously, we want the binding to also update the rest of the application continuously.

   To do this, turn on the Continuously Updates Value checkbox.

8. *Bind the slider to the same property.* Now that the text field has been bound, we'll do the same thing for the slider. Keep the Bindings inspector open and select the horizontal slider.

   Open the Value binding.

   Select App Delegate in the Bind to drop-down list, and set the model key path to **numberValue**.

   Turn Continuously Updates Value on.

You can now see the binding in action. Run the app, and note what happens when you drag the slider back and forth—the text field updates to show the current value of numberValue. If you change the text in the text field, the slider will update.

Binding to Controllers

In the previous example we've bound views directly to properties that are stored in an object, bypassing a controller object. This works just fine for simple cases, but bindings are also capable of much more powerful work.

For example, it's possible to bind views to data stored in the user defaults system—that is, within the NSUserDefaults database. This has a number of useful results, such as being able to quickly and easily build a "settings" screen that binds the controls directly to the data stored in the user preferences system.

However, NSUserDefaults is simply a data storage system, and you can't bind directly to it because its content isn't directly observable by the key-value observing system that bindings rely on. To work with it, you need an object mediating between your views and the model. Sound familiar? That's right—you need a *controller object*!

Apple provides just such an object to let you work with NSUserDefaults in bindings: NSUserDefaultsController. This object provides mechanisms for binding views to defaults stored in NSUserDefaults. It also provides a few more advanced features, such as the ability to make changes and then let the user cancel or apply them—so if you want the user to be able to cancel his changes in your preferences window, you can!

Because NSUserDefaultsController is such a common control, you don't even need to create one to start using it. Simply by binding a control to the defaults makes it appear in the Interface Builder's outline.

To demonstrate how you can use this controller in your app, we'll adapt our application to store user preferences.

1. *Add a checkbox.* First, we'll add a checkbox whose value is stored in the user defaults system, which will also control whether the text field and horizontal slider are enabled (that is, whether the user can interact with them). To do this, simply add a checkbox to the window and change its label to **Enabled**.

2. *Bind the checkbox to the user defaults.* Select the checkbox and open the Bindings inspector.

   Bind its value to the Shared User Defaults Controller, which appears in the list of bindable objects.

   Set the controller key to **values** and the model key path to **controlsEnabled**.

We haven't set up a property in the code called `controlsEnabled`, but that's OK—remember, when you use `NSUserDefaults`, you just set values for preferences you want to store.

3. *Bind the* `Enabled` *property of both the slider and text field.*

   Now that the checkbox has been set up, we'll make the text field and horizontal slider become enabled or disabled based on the value of the `controlsEnabled` property stored in the user defaults. We'll do this by binding the controls' `Enabled` property.

   To do this, select the text field and bind the *Enabled* property to the Shared User Defaults Controller. Set the controller key to **values** and the model key path to **controlsEnabled**.

   Repeat this process for the horizontal slider.

We can now see it in action. Launch the app, and note that changing the state of the checkbox makes the text field and slider become enabled and disabled. Quit and relaunch the application, and note that the checkbox remembers its state.

Quietly marvel at the fact that you wrote no code at all for this feature!

Array and Object Controllers

As we've seen, controllers mediate between views and models, and allow you to make bindings that keep you from having to write lots of laborious code.

We've just seen `NSUserDefaultsController` in action, which allows you to bind views to the user preferences system. In this case, the model object is the `NSUserDefaults` object.

Other controllers exist, which you can use to mediate access to other data in your application. If you want your application to display a collection of data, you need parts of your interface to display the entire collection and other parts to display specific information about the currently selected item in the collection.

This is where `NSArrayController` comes in. `NSArrayController` is a controller object that manages an array (either an `NSArray` or `NSMutableArray`) and provides access to the contents of the array. The array controller also provides the concept of "selected" objects, meaning that your code can display content relevant for only the items that have been selected by the user. Finally, the `NSArrayController` is also capable of adding and removing items from the array that it manages.

Another example of a controller object is `NSObjectController`, which acts as a controller for a single object. The typical use case for this class is where you bind your interface to the `NSObjectController`, and then your code gives an object to that controller. The moment the content object of the controller changes, the interface updates.

A More Complex Bindings App

Controllers allow you to create extremely sophisticated applications with minimal code. To demonstrate how this works, we're going to create an application that lets the user create, edit, view, and delete small text notes, all while doing most of the work with bindings.

The application will work with a class that we'll create called `Note`. This class will contain a number of properties: the note's title, the text contained within it, and the date and time that the note was created and edited. The application will display a list of all notes that the user has created, as well as displaying and allowing the user to edit notes. When the user edits a note, the note will update itself to reflect the date and time that the note was changed.

Let's get started on our app.

1. *Create the application.* Create a new Cocoa application and call it **ControllerBind ings**.

2. *Create the* `Note` *class.* Create a new class by choosing File→New→File or by pressing ⌘-N.

   Create a new Objective-C class called `Note`. Make this class a subclass of `NSObject`.

3. *Add properties to the* `Note` *class.* Now that the class has been created, we'll add the following properties:

   - `title`, an `NSString`
   - `text`, an `NSAttributedString`
   - `created`, an `NSDate`
   - `edited`, an `NSDate`

 `NSAttributedString` is an `NSString` subclass that also stores information like font, style, and color. You can use `NSAttributedString` to store rich text.

Open *Note.h* and add the following code to `Note`'s `@interface` section:

```
@property (strong, nonatomic) NSString* title;
@property (strong, nonatomic) NSAttributedString* text;
@property (strong) NSDate* created;
@property (strong) NSDate* edited;
```

Next, synthesize these properties by opening *Note.m* and adding the following code to the start of Note's @implementation section.

```
@synthesize text = _text;
@synthesize created = _created;
@synthesize edited = _edited;
@synthesize title = _title;
```

You'll notice that the title and text properties have nonatomic in the property descriptions. This is because we'll be overriding the setters for these properties, and it's helpful to let the compiler know that the setters should not be considered thread-safe, which is what nonatomic means.

4. *Update the code for* Note. When the object is created, we want the created property to be set to the current date. Similarly, when the title or text properties are updated, we want the edited property to be updated to the current date. Finally, when the object is created, the note's title text should read "New note."

We'll do this by overriding the init, setText: and setTitle: methods. Add the following methods to *Note.m*, in Note's @implementation section:

```
- (id)init {
    self = [super init];
    if (self) {
        self.title = @"New note";
        self.created = [NSDate date];
    }
    return self;
}

// If the title or text are modified, set the edited date to now
- (void)setTitle:(NSString *)title {
    _title = title;
    self.edited = [NSDate date];
}

- (void)setText:(NSAttributedString *)text {
    _text = text;
    self.edited = [NSDate date];
}
```

We're now done with the Note class. It contains the data that we need it to, and will behave the way we want when it's created and updated.

We now need a place to store the instances of the Note class. Because we don't want to deal with the challenges of storing content on disk, this example project will simply store the Notes in an NSMutableArray inside the application delegate object. This means that no information will be kept around when the app exits.

The NSMutableArray will be stored in a property. This is important, since it means that the array controller object that we'll create later will be able to bind to it.

To add the notes property to AppDelegate, open *AppDelegate.h*. Add the following code to AppDelegate's @interface section:

```
@property (strong) NSMutableArray* notes;
```

Once you've done that, synthesize the property by opening *AppDelegate.m* and adding the following code to the start of AppDelegate's @implementation section:

```
@synthesize notes = _notes;
```

Finally, we need the notes property to be properly set up when the application starts up. In the applicationDidFinishLaunching: method, add the following code:

```
self.notes = [NSMutableArray array];
```

We're now completely done with all the code for this application. From here on out, it's bindings all the way.

The first thing that we want to do is display a list of notes that the user has created, and provide a way to add and remove notes from the list. We need a way to provide access to the Note instances. Unlike in our first application, we can't bind the controls directly to the notes property in the app delegate, because that's an array, and we want to be able to display individual notes.

To enable this, we use an NSArrayController. This class acts as the gateway to the contents of the array. It will be bound to the notes property, and other views will be bound to it.

The list view itself will be an NSTableView. This class is traditionally tricky to set up and requires that your code act as a data source, implementing several methods and providing all kinds of information to the class. Not so with bindings—in this case, we'll be binding the table view's contents directly to the array controller that manages the notes collection.

First, let's create and set up the array controller.

1. *Open the interface and drag in the array controller.*

   Open *MainWindow.xib*. We're going to start by adding the NSArrayController instance, which lives in the Object Library. Search for *array controller*, and you'll find it. Drag one into the outline.

2. *Bind the array controller to the app delegate.* We'll now instruct the array controller to access the notes property when it wants to know where the data it's managing is stored.

   Select the array controller, and open the Bindings inspector.

   Open the Content Array property, and bind it to the App Delegate. Set the model key path to **notes**.

3. *Set the array controller's class.* We also need to let the array controller know about what class of object the array will contain. This is important, since when the array controller is asked to add a new item to the array, it needs to know which class to instantiate.

   With the array controller selected, open the Attributes Inspector. Set the Class Name to **Note**.

   When you provide a content array to an array controller, the array controller is able to be bound to other objects. Some useful bindable properties include:

   - arrangedObjects: The total collection of objects in the array, arranged based on the array controller's settings (such as any filters or sorting options that may have been applied)
   - selection: The currently selected object.
   - canAdd and canRemove: BOOL properties that indicate whether the array controller is currently able to add or remove items.

   These properties can be accessed by using them as controller keys in the Bindings inspector.

The array controller is now set up, and we can start creating the interface. We'll begin by adding the table view that lists all notes, as well as buttons that allow adding and removing items.

1. *Add a table view.* Drag in a table view and place it on the lefthand side of the window. Resize it so that it's about a third of the width of the window.

   When you add a table view, it's placed inside a scroll view. We're going to want to set up several different aspects of the table view, so expand the entire tree by holding down the Option key and clicking the arrow next to Scroll View—Table View in the outline. Select Table View in the items that appear.

   Set the Columns counter in the Attributes inspector to 1.

2. *Bind the table column to the array controller.* We want the table view controller to display note titles in the list. Select the Table Column in the outline and open the Bindings inspector.

Bind the `Value` property to the array controller. Set the controller key to arrange-dObjects and the model key path to **title**.

The table view will now show the value of the `title` property for all items in the notes array. Additionally, the table view will control which item is selected.

3. *Add the add and remove buttons.* We'll now add two buttons to the view to allow adding and removing items.

   Drag in a gradient button from the object library. Resize it to a smallish square shape, and place it underneath the table view.

   In the Attributes inspector, set the button's title to nothing (that is, delete all the text). Set the image to **NSAddTemplate**, which will make the button show a plus icon.

   Hold down the Option key and drag the button to the right. A copy will be made; place it next to the first button. Set the image of this new button to **NSRemove Template**, which shows a minus icon.

4. *Connect the add and remove buttons to the array controller.* We can now make these buttons instruct the array controller to add and remove items.

   Control-drag from the add button to the array controller. Choose "add:" from the menu that appears.

   Control-drag from the remove button to the array controller. Choose "remove:" from the menu that appears.

   Now when these buttons are clicked, the array controller will add a new item to the array that it's managing or delete the currently selected item.

5. *Bind the remove button's* `Enabled` *property to the array controller.* For a finishing touch, we're going to disable the remove button be disabled if there's nothing to remove or if there's no selected object. The array controller exposes a property called canRemove, which we can bind the button's `Enabled` property to.

   Select the remove button and open the Bindings inspector.

   Bind the `Enabled` property to the array controller, using the controller key **can Remove**.

You can now see this in action by launching the app. Clicking on the add and remove buttons will add and remove items from the list, and when nothing is selected, the remove button is disabled.

We'll now make the notes work. All we need to do here is set up views and bind them to the selected object, which is provided to us by the array controller.

1. *Create the interface.* Add a text field to the right side of the window and place it at the top. This text field will show the `title` property in the notes.

Add a text view underneath the text field. Make it rather tall to allow for plenty of room for adding text. This text view will show the text property.

2. *Bind the controls.* Select the text field and bind its value to the array controller. Set the controller key to **selection** and the model key path to **title**. Turn Continuously Updates Value on.

Select the text view (note that it's kept inside a scroll view, so you'll need to expand it in the outline to get to it), and bind its value to the array controller. Set the controller key to "**selection**" and the model key path to **text**. Turn Continuously Updates Value on here too.

3. *Create the date labels.* Finally, we'll create the interface that shows the date and bind it.

Add a label to the window. Set its text to **Created:** and place it under the text view.

Add another label and set its text to **Edited:**. Place it under the Created label.

Add a third label and put it to the right of the Created label. Resize it to the right edge of the window. This label will display the date that the note was created on.

Add a fourth label to the right of the Edited label. Resize it like the last one.

4. *Bind the date labels.* Select the empty label to the right of the Created label and bind it to the array controller. Set the controller key to **selection** and the model key path to **created**.

Select the other label and bind it similarly, but with the model key path set to **edited**.

We're done. You can now see the entire app in action! You can add and remove items, and store any text you like in the text field. Renaming the note updates live in the list, and changing the note's contents updates the **Edited** label.

CHAPTER 11

Table Views and Collection Views

One of the most common tasks for any app, regardless of platform, is displaying lists or collections of data. iOS and OS X provide a number of tools for viewing data, and in this chapter you'll learn how to use them.

Both iOS and OS X feature table views and collection views. A *table view* is designed to provide a list of data, while a *collection view* is designed to show a grid of data. Both table views and collection views can be customized to provide different layouts.

Table views are used all over OS X—Finder and iTunes both use it to show lists of files and songs. Table views are used even more heavily in iOS—any time you see a vertically scrolling list, such as the list of messages in Messages or the options in Settings, you're seeing a table view.

Collection views are used a little less frequently, as they're a newer addition to both platforms. Collection views can be seen (again) in Finder and iTunes, as well as in Launchpad. On the iPad, a collection view appears in the Clock application, which was added in iOS 6.

Data Sources and Delegates

Despite their differences in layout, table and collection views have very similar APIs. When a data display view prepares to show content, it has to know the answers to at least two questions:

1. How many items am I showing?
2. For each item, what do I need to do to display it?

These questions are asked of the view's *data source*, which is an Objective-C object that conforms to the view's *data source protocol*. The data source protocol differs based on the type of view that you're using.

There are other questions that a data view may need to know the answer to, including "How tall should each row in the list be?" and "How many sections should the list contain?" These questions are also answered by the data source, but the view can fall back to some default values in case the data source isn't able to provide this information.

Sometimes displaying information is all you want, but your application usually needs to respond to the user interacting with the view's content. The specific things that the user can do vary depending on the platform, the kind of data view, and how you've configured the view. Some possible interactions include:

- Clicking (or tapping) on an item
- Rearranging content
- Deleting or modifying content

These actions are sent by the view to its *delegate*.

Table Views

Table views are designed for showing lists of information. On OS X, a table view shows data with multiple columns, which can be rearranged and resized, and is generally used to show data. On iOS, table views only show one column and are useful for any kind of vertically scrolling list, as seen in the Settings application.

UITableView on iOS

Table views are implemented on iOS using the `UITableView` class. This is one of the most versatile view classes on iOS: with it, you can create interfaces that range from simple lists of data to complex, multi-part, scalable interfaces.

On iOS, the term "table view" is somewhat of a misnomer. The word "table" usually brings to mind a grid with multiple rows and columns, but on iOS the table view is actually a single column with multiple rows. The reason for this is that the size of the iPhone's screen is too narrow for more than one column to make sense, but the API design for `UITableViewController` was based on `NSTableViewController`, which we'll discuss later in this chapter.

Table views on iOS present a scrolling list of *table view cells*, which are views that can contain any data you like. `UITableView` is designed for speed: one of the most common gestures that the user performs on an iOS device is to flick a finger up and down a scrolling list, which means that the application needs to be able to animate the scrolling of that list at high frame rates (ideally, 60 frames per second, which is the maximum frame rate of iOS).

Sections and Rows

Table views can be divided into multiple *sections*, each of which contains one or more *rows*. Sections allow you to divide your content in a manner that makes sense to you. For example, the Contacts application uses a table view that divides rows by surname, and the Settings application uses a table view that divides rows into categories.

Because table views are divided into sections, specific locations in the table view are identified not by row, but by *index path*. An index path is nothing more complex than a section number and a row number, and is represented using the `NSIndexPath` class:

```
NSIndexPath* indexPath = [NSIndexPath indexPathForRow:2 inSection:1];
```

(Note that you don't usually create `NSIndexPath`s yourself—this example just shows how they're composed.)

Let's imagine that we've got a table view that's divided into two sections: the first section has two rows, and the second section has three (Figure 11-1).

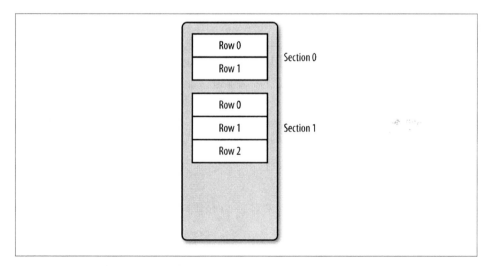

Figure 11-1. A table view, divided into sections

Using index paths, you can refer to the very first cell as section 0, row 0. The second cell is section 0, row 1, and the third cell is section 1, row 0. This allows cells to be numbered independently of their sections, which can be very handy indeed.

Table View Controllers

If you add a `UITableView` to an interface without doing any additional work, you'll see an empty list. By default, `UITableViews` rely on a *data source* object to provide them with information on what content to show.

Any object can be a data source for a `UITableView`; the only requirement is that it must conform to the `UITableViewDatasource` protocol [see "Protocols" (page 29)].

The object is almost always a `UIViewController`, and almost always the view controller of the view that contains the table view. There's nothing stopping you from doing it differently, though.

The two critical methods that the `UITableViewDatasource` protocol defines are:

```
-(NSInteger)numberOfRowsInSection:(NSInteger)section
-(UITableViewCell *)cellForRowAtIndexPath:(NSIndexPath *)indexPath
```

The first, `numberOfRowsInSection:`, returns the number of rows in the specified table section [see "Sections and Rows" (page 177)]. The second, `cellForRowAtIndexPath:`, returns a `UITableViewCell` for the specified index path.

For example, here's how to indicate that every section in the table has two rows:

```
- (NSInteger)numberOfRowsInSection:(NSInteger)section {
    return 2;
}
```

This method is the easier of the two. Here's an example of an implementation of `tableView:cellForRowAtIndexPath:`; we'll talk about exactly what it does in the next section.

```
- (UITableViewCell*) tableView:(UITableView*) tableView
    cellForRowAtIndexPath:(NSIndexPath*) indexPath {

    UITableViewCell* cell = [tableView
        dequeueReusableCellWithIdentifier:@"Cell"];

    cell.textLabel.text = @"Hello";

    return cell;
}
```

Table View Cells

A table view cell represents a single item in the table view. Table view cells are `UITableViewCells`, a subclass of `UIView`. Just like any other `UIView`, table view cells can have any other `UIViews` included as subviews.

When the table view needs to show data, it needs the answer to two questions: how many rows are there to show, and what should be shown for each row. The first question is answered by the `numberOfRowsInSection:` method; the second is answered by `table View:cellForRowAtIndexPath:`.

`cellForRowAtIndexPath:` is called for every visible row in the table view *as it comes into view*. This last part is important, because it enables the table view to not have to worry about displaying content that isn't visible. If, for example, you have a table view that contains a thousand objects, fewer than ten of those objects are likely to be visible. Because it makes no sense for the table view to attempt to display table view cells for rows that may never be shown, `tableView:cellForRowAtIndexPath:` is called only as a cell is about to come onto the screen.

`tableView:cellForRowAtIndexPath:` is responsible for returning a configured `UI TableViewCell`. "Configured," in this case, means making sure that the table view cell is displaying the right content. That content depends on what the table view is being used for: if you're making a shopping list application, each table view cell would contain an item in the shopping list.

Cell reuse

As the user scrolls the table view, some items in the list will go off screen while others come on screen. When a table view cell in the list scrolls off screen, it is removed from the table view and placed in a *reuse queue*. This reuse queue stores `UITableViewCell` objects that have been created but are not currently visible. When a cell is scrolled into view, the table view retrieves an already created `UITableViewCell` object from the reuse queue.

The advantage of this method is that the time taken to allocate and set up a new object is completely removed. All memory allocations take time, and if the user is quickly scrolling through a long list, he would see a noticeable pause as each new cell appeared.

`UITableViewCell` objects are automatically placed into the reuse queue by the table view as the cells scroll off screen; when the table view's data source receives the `table View:cellForRowAtIndexPath:` message, it fetches a cell from the reuse queue and prepares that, rather than creating an entirely new cell.

A table view can have many different kinds of cells—for example, you might have a table view with two sections that show entirely different cells in each section. However, there's only one `tableView:cellForRowAtIndexPath:` method, which is called for all rows in all sections. To differentiate, you can use the index path that is passed to this method to figure out which section and row the table view is wanting a cell for.

Anatomy of a UITableViewCell

A table view cell is a `UIView`, which can contain any additional `UIViews` that you want to include. In addition to this flexibility, `UITableViewCell` objects also support a few basic *styles*, which are similar to the table view cells seen in other parts of iOS. There are four basic table view styles:

Default
A black, bold, left-aligned text label, with an optional image view. As the name suggests, this is the default style for table view cells.

Value 1
A black, left-aligned text label, with a smaller, blue-colored, right-aligned text label on the righthand side. This cell style can be seen in the Settings application.

Value 2
A blue, right-aligned label on the lefthand side, with a black, left-aligned label on the righthand side. This cell style can be seen in the Phone and Contacts applications.

Subtitle
A black, left-aligned label, with a smaller, gray label underneath it. This cell style can be seen in the Music application.

The common theme is that all table view cells have at least one primary text label, and optionally a secondary text label and an image view. These views are `UILabel` and `UIImageView` objects, and can be accessed through the `textLabel`, `detailTextLabel`, and `imageView` properties of the table view cell.

Preparing table views in Interface Builder

Prior to iOS 5, constructing table views and table view cells was a largely programmatic affair, with developers writing code that manually instantiated and laid out the contents of any nonstandard table view cells in code. This wasn't a great idea, since layout code can get tricky. So, from iOS 5 onward, table views and their cells can be designed entirely in Interface Builder.

When you add a table view to an interface, you can also create *prototype cells*. The contents of these cells can be designed by you and completely customized (from changing the colors and fonts to completely changing the layout and providing a custom subclass of `UITableViewCell`). These prototype cells are marked with a *cell identifier*, which allows your code to create instances of the prototypes.

Analyzing tableView:cellForRowAtIndexPath:

With all of the above in mind, we can now take a closer look at the `tableView:cellForRowAtIndexPath:` implementation that we looked at earlier. Here it is again:

```
- (UITableViewCell*) tableView:(UITableView*) tableView
    cellForRowAtIndexPath:(NSIndexPath*) indexPath {

    // 1
    UITableViewCell* cell = [tableView
        dequeueReusableCellWithIdentifier:@"MyCell"];

    // 2
    cell.textLabel.text = @"Hello";

    // 3
    return cell;
}
```

The method performs three actions:

1. The table view is asked to dequeue a table view cell that has a cell identifier of MyCell. This causes the table view to either create an instance of the prototype cell that has this identifier, or dequeue one from the reuse queue if a cell with this identifier has been previously created and is not currently visible.

2. The cell's primary text label is set to display the text Hello.

3. Finally, the cell is returned to the table view, which will display it to the user.

Responding to actions

The most common thing that the user does with table view cells is to tap them. When this happens, the table view will contact its *delegate* and inform it that a cell was selected.

An object must conform to the UITableViewDelegate protocol in order to be a delegate. The table view's delegate can be different from its data source, but in practice the delegate is the same object as the data source (that is, the view controller that manages the table view conforms to both the UITableViewDelegate and UITableViewDatasource protocols).

There are several methods that UITableViewDelegate specifies, all of which are optional. The most important and commonly used method is tableView:didSelectRowAtIndexPath:, which is called when a row is tapped. This is the delegate's opportunity to perform an action like moving to another screen.

```
- (void)tableView:(UITableView *)tableView
    didSelectRowAtIndexPath:(NSIndexPath *)indexPath {
        // The table view cell at 'indexPath' got selected
}
```

Implementing a Table View

To put it all together, we'll build a simple table view application that displays the contents of an array of NSString objects.

1. *Create a new iOS application named* **iOSTableView**. Make it a single-view application for the iPhone.

2. *Delete the* ViewController.h *and* ViewController.m *files.* We'll be creating replacements for them shortly.

3. *Create and set up the table view.* In this example, the view controller will be a UITableViewController, which is a subclass of UIViewController that manages a single UITableView.

   Open *MainStoryboard.storyboard* and delete the existing view controller. Then drag in a Table View Controller from the Objects Library.

4. *Set up the prototype cell.* By default, a UITableViewController that's been dragged in to the storyboard contains a single prototype cell. We're going to configure that to be the cell that we want.

   Select the single cell that appears at the top of the table view.

   Make sure the Attributes inspector is open, and change its identifier to **StringCell**.

   Change the cell's style from Custom to Basic.

The table view is fully configured; it's now time to write the code that will provide the table view with the information it needs.

5. *Create the new table view controller class.* Create a new Objective-C class by choosing File→New→File... and selecting "Objective-C class." Name it TableViewControl ler and make it a subclass of UITableViewController.

6. *Make the table view controller use the new class.* Go back to the storyboard and select the view controller.

   Note that clicking on the table view won't select the view controller—it'll select the table *view.* You can select the table view controller itself from the Outline view on the lefthand side of the Interface Builder.

   Go to the Identity inspector and change the class from UITableViewController to TableViewController.

7. *Open* TableViewController.h *and add the array of strings.*

   We can now write the code that drives the table view. First, we need to create an NSArray that contains the NSString objects that will be displayed.

   Make the class extension at the top of *TableViewController.m* look like this:

```
@interface TableViewController () {
    NSArray* data;
}

@end
```

Next, add the following line of code to the `viewDidLoad` method.

```
data = @[@"Once", @"upon", @"a", @"time"];
```

8. *Make the table view data source return one section.* The table view will contain one section, and this section will contain as many rows as there are entries in the `data` array.

To determine how many sections are present, the table view sends its data source object the `numberOfSectionsInTableView:` message. This method is already implemented in the template code, but returns zero. We just need to change this to return 1.

Find the `numberOfSectionsInTableView:` method in `TableViewController.m` and replace it with the following code:

```
- (NSInteger)numberOfSectionsInTableView:(UITableView *)tableView
{
    return 1;
}
```

9. *Make the table view data source indicate the correct number of rows for the section.* We need to tell the table view that the section has as many rows as there are objects in the `data` array. This is handled by the `tableView:numberOfRowsInSection:` method.

Find the `tableView:numberOfRowsInSection:` method in *TableViewController.m* and replace it with the following code:

```
- (NSInteger)tableView:(UITableView *)tableView
  numberOfRowsInSection:(NSInteger)section
{
    return data.count;
}
```

10. *Implement the* `tableView:cellForRowAtIndexPath:` *method.* We need to prepare the table view cells for each of the rows that the table view will ask for.

Find the `tableView:cellForRowAtIndexPath:` method in *TableViewController.m* and replace it with the following code:

```
- (UITableViewCell *)tableView:(UITableView *)tableView
  cellForRowAtIndexPath:(NSIndexPath *)indexPath
{
    static NSString *CellIdentifier = @"StringCell";
    UITableViewCell *cell = [tableView
        dequeueReusableCellWithIdentifier:CellIdentifier
                         forIndexPath:indexPath];
```

```
        NSString* string = data[indexPath.row];

        cell.textLabel.text = string;

        return cell;
    }
```

11. *Implement the* `tableView:didSelectRowAtIndexPath:` *method*. Finally, we'll make
    the code log the string corresponding to the text that was selected.

    Find the `tableView:didSelectRowAtIndexPath:` method in *TableViewControl
    ler.m* and replace it with the following code:

    ```
    - (void)tableView:(UITableView *)tableView
      didSelectRowAtIndexPath:(NSIndexPath *)indexPath
    {
        NSLog(@"Selected %@", data[indexPath.row]);
    }
    ```

NSTableView on OS X

The process of displaying tables of data on OS X is slightly more complex than on iOS.
Tables on OS X are capable of displaying multiple columns of data, which can be
rearranged and resorted by the user. Table views on OS X are instances of the `NSTable
View` class. However, the fundamental idea behind table views on OS X is the same as
on iOS—a table view uses a data source object to determine how many rows exist and
what content should be shown for each row.

The only significant difference in terms of programming for `NSTableView` is that the
method that returns the content that should be shown for a table view cell needs to take
into account both the row number and column for the data.

The method for returning the view that should be shown in a cell is `tableView:view
ForTableColumn:row:`. This method's parameters are the `NSTableView` that wants to
show content, and the column and row number that are being displayed. The row number is represented as a simple integer, while the table column is an `NSTableColumn`. This
is because columns can be rearranged, and it therefore doesn't make sense to have "column numbers." Rather, `NSTableColumn` objects have *identifiers*, which are used by your
code to figure out what specific piece of information needs to be shown.

To demonstrate how table views work on OS X, we'll build an application that displays
multiple columns of data. This app will display a list of songs, along with their running
times.

1. *Create the project*. Create a new Cocoa application called **CocoaTableView**.

2. *Create the* **Song** *class.* The first thing we'll do is create the data source. Each song that the application displays will be an instance of the class Song, which we'll create ourselves. Each Song object has a `title` string, as well as a duration represented as an `NSTimeInterval` (which is just another way of saying `float`—it's a typedef defined by Cocoa).

To create the class, go to File→New→File… and choose Objective-C class. Create a new class called Song and make it a subclass of `NSObject`.

Once it's been created, open *Song.h* and make its `@interface` look like the following code:

```
@interface Song : NSObject

@property (strong) NSString* title;
@property (assign) NSTimeInterval duration;

@end
```

 You don't need to do anything in *Song.m*, because this class only contains properties and no methods.

3. *Add the* `songs` *and* `songsController` *properties to* `AppDelegate`. Next, we'll make `AppDelegate` store a list of Song objects. This list will be an `NSMutableArray`, which is managed by an `NSArrayController`. This controller will be used as part of the bindings used to drive the table view.

Open *AppDelegate.h* and add the following properties to the `@interface` of App Delegate:

```
@property (strong) NSMutableArray* songs;
@property (strong) IBOutlet NSArrayController *songsController;
```

4. *Populate the songs list.* Finally, we need to make the object populate this list when it appears.

Open *AppDelegate.m* and add the following method to the `@implementation` of AppDelegate:

```
@implementation AppDelegate

- (void)awakeFromNib {

    self.songs = [NSMutableArray array];

    Song* aSong;
```

```
aSong = [[Song alloc] init];
aSong.title = @"Gaeta's Lament";
aSong.duration = 289;

[self.songsController addObject:aSong];

aSong = [[Song alloc] init];
aSong.title = @"The Signal";
aSong.duration = 309;

[self.songsController addObject:aSong];

aSong = [[Song alloc] init];
aSong.title = @"Resurrection Hub";
aSong.duration = 221;

[self.songsController addObject:aSong];

aSong = [[Song alloc] init];
aSong.title = @"The Cult of Baltar";
aSong.duration = 342;

[self.songsController addObject:aSong];

}
```

 Bonus points for those who get the reference!

We'll now prepare the interface for the application.

5. *Add the array controller.* Drag an array controller into the outline.

   Open the Bindings inspector, and bind the content array to the app delegate. Set the model key path to **self.songs**.

   Hold down the Control key and drag from the app delegate to the array controller. Choose songsController from the menu that appears.

6. *Create the table view.* Open *MainMenu.xib* and select the window. It's empty, but we'll soon fix that.

   Drag a table view from the Objects Library into the window. Make it fill the window.

   Select the table header view at the top of the table view. Double-click the first column's header and rename it **Title**. Rename the second column header **Duration**.

7. *Prepare the table columns.* We now need to set up the columns to have the correct identifiers, and to use `NSViews` as their content rather than old-style `NSCells` (which was the previous method prior to OS X 10.7 Lion).

   Select the Table Column—Title object in the outline. Switch to the Identity inspector and set the identifier to Title.

   Then, select the Table Column—Duration object in the outline and change its identifier to **Duration**.

   Finally, select the Table View in the outline and change its content mode from Cell Based to View Based.

8. *Set up the table view's data source and delegate.*

   Control-drag from the table view to the app delegate, and choose "datasource" from the menu that appears. Then control-drag from the table view to the app delegate again, and choose "delegate".

9. *Make `AppDelegate` conform to the protocols.* The `AppDelegate` class needs to conform to the `NSTableViewDataSource` and `NSTableViewDelegate` in order to satisfy the compiler.

   Open *AppDelegate.m.* Add the following class extension above the `@implementa tion` of `AppDelegate`:

   ```
   @interface AppDelegate () <NSTableViewDataSource, NSTableViewDelegate>

   @end
   ```

10. *Add the* `numberOfRowsInTableView:` *method.* Add the following method to `App Delegate`. This method indicates to the table view how many rows should appear:

    ```
    - (NSInteger)numberOfRowsInTableView:(NSTableView *)tableView {
        return self.songs.count;
    }
    ```

11. *Add the* `tableView:viewForTableColumn:row:` *method.* Add the following method to `AppDelegate`. This method returns an `NSView` that will appear in the table view cell, based on the row number and column used:

    ```
    - (NSView *)tableView:(NSTableView *)tableView
        viewForTableColumn:(NSTableColumn *)tableColumn
        row:(NSInteger)row {

        NSTextField* textField = [tableView
            makeViewWithIdentifier:@"TextField" owner:self];

        Song* song = [self.songs objectAtIndex:row];

        if (textField == nil) {
            textField = [[NSTextField alloc] initWithFrame:NSZeroRect];
            [textField setBordered:NO];
    ```

```
        [textField setEditable:NO];
        [textField setDrawsBackground:NO];
        textField.identifier = @"TextField";
    }

    if ([tableColumn.identifier isEqualToString:@"Title"]) {
        textField.stringValue = song.title;
    } else if ([tableColumn.identifier isEqualToString:@"Duration"]) {
        NSString* durationText =
            [NSString stringWithFormat:@"%i:%02i",
                (int)song.duration / 60,
                (int)song.duration % 60];

        textField.stringValue = durationText;
    }

    return textField;
}
```

In this method, the table view is asked to dequeue a reusable view with the identifier
TextField. If one doesn't exist (and it won't, for the first several rows), the method
returns nil and the view must be created manually.

Then, depending on the specific column, the text of the text field is set to either the
song's title or a string representation of the song's duration.

Finally, run the application. Behold the songs!

Sorting a Table View

When you click a table view header, you're indicating to the table view that it should re-
sort the contents of the table. To do this, the table columns need to know what specific
property they're responsible for showing.

This is implemented by providing *sort keys* to each of the columns. Sort keys indicate
what property should be used for sorting.

To add sort keys, select the Table Column—Title in the outline. Open the Attributes
inspector and set the sort key to **title**. Leave the selector as compare: and the order as
Ascending.

Then, select Table Column—Duration in the outline, and change the sort key to
duration.

When a table column header is clicked, the table view's data source receives a table
View:sortDescriptorsDidChange: message. A *sort descriptor* is an instance of the
NSSortDescriptor class, which provides information on how a collection of objects
should be sorted.

The `NSMutableArray` class provides a method called `sortUsingDescriptors:`, which takes an `NSArray` of `NSSortDescriptors` and uses them to re-sort the content.

To implement the `tableView:sortDescriptorsDidChange:` method, add the following method to `AppDelegate`:

```
- (void)tableView:(NSTableView *)tableView
    sortDescriptorsDidChange:(NSArray *)oldDescriptors {
    [self.songs sortUsingDescriptors:tableView.sortDescriptors];
    [tableView reloadData];
}
```

Now, launch the application. Click one of the headings, and note the table view re-sorting.

NSTableView with Bindings

The `NSTableView` class is quite straightforward to use with a code-driven data source, but it's often a lot simpler to use Cocoa bindings (see Chapter 10). So to cap off our coverage of `NSTableView`, we're going to adapt the code to use Cocoa bindings.

When using bindings, we bind both the table view and the specific views in each table view cell. The table view is bound to the array controller so that it knows how many rows exist, and the views in the cells are bound to the specific property that should be displayed.

To bind the table view to the array controller:

1. *Select the table view in the outline.* Go to the Connections inspector and remove the `dataSource` and `delegate` links.

2. *Go to the Bindings inspector, and bind the table view's content to array controller.*

3. *Select the text field in the table view cell in the Title column.* Bind its value to Table Cell View and set the model key path to **objectValue.title**. This will make the cell display the title of the `Song` object that this row is displaying.

4. *Select the text field in the table view cell in the Title column.* Bind its value to "Table Cell View" and set the model key path to **objectValue.durationString**. This a method that we're about to create.

We want to display a human-readable representation of the `Song` object's `duration` property, and the best way to do that is to add a `durationString` method that formats the underlying `NSTimeInterval` appropriately. To add this method to the Song class, add the following to *Song.m*:

```
- (NSString*) durationString {
    return [NSString stringWithFormat:@"%i:%02i",
        (int)self.duration / 60, (int) self.duration % 60];
}
```

Now run the application; you can continue to see the songs.

Collection Views

A collection view is a tool for displaying a collection of objects. While table views are great for tabular displays of data, you often want to display a collection of items in a way that isn't a list.

Collection views exist on both iOS and OS X, though the implementation is better on iOS. In this section, you'll learn how to use UICollectionView, the iOS class that allows you to display a collection of views.

We aren't covering NSCollectionView, the OS X counterpart to UICollectionView, in this book, mostly because the API is a little cumbersome and also because there aren't as many use cases for it. If you're after more information on NSCollectionView, take a look at the *Collection View Programming Guide (http://bit.ly/R1bMJk)*, included as part of the Xcode developer documentation.

UICollectionView on iOS

UICollectionView lets you present a collection of items in a way that doesn't require each item to know how it's being positioned or laid out. UICollectionView behaves rather like UITableView, but it doesn't just lay content out in a vertical list—rather, it supports customizable layout handlers called *layout objects*.

The UICollectionView class makes use of a data source and delegate, much like the UITableView and NSTableView classes. The UICollectionView displays a collection of UICollectionViewCell objects, which are UIViews that know how to be laid out in a collection view. Generally, you create subclasses of these cells and fill them with content.

By default, a UICollectionView displays its content in a grid-like fashion. However, it doesn't have to—by creating a UICollectionViewLayout subclass and providing it to the collection view, you can lay out the UICollectionViewCell objects in any way you want. UICollectionViewLayout subclassing is a little beyond the scope of this chapter, but there's plenty of interesting discussion in the documentation for this class.

To demonstrate collection views in use, we're going to create an application that displays a collection of numbers in a grid.

1. *Create the project.* Create a single-view application for iPad called **AwesomeGrid**.

2. *Create the collection view controller.* Delete the *ViewController.h* and *View Controller.m* files. We'll be replacing them shortly.

   Create a new UICollectionViewController *subclass by choosing* File →New→File... and creating a new Objective-C object named **GridViewControl ler**. Make it a subclass of UICollectionViewController.

3. *Prepare the collection view.* Open *MainStoryboard.storyboard* and delete the view controller. Drag in a collection view controller. With the new view controller selected, open the Identity inspector and change its class from UICollectionView Controller to **GridViewController**.

We'll now create our own subclass of the UICollectionViewCell class, which will contain a label. Unlike UITableViewCell objects, the UICollectionViewCell doesn't provide standard styles for cells, as it doesn't make assumptions about the content your application will be showing.

The actual contents of the UICollectionViewCell will be designed in the Interface Builder.

4. *Create the collection view subclass and use it in the collection view.* Create a new UICollectionViewController subclass by choosing File→New→File... and creating a new Objective-C object named **GridCell**. Make it a subclass of UICollec tionViewCell.

   Go back to *MainStoryboard.storyboard* and select the collection view cell at the top-left of the collection view. Go to the Identity inspector and change its class from UICollectionViewCell to GridCell.

   Go to the Attributes inspector and change the collection view item's identifier to **GridCell**.

   Resize the cell to be about twice the size. Drag a label into the cell. Using the Attributes inspector, make its font larger, and change its color to white. Resize the label to fill the cell and make the text centered.

   Open *GridCell.h* in the assistant. Control-drag from the label into the @inter face of GridCell, and create a new outlet called **label**.

Having set up the collection view, we can now set up the view controller to display the content. The actual "content" to be displayed will be the numbers from 1 to 200, which will be stored as NSNumber objects in an NSArray. For each GridCell that the collection view needs to display, the view controller will convert the number to an NSString and display it in the UILabel.

The first step in this process is to store the array of numbers.

5. *Prepare the data.* Open *GridViewController.m*. Import *GridCell.h* at the top of the file.

   Make the class extension above the @implementation of GridViewController look like the following code.

   ```
   @interface GridViewController () {
       NSArray* numbers;
   }

   @end
   ```

   Next, replace the viewDidLoad method with the following code:

   ```
   - (void)viewDidLoad
   {
       [super viewDidLoad];

       NSMutableArray* numbersToAdd = [NSMutableArray array];

       for (int i = 1; i <= 200; i++) {
           [numbersToAdd addObject:@(i)];
       }

       numbers = numbersToAdd;
   }
   ```

6. *Add the methods that indicate the number of items in the collection view.* The methods for providing data to a UICollectionView are very similar to those for working with a UITableView: you provide the number of sections, the number of items in each section, and a UICollectionViewCell object for each item.

   Add the following methods to GridViewController:

   ```
   - (NSInteger)numberOfSectionsInCollectionView:
   (UICollectionView *)collectionView {
       return 1;
   }

   - (NSInteger)collectionView:(UICollectionView *)collectionView
   numberOfItemsInSection:(NSInteger)section {

       return numbers.count;
   }
   ```

7. *Implement the* `collectionView:cellForItemAtIndexPath:` *method.* Displaying a cell in a collection view is just as simple. Because we have already prototyped the `GridCell` in the Interface Builder, the only thing that needs to happen is for the view controller to prepare the cell when it appears in the collection view.

Add the following method to `GridViewController`:

```
- (UICollectionViewCell*) collectionView:(UICollectionView *)collectionView
  cellForItemAtIndexPath:(NSIndexPath *)indexPath {

    GridCell* cell = [collectionView
      dequeueReusableCellWithReuseIdentifier:@"GridCell"
      forIndexPath:indexPath];

    NSNumber* number = numbers[indexPath.row];

    cell.label.text = [number description];

    return cell;

}
```

Run the application—you should see a scrolling grid of numbers.

Note that when you rotate the iPad (if you're using the simulator, use the ⌘-← and ⌘-→ keys), the collection view lays itself out correctly.

CHAPTER 12

Document-Based Applications

For the user, a computer and the applications that it runs are simply ways to access and work with files. The designers of OS X and iOS understand this, and provide a number of tools for making apps designed around letting the user create, edit, and work with documents.

The idea of a document-based application is simple: the application can create documents, and open previously created documents. The user edits the document and saves it to disk. The document can then be stored, sent to another user, duplicated, or anything else that a file can do.

While both OS X and iOS provide technologies that allow you to make document-based applications, the way in which documents are presented to the user differs.

On OS X, as with other desktop-based OSes, users manage their documents through the Finder, which is the dedicated file management application. The entire filesystem is exposed to the user through the Finder.

On iOS, the filesystem is still there, but the user never sees it. Instead, all documents are presented to the user and managed by the application. All the tasks involved in managing documents—creating new files, renaming files, deleting files, copying files, and so on —must be done by your application.

More than one application may be able to open a document. For example, JPEG images can be opened by both the built-in Preview application and by Photoshop for different purposes. Both OS X and iOS provide ways for applications to specify that they are able to open certain kinds of documents.

In this chapter, you'll learn how to work with documents on both iOS and OS X.

The NSDocument and UIDocument Classes

In both iOS and OS X, documents are represented in your application with the `UIDocu` `ment` and `NSDocument` classes, respectively. These classes represent the document and store its information. Every time a new document is created, a new instance of your application's `NSDocument` or `UIDocument` subclass is created.

Document Objects in MVC

Document objects participate in the model-view-controller paradigm. In your apps, document objects are model objects—they handle the reading and writing of information to disk, and provide that information to other parts of the application.

All document objects, at their core, provide two important methods: one to save the information to disk, and one to load the information from disk. The document object, therefore, is in charge of converting the document information that's held in memory (that is, the Objective-C objects that represent the user's data) into a data representation that can be stored on disk.

For `NSDocument`, the methods are these:

```
- (NSData *)dataOfType:(NSString *)typeName error:(NSError **)outError;
- (BOOL)readFromData:(NSData *)data ofType:(NSString *)typeName
    error:(NSError **)outError;
```

And for `UIDocument`, the methods are these:

```
- (id)contentsForType:(NSString *)typeName error:(NSError **)outError;
- (BOOL)loadFromContents:(id)contents ofType:(NSString *)typeName
    error:(NSError **)outError;
```

The first set of methods is responsible for producing an Objective-C object that can be written to disk, such as an `NSData` object. The second is the opposite—given an Objective-C object that represents one or more files on the disk, the document object should prepare itself for use by the application.

Kinds of Documents

OS X and iOS support three different ways of representing a document on disk:

- *Flat files*, such as JPEG images and text documents, which are loaded into memory wholesale.
- *File packages*, which are folders that contain multiple files, but are presented to the user as a single file. Xcode project files are file packages.
- Databases, which are single files that are partially loaded into memory as needed.

All three of these methods are used throughout OS X and iOS, and there's no single "correct" way to represent files. Each one has strengths and weaknesses.

- A flat file is easy to understand from a development point of view, where you simply work with a collection of bytes in an NSData object. They are also very easy to upload to the web and send via email. However, flat files must be read entirely into memory, which can lead to performance issues if the files are very large.

- File packages are a convenient way to break up a large or complex document into multiple pieces. For example, Keynote presentations are file packages that contain a single file describing the presentation's contents (its slides, text, layout, and so on), and include all images, movies, and other resources as separate files next to the description file. This reduces the amount of data that must be kept in memory, and allows your application to treat each piece of the document as a separate part.

  The downside is that other operating systems besides OS X and iOS don't have very good support for file packages. Additionally, you can't upload a file package to a website without first converting it to a single file (such as by zipping it).

- Databases combine the advantages of single-file simplicity with the random-access advantage of file packages. However, making your application work with databases requires writing more complex code. Some of this is mitigated by the existence of tools and frameworks like sqlite and Core Data, but your code will still be more complex.

The current trend in OS X and iOS is toward flat files and databases, because these are easier to archive and upload to iCloud.

 In this book, we'll be covering flat files. If you want to learn more about file packages or databases, check out the *Document-Based Applications Overview* in the Xcode documentation.

The Role of Documents

A document object—that is, a subclass of NSDocument or UIDocument—is both a model and a model-controller in the model-view-controller paradigm. For simpler applications, the document object is simply a model—it loads and saves data, and provides methods to let controller objects access that information.

For more complex applications, a document object may operate as a model-controller —that is, it would be responsible for loading information from disk and creating a number of subobjects that represent different aspects of the document. For example, a drawing and painting application's documents would include layers, color profiles, vector shapes, and so on.

Document-Based Applications on OS X

OS X was designed around document manipulation, and there is correspondingly strong support for building document-based applications in Cocoa and Xcode.

When you create a document-based application, you specify the name of the NSDocument class used by your application. You also create a nib file that contains the user interface for your document, including the window, controls, toolbars, and other views that allow the user to manipulate the contents of the document.

Both the document class and the document nib file are used by the NSDocumentController to manage the document-related features of your app:

- When you create a new document, a new instance of your document class is created, and copies of the view objects in the document nib file are instantiated. The new document object is placed in charge of the view.
- When the user instructs the application to save the current document, the document controller displays a dialog box that asks the user where she wants to save her work. When the user selects a location, the document controller asks the frontmost document object to store its contents in either an NSData or NSFileWrapper object (for flat files and file packages, respectively; if the document is a database, it saves its contents via its own mechanisms). The document controller then takes this returned object and writes it to disk.
- When the application is asked to open a document, the document controller determines which class is responsible for handling the document's contents. An instance of the document class is instantiated and asked to load its data from disk; the controls are also instantiated from the nib as previously discussed, and the user starts working on the document.

Autosaving and Versions

Starting with OS X 10.7 Lion and iOS 5, the system automatically saves users' work as they go, even if they haven't previously saved it. This feature is built into the NSDocumentController class (and on iOS, the UIDocument class), which means that no additional work needs to be done by your application.

Autosaving occurs whenever the user switches to another application, when the user quits your application, and also periodically. From your code's perspective, it's the same behavior as the user manually saving the document; however, the system keeps all previous versions of the document.

The user can ask to see all the previous versions, which the system handles for you automatically. The user is then able to compare two versions of the document, and copy and paste content from past versions.

Representing Documents with NSDocument

To demonstrate how to make a document-based application in OS X, we'll make an application that works with its own, custom document format. This application will start life as a simple text editor, and we'll then move on to more sophisticated data manipulation.

The first thing to do is create a new Cocoa app for OS X. Make sure that Use Core Data is off and Use Automatic Reference Counting is on.

Turn Create a Document-Based Application on, and set the document extension to `sampleDocument`. When you create the application, it will load and save files named along the lines of *MyFile.sampleDocument*.

When you create a document-based application in Xcode, the structure of the application is different from non-document-based applications. For example, Xcode assumes that the majority of your application's work will be done in the document class, and therefore doesn't bother to create or set up an application delegate class.

It does, however, create a `Document` class, which is a subclass of `NSDocument`. This is used as the document class for the "sampleDocument" type. By default, the `Document` class does nothing except indicate to the application that the interface for manipulating it should be loaded from the Document nib file (see `-windowNibName` in *Document.m*), which Xcode has also already created when setting up the application.

Stubs of `-dataOfType:error:` and `-readFromData:ofType:error:` are also provided, although they do nothing (except throw an exception if you try to save the document, to rather forcefully remind you that you haven't implemented saving yet).

If you open *Document.xib*, you'll find the window that will contain the interface that will represent each document that the user has open. If you select the file's owner in the outline and go to the Identity inspector (the third button from the left at the top of the Utilities pane), you'll note that the object that owns the file is a `Document` object (Figure 12-1). This means that you can create actions and outlets between your `Document` class and the interface.

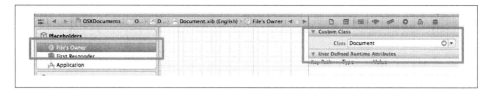

Figure 12-1. The class of the file's owner object can be set using the Identity inspector

Saving Simple Data

The first version of this application will be a plain text editor. We'll now modify the interface for the document to display a text field, and make the `Document` class save and load plain text.

1. *Open* Document.xib *and delete the label in the window.*

   By default, the interface contains a window, which has a label inside it. We'll keep the window, but lose the label.

2. *Add a wrapping text field to the window.*

   Open the Objects Library and scroll until you find "Wrapping text field." Alternatively, search for "wrapping" at the bottom of the library.

   Drag the text field into the window and resize it to make it fill the entire window.

   When you're done, the interface should look like Figure 12-2.

3. *Open the assistant and connect the text field to the class.*

   Once the interface has been built, you need to connect the interface to the document class.

   Open the assistant and *Document.h* should open. If it doesn't, use the jump bar at the top of the assistant editor to select it.

   Control-drag from the text field into `NSDocument`'s `@interface`. Create a new outlet called `textField`.

In addition to having a variable that connects the document class to the text field, we need a variable that contains the document's text. This is because the document loading and interface setup take place at different times—when your `-readFromData :ofType:error:` method is called, the `textField` won't yet exist, so you must store the information in memory. This is also a better design as far as model-view-controller goes, since it means that your data and your views are kept separate.

4. *Add and synthesize an* `NSString` *property called* `text`.

   Add the following code to `Document`'s `@interface`:

   ```
   @property (strong) NSString* text;
   ```

Add the following code to Document's `@implementation`:

```
@synthesize text;
```

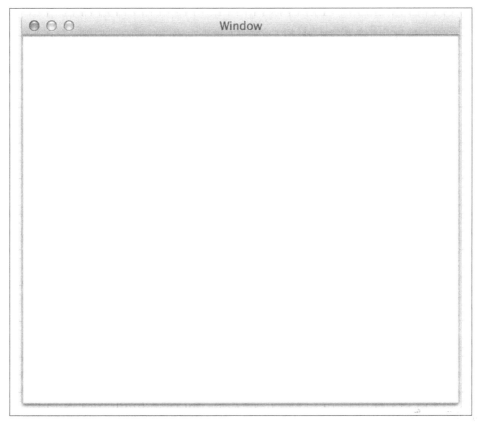

Figure 12-2. The final UI for the document window

Now we'll update the loading and saving methods, and make them load and save the text. We'll also update the `-windowControllerDidLoadNib:` method, which is called when the interface for this document has been loaded and is your code's opportunity to prepare the interface with your loaded data.

5. *Replace methods* `-dataOfType:error:`, `-readFromData:ofType:error:`, *and* `-windowControllerDidLoadNib:` *with the following code:*

```
- (void)windowControllerDidLoadNib:(NSWindowController *)aController
{
    [super windowControllerDidLoadNib:aController];

    if (self.text == nil)
```

```
            self.text = @"";
        textField.stringValue = self.text;
    }

    - (NSData *)dataOfType:(NSString *)typeName error:(NSError **)outError
    {
        self.text = textField.stringValue;
        return [self.text dataUsingEncoding:NSUTF8StringEncoding];
    }

    - (BOOL)readFromData:(NSData *)data ofType:(NSString *)typeName
        error:(NSError **)outError
    {
        if ([data length] > 0) {
            NSString* string = [[NSString alloc] initWithData:data
                encoding:NSUTF8StringEncoding];
            self.text = string;
        } else {
            self.text = @"";
        }

        return YES;
    }
```

Now run the application and try creating, saving, and opening documents. You can also use Versions to look at previous versions of the documents you work with. If you quit the app and relaunch it, all open documents will reopen.

Saving More Complex Data

Simple text is easy to read and write, but more complex applications need more structured information. While you could write your own methods for serializing and deserializing your model objects, it's often the case that the data you want to save is no more complex than a dictionary or array of strings and numbers.

JavaScript Object Notation (JSON) is an ideal method for representing data like this. JSON is a simple, human-readable, lightweight way to represent arrays, dictionaries, numbers, and strings, and both OS X and iOS provide tools for converting certain useful objects into JSON and back.

The NSJSONSerialization class allows you to provide a *property list class*, and get back an NSData object that contains the JSON data that describes that class. A property list class is one of these classes or their mutable variants:

- NSDictionary
- NSArray
- NSString

- NSNumber

In the case of the container classes (dictionaries and arrays), these objects are only allowed to contain other property list classes.

To get JSON data for an object, you do this:

```
NSError* error = nil;
NSData* serializedData = [NSJSONSerialization dataWithJSONObject:dictionary
    options:NSJSONWritingPrettyPrinted error:&error];

// after this call, 'serializedData' is either nil or full of JSON data.
// if there was a problem, the 'error' variable is set to point to an
// NSError object that describes the problem.
```

You can pass other values for the options: parameter as well—check the documentation for NSJSONSerialization. If you don't want to pass an option in, you can pass 0.

To load JSON data in and get back an Objective-C object, you do this:

```
NSDictionary* loadedDictionary =
  [NSJSONSerialization JSONObjectWithData:serialisedData
                                                    options:0
                                                    error:error];
```

Note that the object that gets returned may not be the same class as what was saved. For example, the following will result in an exception being thrown:

```
NSDictionary* someObject = [NSDictionary dictionaryWithObject:@"Hello!"
    forKey:@"greeting"];
NSData* data = [NSJSONSerialization dataWithJSONObject:someObject
    options:0 error:nil];

// .. and then later:

NSArray* anArray = [NSJSONSerialization JSONObjectWithData:data options:0
    error:nil];

NSString* firstObject = [anArray objectAtIndex:0];
// ERROR! anArray is actually an NSDictionary!
```

For this reason, you should check the loaded objects and make sure they're the right type (and if they're dictionaries, contain the right keys; if they're arrays, are of a length that you expect):

```
if ([anArray isKindOfClass:[NSArray class]] [anArray count] >= 1) {
    // we know it's an array, and has at least 1 object in it
}
```

We'll now modify the application to store both a block of text and a Boolean value in a JSON-formatted document. To do this, we'll include a checkbox control in the application's UI, and a BOOL property in the Document.

1. Open *Document.xib*.

2. Resize the text field to make some room at the bottom of the window.

3. Drag a checkbox into the window. The interface should now look something like Figure 12-3.

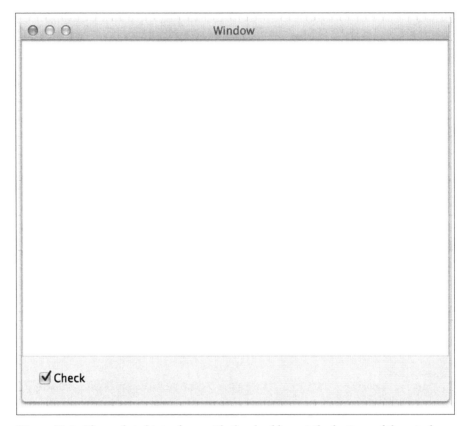

Figure 12-3. The updated interface, with the checkbox at the bottom of the window

4. Open *Document.h* in the assistant.

5. Control-drag from the checkbox into Document's `@interface`, and create a new outlet called **checkbox**.

6. Add and synthesize a `BOOL` property called `checked` to Document.

7. Replace the methods `-dataOfType:error:`, `-readFromData:ofType:error:` and `-windowControllerDidLoadNib:` with the following code:

```
- (void)windowControllerDidLoadNib:(NSWindowController *)aController
{
    [super windowControllerDidLoadNib:aController];
```

```objc
    if (self.text == nil)
        self.text = @"";

    textField.stringValue = self.text;
    checkbox.intValue = self.checked;

}

- (NSData *)dataOfType:(NSString *)typeName error:(NSError **)outError
{
    self.text = textField.stringValue;
    self.checked = checkbox.intValue;

    NSMutableDictionary* dictionary = [NSMutableDictionary dictionary];

    [dictionary setValue:[NSNumber numberWithBool:self.checked]
        forKey:@"checked"];
    [dictionary setValue:self.text forKey:@"text"];

    NSError* error = nil;
    NSData* serializedData = [NSJSONSerialization
        dataWithJSONObject:dictionary options:NSJSONWritingPrettyPrinted
                    error:error];

    if (serializedData == nil || error != nil)
        return nil;

    return serializedData;
}

- (BOOL)readFromData:(NSData *)data ofType:(NSString *)typeName
    error:(NSError **)outError
{

    NSDictionary* loadedDictionary;

    NSError* error = nil;

    loadedDictionary = [NSJSONSerialization JSONObjectWithData:data
        options:0 error:error];

    if (loadedDictionary == nil || error != nil)
        return NO;

    self.text = [loadedDictionary valueForKey:@"text"];
    self.checked = [[loadedDictionary valueForKey:@"checked"] boolValue];

    return YES;
}
```

This new saving code stores the document information in an `NSDictionary`, and returns the JSON in the `NSData`.

> If you're curious, the JSON representation of this dictionary looks like this:
>
> ```
> {
>     "checked" : true,
>     "text" : "Hello!!"
> }
> ```

The loading code does the same in reverse—it takes the `NSData` that contains the JSON, and converts it to an `NSDictionary`. The loaded dictionary then has the data copied out of it.

Now run the application and create, load, and save some new documents!

Document-Based Applications on iOS

In contrast to apps on OS X, apps on iOS generally only have one document open at a time. This means that the document API is simpler, since an `NSDocumentController` is not needed—the concept of "frontmost document" doesn't apply.

In iOS, instead of using `NSDocument`, you use `UIDocument`. However, instead of users selecting which document to open via the Finder, you instead present a list of the user's documents and allow the user to select a file. When she chooses a file, you create an instance of your document class and instruct the document object to load from the appropriate URL.

You also provide the interface for letting the user create a new document; when she does so, you again create an instance of your document class and immediately save the new document. Generally, you then immediately open the newly created file.

Representing Documents with UIDocument

We're going to create an application for iPhone that acts as a simple text editor. Creating document-based applications on iOS is less automated than on OS X, but is still fairly straightforward.

This application will present its interface with two view controllers: a master view controller that lists all available documents, and a detail view controller that displays the contents of the currently open document and allows the user to edit it.

The built-in master-detail application template for iOS is ideal for this, and we'll use that. We'll also have to create our `UIDocument` subclass manually.

---

1. *Create a new master-detail app for iOS.* Make this application designed for iPhone, and turn Automatic Reference Counting and Storyboards on.

   We'll start by creating the interface.

2. *Open* MainStoryboard.storyboard *and go to the master view controller.*

3. Add a bar button item to the navigation bar.

 This button will be the "create new document" button. Select it and set its identifier to Add to make it display a + symbol.

4. *Open* MasterViewController.h *in the assistant.*

5. *Connect the button to the* MasterViewController *class.*

   Control-drag from the button to MasterViewController's @interface.

   Create an action named **createDocument**.

6. *Select the table view and make it use dynamic prototype cells.*

7. *Update the prototype cell.*

   Select the prototype cell that now appears in the table view. Set its style to basic and its identifier to **FileCell**.

   Set its accessory to Disclosure Indicator.

8. *Create a segue from the master view controller to the detail view controller.*

   Control drag from the master view controller to detail view controller. Create a push segue, and name the new segue **OpenDocument**.

   We'll now create the UI for the documents.

9. *Open the detail view controller and delete the label in the middle of the view.*

10. *Add a text view.*

    Drag a UITextView into the view controller's view. Make the text view fill the entire screen.

11. *Open* DetailViewController.h *in the assistant.*

12. *Connect the text view to the detail view controller.*

    Control-drag from the text view into *DetailViewController.h*+'s +@interface section.

    Create a new outlet called **textView**.

13. *Add a Done button to the navigation bar in the detail view controller.*

Drag a bar button item into the lefthand side of the navigation bar and set its identifier to **Done**. (We'll make the code not display the Back button.)

14. *Make the view controller the delegate for the text view.*

    We want the detail view controller to be notified when the user makes changes. Control-drag from the text view to the view controller, and select *delegate* from the menu that pops up.

We'll now make the code for our UIDocument subclass, called SampleDocument. This document class will manage its data in a flat file, which means that it will work by loading and saving its content in an NSData.

15. *Create a new Objective-C class.* Name the new class **SampleDocument** and make it a subclass of UIDocument.

16. *Update* SampleDocument.h. Make *SampleDocument.h* look like the following code:

```
#import <UIKit/UIKit.h>

@interface SampleDocument : UIDocument

@property (nonatomic, strong) NSString* text;

@end
```

17. *Update* SampleDocument.m. Make *SampleDocument.m* look like the following code:

```
#import "SampleDocument.h"

@implementation SampleDocument

@synthesize text;

// Called when a document is opened.
- (BOOL)loadFromContents:(id)contents ofType:(NSString *)typeName
    error:(NSError *__autoreleasing *)outError {

    // Cast the contents variable to an NSData, for convenience
    NSData* data = contents;

    if ([data length] > 0) {
        // The file isn't empty, so create a string from its contents
        self.text = [[NSString alloc] initWithData:data
        encoding:NSUTF8StringEncoding];
    } else {
        self.text = @"";
    }

    return YES;
}
```

```
    // Called when the system needs a snapshot of the current state of
        the document, for autosaving.
    - (id)contentsForType:(NSString *)typeName
        error:(NSError *__autoreleasing *)outError {

        if (self.text == nil)
            self.text = @"";

        return [self.text dataUsingEncoding:NSUTF8StringEncoding];
    }

    @end
```

We'll now update the code for *MasterViewController.m* to display a list of files. Make it look like the following:

```
#import "MasterViewController.h"
#import "DetailViewController.h"
#import "SampleDocument.h"

@interface MasterViewController () {
    NSArray* _files;
}
@end

@implementation MasterViewController

- (NSURL*)URLforDocuments {
    return [[[NSFileManager defaultManager]
        URLsForDirectory:NSDocumentDirectory inDomains:NSUserDomainMask]
            lastObject];
}

- (void) updateFileList {
    _files = [[NSFileManager defaultManager]
        contentsOfDirectoryAtURL:[self URLforDocuments]
        includingPropertiesForKeys:nil options:0 error:nil];

    [self.tableView reloadData];
}

#pragma mark - View lifecycle

- (void)viewWillAppear:(BOOL)animated
{
    [super viewWillAppear:animated];
    [self updateFileList];
}


- (BOOL)shouldAutorotateToInterfaceOrientation:
```

```
            (UIInterfaceOrientation)interfaceOrientation
{
    // Return YES for supported orientations
    return (interfaceOrientation != UIInterfaceOrientationPortraitUpsideDown);
}


- (void)prepareForSegue:(UIStoryboardSegue *)segue sender:(id)sender {

    DetailViewController* detailViewController =
        segue.destinationViewController;

    if ([segue.identifier isEqualToString:@"OpenDocument"]) {
        SampleDocument* document = sender;
        detailViewController.detailItem = document;
    }
}

#pragma mark - Table View Controller


- (NSInteger)numberOfSectionsInTableView:(UITableView *)tableView {
    return 1;
}

- (NSInteger)tableView:(UITableView *)tableView
    numberOfRowsInSection:(NSInteger)section {
    return [_files count];
}

- (UITableViewCell*) tableView:(UITableView *)tableView
    cellForRowAtIndexPath:(NSIndexPath *)indexPath {

    UITableViewCell* cell = [tableView
        dequeueReusableCellWithIdentifier:@"FileCell"];

    NSURL* url = [_files objectAtIndex:indexPath.row];

    cell.textLabel.text = [url lastPathComponent];

    return cell;

}

- (void)tableView:(UITableView *)tableView
    didSelectRowAtIndexPath:(NSIndexPath *)indexPath {

    NSURL* url = [_files objectAtIndex:indexPath.row];

    SampleDocument* document = [[SampleDocument alloc] initWithFileURL:url];
```

```objc
    [document openWithCompletionHandler:^(BOOL success) {
        [self performSegueWithIdentifier:@"OpenDocument" sender:document];
    }];
}

- (IBAction)createDocument:(id)sender {

    NSDateFormatter* formatter = [[NSDateFormatter alloc] init];
    [formatter setDateFormat:@"yyyy-MM-dd HH:mm:ssZZZ"];
    NSString* fileName = [NSString stringWithFormat:
        @"Document %@.sampleDocument",
        [formatter stringFromDate:[NSDate date]]];

    NSURL* url = [[self URLforDocuments]
     URLByAppendingPathComponent:fileName];


    SampleDocument* document = [[SampleDocument alloc] initWithFileURL:url];

    [document saveToURL:url
        forSaveOperation:UIDocumentSaveForCreating
        completionHandler:^(BOOL success) {
        [self performSegueWithIdentifier:@"OpenDocument" sender:document];
    }];

}
@end
```

Finally, we'll update the code for DetailViewController to make it display the content from the loaded SampleDocument object and send the user's changes to the document. The *DetailViewController* will also notice when the user taps the Done button that was added earlier, and signal to the document that it should be saved and closed.

We also want to make the class conform to the UITextViewDelegate protocol, so that we receive changes from the user as she types them.

To make DetailViewController conform to UITextController, go to *DetailView Controller.h* and update the declaration of DetailViewController to look like the following code:

```objc
@interface DetailViewController : UIViewController <UITextViewDelegate>
```

Finally, make *DetailViewController.m* look like the following code:

```objc
#import "DetailViewController.h"
#import "SampleDocument.h"

@interface DetailViewController ()
- (void)configureView;
@end

@implementation DetailViewController
```

```
@synthesize textView = _textView;
@synthesize detailItem = _detailItem;
@synthesize detailDescriptionLabel = _detailDescriptionLabel;

#pragma mark - Managing the detail item

- (void)setDetailItem:(id)newDetailItem
{
    if (_detailItem != newDetailItem) {
        _detailItem = newDetailItem;

        // Update the view.
        [self configureView];
    }
}

- (void)configureView
{
    // Update the user interface for the detail item.

    if (self.detailItem) {
        SampleDocument* document = self.detailItem;
        self.textView.text = document.text;
    }
}

- (void)textViewDidChange:(UITextView *)textView {
    SampleDocument* document = self.detailItem;
    document.text = self.textView.text;

}

#pragma mark - View lifecycle

- (void)viewDidLoad
{
    [super viewDidLoad];
    [self configureView];
    self.navigationItem.hidesBackButton = YES;
}

- (void)viewDidUnload
{

    [self setTextView:nil];
    [super viewDidUnload];
}

- (BOOL)shouldAutorotateToInterfaceOrientation:
    (UIInterfaceOrientation)interfaceOrientation
{
```

```
    // Return YES for supported orientations
    return (interfaceOrientation != UIInterfaceOrientationPortraitUpsideDown);
}

- (IBAction)done:(id)sender {
    SampleDocument* document = self.detailItem;
    [document saveToURL:document.fileURL
        forSaveOperation:UIDocumentSaveForOverwriting
        completionHandler:^(BOOL success) {
          [self.navigationController popViewControllerAnimated:YES];
    }];

}
@end
```

In this code, the DetailViewController object has received the SampleDocument object loaded by the MasterViewController, and makes the text view display the text that it contains. Every time the user makes a change to the text field, the text in the Sample Document is updated; the SampleDocument will automatically save the document's contents in order to prevent data loss if something bad happens (like a crash or the device running out of battery).

When the Done button is tapped, the document is told to close, which saves any unsaved changes. Once this process is complete, the view controller dismisses itself.

CHAPTER 13

Networking

Many chapters in books like this begin with something like, "The ability to talk to computers over the network is an increasingly popular feature." We won't bore you with that. Suffice to say—it's the 21st century, networking is huge, and you need your app to send and receive data. Let's learn how.

In this chapter, you'll learn how to make connections over the network and access resources with URLs. You'll also learn how to use Bonjour to discover nearby network services so that you can connect to them. Finally, you'll learn how to create your own network service and receive connections from other devices.

All of the content in this chapter applies to both OS X and iOS.

Connections

At the lowest level, network connections in Cocoa are the same as in every other popular OS. The Berkeley sockets API, the fundamental networking and connectivity API used on Windows and almost every Unix OS (which includes OS X and iOS), is available, allowing you to make connections to any computer on the network and send and receive data.

However, working with such a low-level API can be cumbersome, especially when you want to use popular, higher-level protocols like HTTP. To make things more fun for developers like us, Cocoa provides a higher-level API that provides a simple interface for accessing content via URLs on the Internet.

A URL is a *Uniform Resource Locator*. It's a location on the Internet, and specifies the location of the server to connect to, the protocol to use, and the location of the resource on the server. Consider the following URL:

```
http://oreilly.com/iphone/index.html
```

In this case, *oreilly.com* is the location of the computer on the Internet, *http* is the scheme (here, *HyperText Transfer Protocol*), and */iphone/index.html* is the location of the specific resource hosted by this computer.

When working with network requests, there are three primary classes that you interact with: `NSURL`, `NSURLRequest`, and `NSURLConnection`.

NSURL

The `NSURL` class represents a URL. `NSURL`s are just model objects—they contain information about the location of the resource they point to, and provide a number of useful methods for retrieving specific components of the URL, as well as creating URLs relative to other URLs.

The easiest way to create an `NSURL` is to create one with `+URLWithString:` like this:

```
NSURL* myURL = [NSURL URLWithString:@"http://oreilly.com"];
```

 If you use `URLWithString:`, the string you provide must be a complete, well-formed URL. If it isn't well-formed, the method will return `nil`. This applies to any other method that creates new URLs—if you ask `NSURL` to create a URL that doesn't make sense, `NSURL` will return `nil`.

You can also create URLs that are relative to other URLs:

```
// creates http://oreilly.com/resources/index.html
NSURL* relativeURL = [NSURL URLWithString:@"resources/index.html"
    relativeToURL:[NSURL URLWithString:@"http://oreilly.com/"]];
```

Once you have an `NSURL`, you can retrieve information about it. For example, to retrieve the host (the computer name), you can do the following:

```
NSString* host = [relativeURL host]; // @"oreilly.com"
```

 `NSURL` is an immutable class. If you want to create a URL object that you can later modify, use `NSMutableURL`.

URLs are also useful for indicating the location of a file or folder on the local disk, and both iOS and OS X are increasingly trending toward using them instead of using strings that contain paths.

A file URL is a regular NSURL, but uses the scheme file:. A file URL, therefore, looks like this:

```
file://localhost/Applications/
```

There are special methods in NSURL that make it easier to create file URLs. For example, you can create one using the fileURLWithPath: method:

```
NSURL* myFileURL = [NSURL fileURLWithPath:@"/Applications/"];
```

NSURLRequest

Once you have an NSURL object that points to where your resource is located, you construct an NSURLRequest. While NSURL points to *where* the resource is on the network, NSURLRequest describes *how* it should be accessed.

NSURLRequest takes an NSURL and adds information about things like how long the request should go without an answer before timing out, whether (and how) to use caching, and, if the request is an HTTP request, which request method (GET, POST, PUT and so on) to use and what the HTTP request's body should be.

For most cases, you can use the requestWithURL: method to create an NSURLRequest given an NSURL:

```
NSURLRequest* request = [NSURLRequest requestWithURL:myURL];
```

If you want to have more control over how the request is performed, you can use requestWithURL:cachePolicy:timeoutInterval:. This method is the same as the previous one, but you specify how the request should cache content that it downloads and how long the request should wait before giving up.

requestWithURL: creates a request that caches content according to the default caching policy of the protocol you're using (for example, HTTP caches depending on whether the server instructs it to, while FTP never caches) and times out after 60 seconds.

If you want to send a POST request or make changes to the request, you can use NSMutableURLRequest. This is the mutable version of the NSURLRequest class, and allows you to configure the request after you create it. To create a POST request, for example, you use the setHTTPMethod: method:

```
NSMutableURLRequest* mutableRequest = [NSMutableURLRequest
    requestWithURL:myURL];
[mutableRequest setHTTPMethod:@"POST"];
```

NSURLConnection

Once you have an NSURLRequest to use, you can go ahead and execute that request on the network.

Because network requests aren't instant, your code needs to be able to manage the life-cycle of the connection. This is done for you by the NSURLConnection object, which represents a connection in progress.

NSURLConnection takes an NSURLRequest and goes off to the network to perform the request. When the request is done, a block of code is run, which is passed the server's response, the loaded data, and any error that might have occurred. The data is provided as an NSData object, so it's up to you to convert it to something your application can use, such as text or an image.

NSURLConnection is a slightly more complex class than NSURL and NSURLRequest. We'll go into more detail on how it works in the sample code in the section "Building a Net-worked Application" (page 218).

NSURLResponse and NSHTTPURLResponse

The response classes describe the initial response from the server about the request. This information includes the expected size of the downloaded file (in bytes), and the suggested filename that the server wants to call it. If you're making an HTTP request, the server response is an instance of the NSHTTPURLResponse, which also includes the HTTP status code and the headers that the server sends down.

You don't generally create your own NSURLResponse instances, but rather get them from an NSURLConnection object when it first successfully gets a response from the server and starts downloading content.

Building a Networked Application

To put all of this together, we'll build a simple application that downloads an image from the Internet and displays it in an NSImageView.

The exact same networking code will work on iOS, but using UIImageView rather than NSImageView.

This application will download an image from Placekitten, the world's most adorable placeholder image service. Of course, web services come and go, so if you're living in the World of Tomorrow and Placekitten is long since history, find another image URL to use instead. And then eat another meal in pill form and catch a space-taxi to the moon.

1. *Create the project.* Make a new Cocoa application called **Networking**.

2. *Build the interface.* Open *MainWindow.xib*. Drag in an NSImageView.

3. *Connect the interface.* Open *AppDelegate.h* in the assistant.

   Control-drag from the image view to AppDelegate's interface. Create a new outlet called imageView.

4. *Add the code that performs the network request.* Open *AppDelegate.m* and replace the -applicationDidFinishLaunching: method with the following code:

```
- (void)applicationDidFinishLaunching:(NSNotification *)aNotification
{

    // PlaceKitten.com URLs work like this:
    // http://placekitten.com/<width>/<height>

    NSInteger width = (int)self.imageView.bounds.size.width;
    NSInteger height = (int)self.imageView.bounds.size.height;

    NSString* urlString = [NSString
        stringWithFormat:@"http://placekitten.com/%i/%i", width, height];

    NSURL* url = [NSURL URLWithString:urlString];
    NSURLRequest* request = [NSURLRequest requestWithURL:url];

    [NSURLConnection sendAsynchronousRequest:request
        queue:[NSOperationQueue mainQueue]
        completionHandler:^(NSURLResponse * response,
            NSData * data,
            NSError * error) {
        NSImage* image = [[NSImage alloc] initWithData:data];
        self.imageView.image = image;
    }];

}
```

This code creates the URL based on the size of the image view, and then creates an NSURLRequest for that URL. It then asks the NSURLConnection class to go and perform the request; the completion block takes the loaded data, converts it to an NSImage, and provides the image to the image view.

Now test the application. Run the app, and feel free to squeal in delight when you see a cute kitten.

Discovering Nearby Services

If you're writing networking code that deals with resources on the local network, your code needs a way to figure out where they are.

Bonjour is a protocol based on multicast DNS that allows a network service to advertise its presence on a network, and provides a method for clients to find services. Bonjour doesn't handle the actual connection, just the discovery.

When you want to find local services via Bonjour, you use an NSNetServiceBrowser object. This object, once created and started, looks for network services that match the description that you provide it. Because network services come and go, the NSNet ServiceBrowser continuously notifies its delegate object when services become available and when they stop being available.

Once NSNetServiceBrowser locates a network service, you can ask for additional information about the service such as the hostname of the computer providing the service and the port number that the service is running on. This is called *resolving* the service, and takes a bit of extra time (which is why the service browser doesn't do it for every service it discovers). When the service resolves (or fails to resolve), the NSNetService object informs its delegate.

To be notified of when NSNetServiceBrowser notices when services appear and disappear, your object needs to conform to the NSNetServiceBrowserDelegate protocol. To be notified of when an NSNetService resolves, your object also needs to conform to the NSNetServiceDelegate protocol.

Browsing for Shared iTunes Libraries

If you have "Share my library on the local network" turned on in iTunes, iTunes will broadcast the library via Bonjour. Specifically, it will advertise that your computer is hosting a DAAP (Digital Audio Access Protocol) server.

To discover services of this type, you get an NSNetServiceBrowser to search for _daap._tcp services. We'll make a simple application that browses for, resolves, and logs any shared iTunes libraries it finds.

All you need to do is create a new Cocoa application called **iTunesDetector** and update *AppDelegate.m* so that it looks like the following code:

```
#import "AppDelegate.h"

@interface AppDelegate () <NSNetServiceBrowserDelegate, NSNetServiceDelegate> {
```

```
    NSNetServiceBrowser* browser;
    NSMutableArray* services;
}

@end

@implementation AppDelegate

@synthesize window = _window;

- (void)applicationDidFinishLaunching:(NSNotification *)aNotification
{

    services = [NSMutableArray array];

    browser = [[NSNetServiceBrowser alloc] init];

    browser.delegate = self;
    [browser searchForServicesOfType:@"_daap._tcp" inDomain:nil];
}

- (void)netServiceBrowser:(NSNetServiceBrowser *)aNetServiceBrowser
    didFindService:(NSNetService *)aNetService moreComing:(BOOL)moreComing {

    [services addObject:aNetService];

        aNetService.delegate = self;
    [aNetService resolveWithTimeout:5];

    NSLog(@"Found a service: %@", aNetService);

}

- (void)netServiceBrowser:(NSNetServiceBrowser *)aNetServiceBrowser
    didRemoveService:(NSNetService *)aNetService moreComing:(BOOL)moreComing {

    [services removeObject:aNetService];
    NSLog(@"A service was removed: %@", aNetService);

}

- (void)netServiceDidResolveAddress:(NSNetService *)sender {
    NSURL* serviceURL = [NSURL URLWithString:[NSString
        stringWithFormat:@"http://%@:%i", sender.hostName, sender.port]];

    NSLog(@"Resolved address for service %@: %@", sender, serviceURL);

}
```

```
-(void)netService:(NSNetService *)sender
    didNotResolve:(NSDictionary *)errorDict {
    NSLog(@"Couldn't resolve address for service %@: %@", sender, errorDict);
}
```

This code does the following things:

1. It adds a class extension to the AppDelegate class, which makes the class conform to the NSNetServiceBrowserDelegate and NSNetServiceDelegate protocols, and adds two instance variables: an NSNetServiceBrowser and an NSMutableArray. The net service browser variable is needed to keep the net service browser in memory while it does its work; the array will be used to keep the discovered network services around.

2. In the applicationDidFinishLaunching: method, the NSNetServiceBrowser is created and told to start browsing for _daap._tcp services.

3. The rest of the methods handle the cases of services being discovered, removed, resolved, or failing to be resolved.

Now run the application and watch the log to see your iTunes library get discovered. If you don't see anything appear, make sure that iTunes is open and that you're sharing your library. Do this by opening Preferences, going to Sharing, and turning on "Share my library on my local network.")

CHAPTER 14

Working with the Real World

Desktops, laptops, iPhones, and iPads are all physical devices and exist in the real world —either on your desk, on your lap, or in your hand. For a long time, your apps were largely confined to your computer, and weren't able to do much with the outside world besides instructing a printer to print a document.

Starting with iOS and OS X 10.6, however, things began to change, and your code is now able to learn about the user's location, how the device is moving and being held, and how far away the computer is from landmarks.

In this chapter, you'll learn about how your programs can interact with the outside world. Specifically, you'll learn about how to use Core Location to determine where your computer or device is on the planet, how to use Core Motion to learn about how the user is holding the device, and how to use the printing services available on OS X and iOS to work with printers.

 Most of the technology discussed in this chapter works on both OS X and iOS. Some of the technology has an identical API on both platforms (Core Location), some has different APIs on the two platforms (print services) and some is only available on iOS (Core Motion). We'll let you know which technology is available where.

Working with Location

Almost every user of your software will be located on Earth.[1]

---

1. Unless, of course, you're taking your iPhone to space (*http://bit.ly/TKgycl*).

Knowing where the user is on the planet is tremendously useful, because it enables you to provide more relevant information. For example, while the recommendations service Yelp works just fine as a search engine for businesses and restaurants, it only becomes truly useful when it limits its results to businesses and restaurants near the user.

Location awareness is a technology that is at its most helpful when on a mobile device (like an iPhone or iPad), since its location is more likely to change. However, it's also applicable to a more fixed-location device (like a desktop or, to a lesser extent, laptops) to know where it is in the world. A great example of this is the time-zone system in OS X—if you get off a plane, your time zone will have likely changed, and OS X uses its built-in location systems to work out how to set the clock to local time.

In this section, the exercises we'll be building will run on iOS, but the techniques apply equally well to OS X.

Location Hardware

There are a number of different techniques for determining where a computer is on the planet, and each requires different hardware. The ones in use by iOS and OS X are:

- GPS, the Global Positioning System
- WiFi base station lookups
- Cell tower lookups

GPS

GPS devices became popular first as navigation assistants for cars, and later as features built into smartphones. Initially developed by the US military, the GPS is a constellation of satellites that contain extremely precise clocks and continuously broadcast time information. A GPS receiver is able to listen for these time signals and compare them to determine where on the planet the user is.

Depending on how many satellites the GPS receiver can see, GPS is capable of working out a location to less than one meter of accuracy.

The GPS receiver is only included on the iPhone, and on iPad models that contain 3G or 4G cellular radios. It's not included on any desktop, laptop, or iPod touch, or on WiFi-only iPads.

WiFi base station lookups

While a device that uses WiFi to access the Internet may move around a lot, the base stations that provide that connection generally don't move around at all. This fact can be used to determine the location of a user if a GPS receiver isn't available.

Apple maintains a gigantic database of WiFi hotspots, along with rough coordinates that indicate where those hotspots are. If a device can see any WiFi hotspots and is also connected to the Internet, it can tell Apple's servers, "I can see hotspots A, B, and C." Apple's servers can then reply, "If you can see them, then you must be near them, and therefore you must be near location X." The device keeps a subset of this database locally, in case a wifi lookup is necessary when the device has no access to the internet.

This method of locating the user isn't terribly precise, but it's able to get within 100 meters of accuracy. Because it uses hardware that's built into all devices that can run OS X and iOS, this capability is available on every device.

Cell tower lookups

If a device uses cell towers to communicate with the Internet, it can perform a similar trick with the towers as with WiFi base stations. The exact same technique is used, although the results are slightly less accurate—because cell towers are less numerous than WiFi stations, cell tower lookups can only get within a kilometer or so of accuracy.

Cell tower lookups are available on any device that includes a cell radio, meaning the iPhone and the 3G and 4G models of iPad.

The Core Location Framework

As you can see, not every piece of location-sensing hardware is available on all devices. Because it would be tremendously painful to have to write three different chunks of code for the three different location services and then switch between them depending on hardware availability, OS X and iOS provide a single location services API that handles all of the details of working with the location hardware.

Core Location is the framework that your applications use to work out where they are on the planet. Core Location accesses whatever location hardware is available, puts the results together, and lets your code know its best guess for where the user is on the planet. It's also able to work out the user's altitude and speed.

When you work with Core Location, you work with an instance of CLLocation Manager. This class is your interface to the Core Location framework—you create a manager, optionally provide it with additional information on how you want it to behave (such as how precise you want the location information to be), and then provide it with a delegate object. The location manager will then periodically contact the delegate object and inform it of the user's changing location.

CLLocationManager is actually a slightly incomplete name for the class, since it doesn't just provide geographic location information. It also provides heading information—

that is, the direction the user is facing relative to magnetic north or true north. This information is only available on devices that contain a magnetometer, which acts as a digital compass. At the time of writing, all currently shipping iOS devices contain one, but devices older than the iPhone 3GS, iPod touch 3rd generation, and iPad 2 don't.

To work with Core Location, you create the `CLLocationManager` delegate, configure it, and then send it the `startUpdatingLocation` message. When you're done needing to know about the user's location, you send it the `stopUpdatingLocation` message.

 You should always turn off a `CLLocationManager` when you're done, since location technologies are both CPU intensive and can require the use of power-hungry hardware. Think of the user's battery!

To work with Core Location, you provide it with an object that conforms to the `CLLocationManagerDelegate` protocol, which it uses as a delegate. The key method in this protocol is -`locationManager:didUpdateToLocation:fromLocation:`, which is sent periodically by the location manager.

This method receives both the location that the user is now at (as far as Core Location can tell) and his previous location. These two locations are represented as `CLLocation` objects, which contain information like the latitude and longitude, altitude, speed, and accuracy.

Core Location may also fail to get the user's location at all. If, for example, GPS is unavailable and neither WiFi base stations nor cell towers can be found, no location information will be available. If this happens, the `CLLocationManager` will send its delegate the -`locationManager:didFailWithError:` message.

Working with Core Location

To demonstrate Core Location, we'll create a simple application that attempts to display the user's location. This will be an OS X application, but the same API applies to iOS.

To get started with Core Location, you first need to make your application use the Core Location framework. Start by creating a new Cocoa application called **Location**.

Next, select the project at the top of the project navigator. The project will appear in the main editor. Select the `Locations` target, and click the + button at the bottom of Linked Frameworks and Libraries. The frameworks window will appear.

Browse or search for "*CoreLocation.framework*". When you find it, click the Add button.

Now that the framework has been added to the application, we'll build the interface. The interface for this app will be deliberately simple—it will show the user's latitude and longitude coordinates, as well as the radius of uncertainty that Core Location has about the user.

No location technology is completely precise, so unless you're willing to spend millions of dollars on (classified) technology, the best any consumer GPS device will get is about 5 to 10 meters of accuracy. If you're not using GPS, which is the case when using a device that doesn't have it built in, Core Location will use less-accurate technologies like WiFi or cell tower triangulation.

This means that Core Location is always inaccurate to some extent. When Core Location updates its delegate with the location, the latitude and longitude provided are actually the center of a circle that the user is in, and the value of the `CLLocation` property `horizontalAccuracy` indicates the radius of that circle, represented in meters.

The interface of this demo application, therefore, will show the user's location as well as how accurate Core Location reports it is.

To start out, open *MainWindow.xib* and select the window.

You'll now add the latitude, longitude, and accuracy labels. Drag in three labels and make them read **Latitude**, **Longitude**, and **Accuracy**. Lay them out vertically.

Drag in another three labels, and lay them out vertically next to the first three.

Finally, drag in a circular progress indicator and place it below the labels.

When you're done, your interface should look like Figure 14-1.

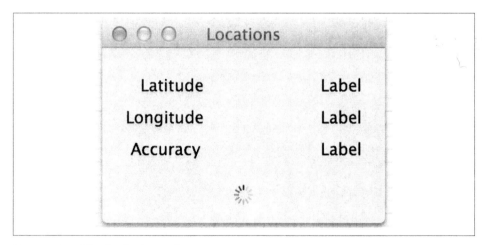

Figure 14-1. The finished interface

You'll now connect the interface to the app delegate. Open *AppDelegate.h* in the assistant and control-drag from each of the labels on the right. Create outlets for each of them called **latitudeLabel**, **longitudeLabel**, and **accuracyLabel**, respectively. Control-drag from the progress indicator, and create an outlet for it called **spinner**.

Now make the app delegate conform to the CLLocationManagerDelegate protocol and import the Core Location framework header. When you're done, *AppDelegate.h* should look like the following code:

```
#import <Cocoa/Cocoa.h>
#import <CoreLocation/CoreLocation.h>

@interface AppDelegate : NSObject <NSApplicationDelegate,
  CLLocationManagerDelegate>

@property (assign) IBOutlet NSWindow *window;
@property (weak) IBOutlet NSTextField *latitudeLabel;
@property (weak) IBOutlet NSTextField *longitudeLabel;
@property (weak) IBOutlet NSTextField *accuracyLabel;

@property (weak) IBOutlet NSLayoutConstraint *spinner;
@end
```

Create the CLLocationManager and make it start updating the user's location by making *AppDelegate.m* look like the following code:

```
#import "AppDelegate.h"

@interface AppDelegate () {
    CLLocationManager* _locationManager;
}

@end

@implementation AppDelegate

@synthesize window = _window;
@synthesize latitudeLabel = _latitudeLabel;
@synthesize longitudeLabel = _longitudeLabel;
@synthesize accuracyLabel = _accuracyLabel;
@synthesize spinner = _spinner;

- (void)applicationDidFinishLaunching:(NSNotification *)aNotification
{
    _locationManager = [[CLLocationManager alloc] init];
    _locationManager.delegate = self;
    [_locationManager startUpdatingLocation];
}

- (void)locationManager:(CLLocationManager *)manager
    didUpdateToLocation:(CLLocation *)newLocation
    fromLocation:(CLLocation *)oldLocation {
```

```
    self.latitudeLabel.stringValue = [NSString stringWithFormat:@"%.2f",
        newLocation.coordinate.latitude];
    self.longitudeLabel.stringValue = [NSString stringWithFormat:@"%.2f",
        newLocation.coordinate.longitude];
    self.accuracyLabel.stringValue = [NSString stringWithFormat:@"%.1fm",
        newLocation.horizontalAccuracy];

    [self.spinner stopAnimation:nil];

}

- (void)locationManager:(CLLocationManager *)manager
    didFailWithError:(NSError *)error {

    self.latitudeLabel.stringValue = @"-";
    self.longitudeLabel.stringValue = @"-";
    self.accuracyLabel.stringValue = @"-";

    [self.spinner startAnimation:nil];
}

@end
```

This code does the following things:

1. Adds a class extension to the `AppDelegate` class that adds a variable for storing the `CLLocationManager`.

   The location manager object must be stored in an instance variable, or else it will be removed from memory before it has a chance to update the app with the user's location.

2. In the `applicationDidFinishLaunching:` method, the `CLLocationManager` is created and given a delegate. It's then told to start updating the user's location.

3. In the `locationManager:didUpdateToLocation:fromLocation:` method, the labels are updated to show the appropriate information, and the spinner is stopped.

4. In the `locationManager:didFailWithError:` method, the labels are updated to show dashes, and the spinner is started again.

It's possible for the location manager to successfully determine the user's location and then later fail (or vice versa). This means that a failure isn't necessarily the end of the line—the location manager will keep trying, so your application should keep this in mind.

Now run the application. On its first run, it will ask the user if it's allowed to access his location. If the user grants permission, the application will attempt to get the user's location. If it can find it, the labels will be updated to show the user's approximate location, and how accurate Core Location thinks that it is.

Geocoding

When you get the user's location, Core Location returns a latitude and longitude coordinate pair. This is useful inside an application and great for showing on a map, but isn't terribly helpful for a human being. Nobody looks at the coordinates "-37.813611, 144.963056" and immediately thinks, "Melbourne, Australia."

Because people deal with addresses, which are composed of a sequence of decreasingly precise place names ("1 Infinite Loop," "Cupertino," "Santa Clara," "California," and so on), Core Location includes a tool for converting from coordinates to addresses and back again. Converting an address to coordinates is called *geocoding*; converting coordinates to an address is called *reverse geocoding*.

Core Location implements this via the CLGeocoder class, which allows for both forward and reverse geocoding. Because geocoding requires contacting a server to do the conversion, it will only work when an Internet connection is available.

To geocode an address, you create a CLGeocoder and then use one of its built-in geocoding methods. You can provide either a string that contains an address (like "1 Infinite Loop Cupertino California USA") and the geocoder will attempt to figure out where you mean, or you can provide a dictionary that contains more precisely delineated information. Optionally, you can restrict a geocode to a specific region (to prevent confusion between, say, Hobart, Minnesota and Hobart, Tasmania).

We're going to add reverse geocoding to the application, which will show the user her current address. To do this, we'll add a CLGeocoder to the AppDelegate class. When Core Location gets a fix on the user's location, we'll ask the geocoder to perform a reverse geocode with the CLLocation provided by Core Location.

When you reverse geocode, you receive an NSArray that contains a number of CLPlacemark objects. An NSArray is used because it's possible for the reverse geocode to return with a number of possible coordinates that your address may resolve to. CLPlacemark objects contain a number of properties that contain address information. Note that not all of the properties may contain information; for example, if you reverse geocode a location that's in the middle of a desert, you probably won't receive any street information.

The available properties you can access include:

- The name of the location (for example, "Apple Inc")
- The thoroughfare (for example, "1 Infinite Loop")
- The locality (for example, "Cupertino")
- The sublocality (the neighborhood or name for that area; for example, "Mission District")

- The administrative area (the state name or other main subdivision of a country; for example, "California")
- The subadministrative area (for example, "Santa Clara")
- The postal code (for example, "95014")
- The ISO country code (a two- or three-letter code for that country; for example, "US")
- The country name (for example, "United States")

Some placemarks may contain additional data, if relevant:

- The name of the inland body of water that the placemark is located at or very near to (for example, "Derwent River")
- The name of the ocean that the placemark is at (for example, "Pacific Ocean")
- An NSArray containing any additional areas of interest (for example, "Golden Gate Park").

You can use this information to create a string that can be shown to the user.

We'll start by creating a label that will display the user's address.

Open *MainMenu.xib* and drag in a new label underneath the current set of labels. The updated interface should look like Figure 14-2. Then open *AppDelegate.h* in the assistant and control-drag from the new label into AppDelegate's interface. Create a new outlet for the label called addressLabel.

Then add CLGeocoder to the app delegate by updating *AppDelegate.m* to make the class extension at the top of the file look like the following code:

```
@interface AppDelegate () {
    CLLocationManager* _locationManager;
    CLGeocoder* _geocoder;
}
@end
```

When the user's location is determined, perform a reverse geocode by adding the following code to the end of the locationManager:didUpdateToLocation:fromLocation: method:

```
[_geocoder reverseGeocodeLocation:newLocation
    completionHandler:^(NSArray *placemarks, NSError *error) {

        if (error != nil) {
            self.addressLabel.stringValue = @"Can't find address!";
            return;
        }
```

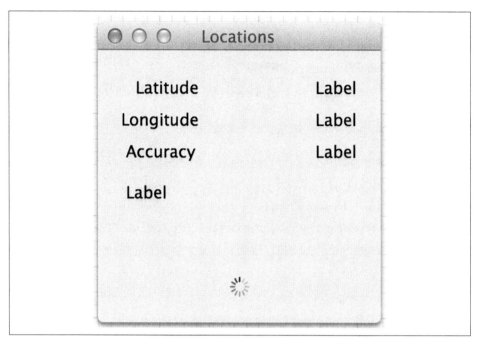

Figure 14-2. The updated interface for the Locations application

```
CLPlacemark* placeMark = [placemarks lastObject];

NSString* addressString = [NSString stringWithFormat:@"%@ %@, %@, %@ %@",
    placeMark.subThoroughfare,
    placeMark.thoroughfare,
    placeMark.locality,
    placeMark.administrativeArea,
    placeMark.country];

self.addressLabel.stringValue = addressString;
}];
```

Now run the application. Shortly after the user's location is displayed, the approximate address of your location will appear. If it doesn't, check to make sure that you're connected to the Internet.

Locations and Privacy

The user's location is private information, and your application must be granted explicit permission by the user on at least the first occasion that it tries to access it.

People are understandably wary about software knowing about where they are—it's a privacy issue and potentially a safety risk. To avoid problems, follow these guidelines in your application:

- Be very clear about what your application is using location information for.
- Never share the user's location with a server or other users unless the user has explicitly given permission.
- The user can always see when an application is accessing location information, because a small icon appears at the top of the screen (on both iOS and OS X). Once your app has performed the task that location information is needed for, turn off Core Location—both to save power and to let the user know that he's no longer being tracked.

Device Motion

An iOS device is often held in the user's hands, which means that it's subject to movement and rotation. iOS allows your code to receive information about how the device is moving, how it's being rotated, and how it's oriented. All of this information is available through the Core Motion framework, which provides a unified interface to the various relevant sensors built into the device.

 Core Motion is only available on iOS, since laptops and desktops don't generally get shaken around while being used. While some Mac laptops include an accelerometer, it isn't available to your code through any publicly accessible APIs.

Core Motion provides *device motion* information to your application by measuring data from the sensors available to the device:

- The accelerometer, which measures forces applied to the device
- The gyroscope, which measures rotation
- The magnetometer, which measures magnetic fields

The first iOS devices only included an accelerometer, which is actually sufficient for getting quite a lot of information about device motion. For example, based on the forces being applied to the device over time, you can determine the direction of gravity, which gives you information about how the device is being held, as well as determine if the device is being shaken. If a gyroscope is available, you can refine this information and determine if the device is rotating around an axis of gravity. If a magnetometer is available, it's possible to determine a frame of reference.

Core Motion collects data from all the available sensors and provides direct access to the sensor information. You can therefore ask Core Motion to give you the angles that define the device's orientation in space, as well as get raw accelerometer information.

Raw sensor data can lead to some very cool tricks. For example, the magnetometer measures magnetic fields, which means that the device can actually be used as a metal detector by measuring changes in the magnetic field.

Working with Core Motion

Core Motion works in a very similar manner to Core Location: it provides a manager object that provides periodic updates on device motion. However, the means by which the manager object provides these updates differs from how `CLLocationManager` does —instead of providing a delegate object, you instead instruct the motion manager to call a block that you provide. In this block, you handle the movement event.

The iOS Simulator doesn't simulate any of the motion hardware that Core Motion uses. If you want to test Core Motion, you need to use a real iOS device.

The motion manager class is called `CMMotionManager`. To start getting motion information, you create an instance of this class and instruct it to begin generating motion updates. You can also optionally ask for only accelerometer, gyroscope, or magnetometer information.

You can also get information from the `CMMotionManager` by querying it at any time. If your application doesn't need to get information about device motion very often, it's more efficient to simply ask for the information when it's needed. To do this, you send the `CMMotionManager` object the `startDeviceMotionUpdates` method (or `startAccelerometerUpdates` or `startGyroUpdates`), and then, when you need the data, you access the `CMMotionManager`'s `accelerometerData`, `gyroData`, or `deviceMotion` properties.

The fewer devices that Core Motion needs to activate in order to give you the information you need, the more power is saved. As always, consider the user's battery!

Forces and Orientation and Gravity, Oh My!

Core Motion separates out "user motion" from the sum total of forces being applied to the device. There's still only one accelerometer in there, though, so what Core Motion does is use a combination of low- and high-pass filtering to separate out parts of the signal, with the assistance of the gyroscope, to determine which forces are gravity and which forces are "user motion"—forces like shaking or throwing your device. (Note: The authors do not recommend throwing your device, no matter how much fun it is. The authors specifically do not recommend making an awesome app that takes a photo at the peak of a throw. You will break your phone.)

You can also configure how often the CMMotionManager updates the accelerometer and gyro—the less often it uses it, the more power you save (and, as a tradeoff, the more imprecise your measurements become).

To work with Core Motion, you'll need to add the Core Motion framework to your project. We'll now build a small iPhone app that reports on how it's being moved and how the device is oriented.

1. *Create the project.* Create a new single-view application for iPhone. Call it **Motion** and use storyboards.

2. *Add the Core Motion framework.* Select the project at the top of the project navigator. The project settings will appear in the main editor; select the **Motion** target.

   a. Scroll down to Linked Frameworks and Libraries, and click the + button.

   b. The frameworks sheet will appear; browse or search for *CoreMotion.frame work* and add it to the project.

3. *Build the interface.* Once the framework has been added, we'll begin building the interface for the app. This will be similar to the Core Location app: it will report on the numbers being sent by Core Motion. However, you can (and should!) use the information for all kinds of things—game controls, data logging, and more. The authors once used Core Motion to build an app that tracks human sleeping activity. It's a tremendously flexible framework.

   a. Open *MainStoryboard.storyboard*.

   b. First, we'll create the labels that display the user motion.

   c. Drag in three labels and lay them out vertically on the lefthand side of the screen. Make their text **X**, **Y**, and **Z**, respectively.

   d. Drag in another three labels and lay them out vertically to the right of the first three.

e. Next we'll create the labels that display orientation.

f. Drag in another three labels and lay them out vertically on the lefthand side of the screen, underneath the existing set of labels. Make their text **Pitch**, **Yaw**, and **Roll**, respectively.

g. Drag in a final set of three labels and lay them out vertically and to the right.

h. Once you're done, your interface should look like Figure 14-3.

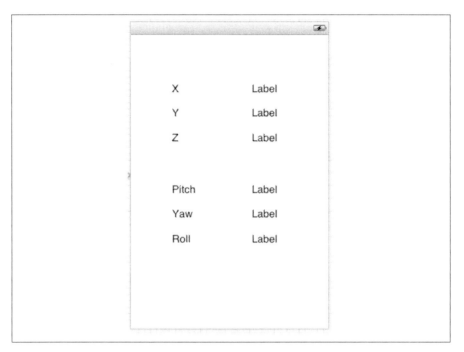

Figure 14-3. The motion application's interface

4. *Connect the interface to the view controller.* Open *ViewController.h* in the assistant.

a. Control-drag from each of the labels on the right and create outlets for each of them.

b. From top to bottom, the labels should be called **xLabel**, **yLabel**, **zLabel**, **pit chLabel**, **yawLabel**, and **rollLabel**.

c. While you have *ViewController.h* open, import *<CoreMotion/CoreMotion.h>*.

When you're done, *ViewController.h* should look like the following:

```
#import <UIKit/UIKit.h>
#import <CoreMotion/CoreMotion.h>

@interface ViewController : UIViewController

@property (strong, nonatomic) IBOutlet UILabel *xLabel;
@property (strong, nonatomic) IBOutlet UILabel *yLabel;
@property (strong, nonatomic) IBOutlet UILabel *zLabel;
@property (strong, nonatomic) IBOutlet UILabel *pitchLabel;
@property (strong, nonatomic) IBOutlet UILabel *yawLabel;
@property (strong, nonatomic) IBOutlet UILabel *rollLabel;
@end
```

5. *Add the code that starts, stops, and handles device motion updates.* Now that the view controller's header file has been set up, we'll write the code that actually creates the motion manager and then starts updating the labels as device motion updates arrive.

We'll store a reference to the CMMotionManager as an instance variable in the class, and start and stop the device motion updates when the view controller appears and disappears.

Update *ViewController.m* so that it looks like the following code:

```
#import "ViewController.h"

@interface ViewController () {
    CMMotionManager* _motionManager;
}

@end

@implementation ViewController
@synthesize xLabel;
@synthesize yLabel;
@synthesize zLabel;
@synthesize pitchLabel;
@synthesize yawLabel;
@synthesize rollLabel;

- (void)viewDidLoad
{
    [super viewDidLoad];
    _motionManager = [[CMMotionManager alloc] init];
}

- (void)viewWillAppear:(BOOL)animated {
    [_motionManager startDeviceMotionUpdatesToQueue:
        [NSOperationQueue mainQueue]
        withHandler:^(CMDeviceMotion *motion, NSError *error) {

        self.xLabel.text = [NSString stringWithFormat:@"%.1f",
```

```
            motion.userAcceleration.x];
        self.yLabel.text = [NSString stringWithFormat:@"%.1f",
            motion.userAcceleration.y];
        self.zLabel.text = [NSString stringWithFormat:@"%.1f",
            motion.userAcceleration.z];


        // Convert the angles to degrees
        CGFloat pitchDegrees = motion.attitude.pitch * 180 / M_PI;
        CGFloat yawDegrees = motion.attitude.yaw * 180 / M_PI;
        CGFloat rollDegrees = motion.attitude.roll * 180 / M_PI;


        self.pitchLabel.text = [NSString stringWithFormat:@"%.1f",
            pitchDegrees];
        self.yawLabel.text = [NSString stringWithFormat:@"%.1f",
            yawDegrees];
        self.rollLabel.text = [NSString stringWithFormat:@"%.1f",
            rollDegrees];


    }];
}

- (void)viewWillDisappear:(BOOL)animated {
    [_motionManager stopDeviceMotionUpdates];
}

- (void)viewDidUnload
{
    [self setXLabel:nil];
    [self setYLabel:nil];
    [self setZLabel:nil];
    [self setPitchLabel:nil];
    [self setYawLabel:nil];
    [self setRollLabel:nil];
    [super viewDidUnload];
    // Release any retained subviews of the main view.
}

- (BOOL)shouldAutorotateToInterfaceOrientation:
    (UIInterfaceOrientation)interfaceOrientation
{
    return (interfaceOrientation != UIInterfaceOrientationPortraitUpsideDown);
}

@end
```

Finally, connect an iOS device and run the application on it. Watch the numbers on the screen change as you shake and rotate the device.

Printing Documents

Despite decades of promises, the "paperless office" has never really materialized. Users like having documents on paper, and both OS X and iOS provide ways of getting stuff printed on dead trees.

The APIs and methods for printing on OS X and iOS are completely different. On OS X, individual NSViews are printed, either directly or via an intermediary system. On iOS, you print via a separate system of print renderer and formatter objects.

We'll build two demo apps that show how to print documents on OS X and iOS.

Printing on OS X

One of the happy quirks of OS X's development is that the entire graphics system traces its lineage to PostScript, the language of printers. On OS X, drawing graphics is very easily translatable to printer commands—so much so, in fact, that the translation is done for you by the OS.

Given any NSView, you can print it by sending it the print message. OS X takes over from that point—the print panel appears, the user chooses which printer to use and how, and the printer prints the document.

When a view is printed, its drawRect: method is called—however, the graphics context prepared before the method is called is one designed for generating printer commands (specifically EPS or PDF content). This means that any custom NSView subclass that you make is already set up for printing.

To demonstrate printing, we'll build a small sample application that prints an NSText View.

1. *Create the project.* Create a new Cocoa application named **OSXPrinting**.
2. *Create the interface.* Open *MainWindow.xib*.
   a. Drag an NSTextView into the app's main window. Make it fill the window, but leave some room at the bottom.
   b. Drag in an NSButton and place it at the bottom-right of the window. Change its label to **Print**.
3. *Connect the interface.* We don't need to write any code for this, since the button can be directly connected to the print: of the view.
   a. Control-drag from the print button to the text view.
   b. Choose "print:" from the list that pops up.

4. *Test the application.* Run the application and type some text into the text view. Click the Print button and try printing the document. (If you don't want to waste paper, you can print to PDF by choosing "Save as PDF" in the PDF menu, just like in all applications on OS X.)

 You can also choose Print from your application's File menu, or press ⌘-P. The reason this works without having connected the views up is that the Print menu item is connected to the First Responder, which is the object that corresponds to whichever view is currently responding to user input.

Printing on iOS

While OS X machines are often connected to a computer (usually via USB, and sometimes over the network), iOS printing is much more ad hoc and on-the-fly. In iOS, all printing is done over AirPrint, the WiFi-based printer discovery system. When you print a document, iOS shows you a list of printers nearby, and you send your print work to the printer you want to use.

The printing system is more complex than on OS X, but more flexible. When you want to print a document, you ask iOS for the shared instance of the UIPrintInteraction Controller, which is a view controller that allows the user to configure the print job and works in the same way as the print panel on OS X. You then provide the print interaction controller with the items you want to have printed.

There are several ways you can indicate to the print interaction controller what should be printed. If you have a UIImage, or an NSData that contains PDF or image data, you can give it directly to the print controller. You can also provide an NSArray of these objects if you have multiple things you want to print.

If you want to print content like text, markup, or custom views, you create a UIPrint Formatter object for each piece of content. For example, if you have a block of text, you can create an instance of UISimpleTextPrintFormatter, give it the NSString that contains your text, and then provide the print formatter to the print controller.

If you want to have total control over what gets printed, you can also use the UIPrint PageRenderer class, which allows for advanced customization and drawing.

In this section, we'll create a simple iOS application that does the same thing as the OS X application in the previous section—a simple text box, plus a print button.

1. *Create a new application.* Create a new single-view application for iOS named **Prin tingiOS**.

2. *Create the interface.*

   a. Open *MainStoryboard.storyboard.*

   b. Drag a `UINavigationBar` into the window and place it at the top.

   c. Drag a `UIBarButtonItem` into the navigation bar. Change its label to **Print**.

   d. Finally, drag in a `UITextView` and make it fill the rest of the space.

3. *Connect the interface to the view controller.*

   a. Open *ViewController.h* in the assistant.

   b. Control-drag from the text view into `ViewController`'s interface, and create an outlet called textView.

   c. Control-drag from the Print button into `ViewController`, and create an action called **print**.

We're done with the interface. The next step is to make the print button actually print.

4. *Add the printing code.* Open *ViewController.m.* Replace the `print:` method with the following code:

```
- (IBAction)print:(id)sender {
    UIPrintInteractionController* printInteraction =
        [UIPrintInteractionController sharedPrintController];

    UISimpleTextPrintFormatter* textFormatter =
        [[UISimpleTextPrintFormatter alloc] initWithText:textView.text];

    printInteraction.printFormatter = textFormatter;

    [printInteraction presentAnimated:YES
        completionHandler:^(UIPrintInteractionController
            *printInteractionController, BOOL completed, NSError *error) {
    }];
}
```

In order to test the printing system without using up actual paper, Xcode provides a tool called the Printer Simulator that simulates printers on the network. It's not a substitute for actually printing on paper—if you're doing anything with graphics, for example, the colors will likely be quite different, and a simulated printer won't demonstrate effects like ink bleed—but it's sufficient for demonstrating that it actually works.

5. *Launch the Printer Simulator.* Open the iOS Simulator, if it isn't open already, and choose Open Printer Simulator from the File menu. The Print Simulator will open.

6. *Test the application.* Launch the application and hit the Print button. Choose one of the simulated printers and tap Print. The Print Simulator will simulate printing and show you the final result.

CHAPTER 15

Event Kit

The user's life isn't confined to the use of computers and phones, and many people even use technology to interact with other human beings. One capability of Apple devices is calendaring and scheduling, which is usually managed through built-in applications (the Calendar app on iOS and OS X).

However, it can be very useful for third-party applications to be able to access the calendar, either to create new appointments or to view what the user has lined up for the day. This information is exposed via Event Kit, the calendar data store API.

In this chapter, you'll learn how to work with Event Kit to access the user's calendar. The same API applies to both OS X and iOS; in this chapter, the sample code will be written for OS X.

Understanding Events

All of the information that relates to the user's calendars comes from the *Event Kit event store*. This object, which is an instance of the `EKEventStore`, acts as the database of all calendars, which themselves contain events.

The event store stores multiple calendars, which are `EKCalendar` objects. Each calendar has information like its name, whether it's editable, whether it's a subscribed calendar, and so on.

An "event" is an entry in the user's calendar, and is represented as an `EKEvent` object. Events contain several key pieces of information, including:

- A text label describing what the event is
- The date and times that the event begins and ends
- The location of the event
- When the event was created and last modified

EKEvent is actually a subclass of the EKCalendarItem class. That's because EKCalen dars don't just contain events—they can also contain reminders, which are scheduled alerts.

 Reminders are only available on OS X and iOS 6.

Events can also be set to repeat, and the rules for this repetition can be complex. For example, you can have an event that repeats every day, every second day, on the second Tuesday of every month, and so on.

In addition to this repeating behavior, it's possible to *detach* a specific instance of a repeating event. For example, imagine you have an event on the calendar that repeats every week on Monday morning, and one week you need to push it back. However, you only want to move this one instance, not the entire repeating set. When you move the event, your calendaring application asks if you want to move all future events, or just the specific one you just moved. Your answer indicates to the system whether you want to create a detached event or modify the entire repeating event.

Accessing the Event Store

To get access to the calendar system, you create an instance of EKEventStore, indicating what kinds of calendar items you want to get from the store (either events or reminders).

To connect to the store and request access to events, you allocate an EKEventStore object and initialize it with the initWithAccessToEntityTypes: method:

```
EKEventStore* store = [[EKEventStore alloc]
    initWithAccessToEntityTypes:EKEntityMaskEvent];
```

If the user hasn't already granted permission to access calendar events of that type, an alert box will pop up asking the user if it's OK for your application to access the calendar. Until the user grants permission, any requests for data will return nil.

The event store might not have permission at the moment you create the EKEvent Store object, but it might gain permission later. When the user grants (or revokes) permission, an `EKEventStoreChangedNotification` is broadcast by the object. This notification is also sent when the contents of the event store changes; in both cases, it's a signal to refresh whatever views you have that are displaying the contents of the calendar.

Once you have access to the data store, you can retrieve the list of calendars.

Accessing Calendars

To get the list of calendars available to the user, simply ask the event store. Because a calendar can support only events, only reminders, or both, you need to specify what you want the calendars that you get back to support.

To get the user's calendars that support storing events, you use the `calendarsForEnti tyType:` method, and pass in the `EKEntityTypeEvent` value as the type parameter:

```
[store calendarsForEntityType:EKEntityTypeEvent];
```

This returns an `NSArray` of `EKCalendars`, which you can get events out of.

Getting the array of calendars that support reminders is just as easy—you just pass in the `EKEntityTypeReminder` parameter:

```
[store calendarsForEntityType:EKEntityTypeReminder];
```

Once you have a calendar, you can start working with events inside it.

Accessing Events

A calendar is a potentially infinitely large collection of data. If a calendar contains any repeating events that don't have an end date, such as a weekly meeting or someone's birthday, then it's not possible to ask for "all events," since that collection is of an infinite size. Instead, you need to specify the date range that you're interested in receiving events for.

While you're filtering based on date range, it's also useful to filter based on other properties as well, including time of day, event name, and so on. The standard filtering tool in Cocoa and Cocoa Touch is `NSPredicate`, which allows you to specify parameters for finding events in a data set.

 `NSPredicate` is also useful outside of Event Kit. In "Blocks" (page 89), we talked about how to use `NSPredicate` to filter an `NSArray` to only contain objects that match certain parameters.

To construct an event-finding predicate, ask your `EKEventStore` to provide you with a predicate that finds events between a start date and an end date, as well as the calendars that the events should be in. This is done with the `predicateForEventsWithStart Date:endDate:calendars:` method:

```
NSDate* startDate = ...
NSDate* endDate = ...

NSPredicate* predicate = [store predicateForEventsWithStartDate:startDate
                                 endDate:endDate
                                 calendars:self.calendars];
```

Once you have this `NSPredicate`, you can give it back to the `EKEventStore` and it will retrieve all matching calendar items:

```
NSArray* events = [store eventsMatchingPredicate:predicate];
```

This array contains all matching events, from which you can extract information.

Working with Events

Modifying an event or reminder is as simple as modifying its properties. For example, to modify an event's title, you just change its `title` property:

```
EKEvent* event = ...
event.title = @"Party Times";
```

 `title` is actually a property on `EKCalendarItem`, `EKEvent`'s superclass. This means that it exists in both `EKEvent` and `EKReminder`.

However, changing properties on an event or reminder does not update the shared calendar system immediately. When the calendar item has finished being modified, it must be explicitly saved back to the event store. You do this by using the method `save Event:span:error:`, which takes as its parameters the event that you're saving, the span of time that the changes should apply for, and a reference to an `NSError` variable that the method will store error information in if anything goes wrong.

The span of time is represented as an `EKSpan`, which is simply an enumeration with two options: this event or future events. When you modify a repeating event and choose to make those changes apply only to one specific instance, the instance will become detached:

```
EKEvent* event = ...
NSError* error = nil;
[store saveEvent:event span:EKSpanThisEvent error:&error];
```

The EKEventStore that you use to save the event needs to be the same as the one you got the event from. If you get an EKEvent from one EKEventStore and try to save it in a different one, your app will throw an exception.

It's possible that an EKEvent that you're working with might have changed while your code was modifying it. Whenever the calendar changes, the EKEventStore that you're working with posts an EKEventStoreChangedNotification to let you know that the contents of the event store have been modified. To ensure that an EKEvent is up to date with the most recent information inside the calendar, use the refresh method:

```
EKEvent* event = ...
[event refresh];
```

Refreshing an event means that properties that have changed since you got the event from the event store will be updated to match the most recent version. Note that any properties that *you* have changed will *not*.

For example, say you get an EKEvent and change its title to Excellent Party Times, but don't save it. You then modify the title of that same event using the Calendar application, and *then* save your modified EKEvent object. In this case, it will be *your* version that is written to the event store.

This means that if you want to revert any changes that you've made to an EKEvent, all you have to do is not save them.

You can also call the reset method on your EKEventStore to reset the entire event store to its last saved state.

You can also delete events. Removing an event is rather straightforward: all you need to do is call the removeEvent:span:error: method on your EKEventStore. This behaves much like the method used for saving events—you simply provide the event to be removed, indicate whether you want to remove a single event or all future events (if the event is a repeating one), and provide a reference to a variable for an NSError to be placed in if something goes wrong:

```
EKEvent* event = ....
NSError* error = nil;
[store removeEvent:event span:EKSpanFutureEvents error:&error];
```

Building an Events Application

To wrap things up, we're going to build an app that displays events for the user, depending on which day they've selected.

This app presents a date picker and a list of events. When the date picker's selected date changes, the list updates to show the user's events for that day.

1. *Create the project.* Create a new Cocoa application called **Events**.

To work with Event Kit, we need to add the Event Kit framework.

2. *Add* EventKit.framework *to the project.* Select your project at the top of the project navigator. The project will appear in the main editor. Select the `Locations` target and click the + button at the bottom of Linked Frameworks and Libraries. The frameworks window will appear.

   Browse or search for *EventKit.framework.* Click the Add button.

First, we'll write the code that will expose the calendar information. We're going to create several properties, some of which will be backed by instance variables and some of which will not.

Specifically, the application will keep track of the following information:

- The currently selected date
- The event store used to access the calendar
- The available calendars
- The events for the currently selected date

The event store and date properties will be backed by an instance variable, while the available calendars and events properties will be dynamically computed when needed (based on the selected date and event store).

First, we'll create the properties.

1. *Open* AppDelegate.m. Add the following code to the file, before the line `@implementation`:

   ```
   @interface AppDelegate () {

   }

   @property (nonatomic, strong) NSDate* date;
   @property (readonly) EKEventStore* store;
   @property (readonly) NSArray* calendars;
   @property (readonly) NSArray* events;

   @end
   ```

2. *Implement the properties.* Add the following code to `AppDelegate`'s implementation:

```
@synthesize store = _store;
@synthesize date = _date;
@dynamic calendars;
@dynamic events;
```

The store property will be lazily loaded. That is, the first time the property is accessed, an EKEventStore object will be created and assigned to the property. This keeps us from having to do any deliberate setup in the application's init or awakeFromNib methods.

3. *Add the* store *method.* Add the following code to AppDelegate's implementation:

```
- (EKEventStore*) store {
    if (_store == nil) {
        _store = [[EKEventStore alloc]
            initWithAccessToEntityTypes:EKEntityMaskEvent];
    }
    return _store;
}
```

We can now add the calendars and events accessors. These don't have any instance variables, since all they'll do is retrieve information from the event store.

4. *Add the* calendars *and* events *methods.* Add the following code to AppDelegate's implementation:

```
- (NSArray*) calendars {
    return [[self store] calendarsForEntityType:EKEntityTypeEvent];
}


- (NSArray *)events {

    NSDate* endDate = [self.date dateByAddingTimeInterval:24 * 60 * 60];

    NSPredicate* predicate = [self.store
        predicateForEventsWithStartDate:self.date
        endDate:endDate calendars:self.calendars];

    NSArray* events = [self.store eventsMatchingPredicate:predicate];
    return events;
}
```

The calendars method simply returns the array of calendars that support events.

The events method is a little more complex. Because a request to the event store requires that we provide a start date and an end date for our query, we need to create an end date that's one day after our start date (which we'll set up in a moment).

Because there are 24 hours in a day, 60 minutes in an hour, and 60 seconds in a minute, we can create an `NSDate` that's one day after the start date with the `dateByAdding TimeInterval:` method on `NSDate`. This method takes as its sole parameter the number of seconds in the future the new date should be; thus, we want a date that's 86400 seconds in the future, which is 24 times 60 times 60.

Given these two dates, we call `predicateForEventsWithStartDate:endDate:predi cate:` and provide the start date, end date, and the calendars to check. We then get the array of events that matched that predicate, and return it.

The final methods to set up are the methods for the `date` property. The getter method will be another lazy loader—if there is no current date set, the current date should be today.

Additionally, we want to disregard the time information from the date; when you ask `NSDate` for the current date, it returns an `NSDate` corresponding to the current date *and time*. We don't want that, so we need to do some calendar calculation to make the time value correspond to midnight on the provided day, thus ensuring that the time value is consistent no matter which date we select.

5. *Add the* `setDate:` *and* `date` *methods to* `AppDelegate`. Add the following code to `AppDelegate`'s implementation:

```
- (NSDate *)date {
    if (_date == nil) {
        [self setDate:[NSDate date]];
    }
    return _date;
}

- (void)setDate:(NSDate *)date {
    NSDateComponents* dateComponents =
      [[NSCalendar currentCalendar] components:NSDayCalendarUnit
        | NSMonthCalendarUnit | NSYearCalendarUnit fromDate:date];
    _date = [[NSCalendar currentCalendar] dateFromComponents:dateComponents];
}
```

`NSDateComponents` is a class that is able to perform calculations on dates, given a calendar. In this case, we're asking the class to get the day, month, and year from a date, and then create a date from that—thereby creating an `NSDate` object on the same date as the provided one, but with a time value set to midnight on that day.

There's one last method to create: one that will be used to indicate to the system that when the date changes, the list of events will also change.

6. *Add the* `keyPathsForValuesAffectingEvents` *method to* `AppDelegate`. Add the following code to `AppDelegate`'s implementation:

```
+ (NSSet *)keyPathsForValuesAffectingEvents {
    return [NSSet setWithObject:@"date"];
}
```

This method returns an NSSet containing the list of properties that, when modified, cause the events property to change. This method is checked by the Cocoa bindings system whenever a property changes on the AppDelegate object, and helps us bind the code to the view with minimal additional work.

With all of that out of the way, it's finally time to create the interface. Fortunately, because of the work we've done in the code, it's very simple to set up.

7. *Open* MainMenu.xib. Drag an array controller into the outline. Bind its content array to the app delegate, with the model key path *self.events*. Open the Identity inspector, and change its label to **Events**.

   Drag in a date picker and a table view. Select the date picker, and change its style to Graphical. This creates a nice calendar control.

   When you're done, the finished interface should look something like Figure 15-1.

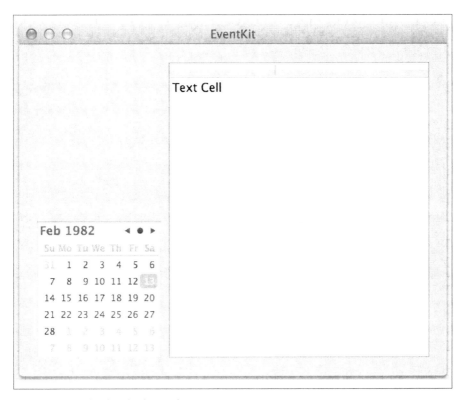

Figure 15-1. The finished interface

8. *Bind the date picker.* The date picker needs to control the `date` property on the app delegate. To make this happen, select the date picker, open the Bindings inspector, and bind the `Value` property to the app delegate, with the model key path *self.date*.

   All we need to do now is bind the table view to the list of events for the selected date. Because this is exposed as the `events` property on the app delegate, and this property will automatically update its contents as the date is changed, the table view will always show the events for the selected date, even as the user changes it.

9. *Bind the table view.* Select the table view in the outline (it's inside the scroll view), and bind its content to the Events array controller that you set up earlier. Set the controller key to `arrangedObjects`.

   Select the table column (inside the table view in the outline), and bind its Value to the Events array controller. Set the controller key to `arrangedObjects` and the model key path to `self.title`.

You're done! Run the app, and try selecting different dates in the date picker.

 If nothing is appearing in the table view, you should double-check to make sure that there is actually an event on the date you're trying to look at. One of the authors, who shall remain nameless (although it was Jon), spent over 10 minutes trying to debug the app before realizing his mistake.

 If you've got any CalDAV delegates set up, they won't appear in the list of calendars returned from the event store. They don't appear to be exposed to apps using Event Kit. Your guess is as good as ours.

User Privacy

Just like a user's location (see Chapter 14) and contacts, the events on the user's calendar are considered private and sensitive information. Apps aren't allowed to access the calendar unless the user explicitly grants them permission, and they are expected to behave properly when they don't receive this permission. Additionally, the user can revoke access to the calendar (or any of the other private data stores) at any time.

This means that you can't write code and assume that you'll get access to the information your application needs. Instead, your code needs to gracefully fail—if your app can get any useful work done without access to the calendar, it should go ahead and do so, and if it is rendered inoperable by not having access, it should tell the user in a friendly manner (don't pop up a scary "error!" dialog box).

If you're writing an application to be submitted to the App Store, you can expect that whoever reviews your application will disallow calendar access and see how the app behaves. If your application doesn't cope, expect it to be rejected.

CHAPTER 16

Instruments and the Debugger

As anyone who's written software knows, designing and implementing the features of an application is only a fraction of the work. Once the app's done and performs all the tasks it's meant to do, you need to make sure that it runs *well*.

Performance is a feature that many developers neglect, but it's something that influences people's decisions to buy your software or not. Many of our friends and family prefer to use Pages instead of Microsoft Word, because despite Page's relative lack of features, it's a more nimble and zippy application.

Not paying attention to performance also has more tangible implications for your code. For example, an application that is careless with memory will end up being force-quit by the system on iOS, and an app that consumes lots of CPU time will exhaust your user's battery and make the system run hot. There are other resources as well that your application needs to be careful with, including network bandwidth and disk space.

To help monitor your application's performance and use of resources, the developer tools include *Instruments*, an application that's able to inspect and report on just about every aspect of an application.

Instruments works by inserting diagnostic hooks into a running application. These hooks are able to do things like analyze the memory usage of an application, monitor how much time the app spends in various methods, and examine other data. This information is then collected, analyzed, and presented to you, allowing you to figure out what's going on inside your application.

In this chapter, you'll learn how to get around in Instruments, how to analyze an application, and how to spot and fix memory issues and performance problems using the information that Instruments gives you. You'll also learn how to use Xcode's debugger to track down problems and fix them.

Getting Started with Instruments

To get started with Instruments, we'll load a sample application and examine how it works.

The application that we'll be examining is *TextEdit*, which is the built-in text editor that comes with OS X. TextEdit is a great sample app to modify, because it's a rather complex little app—it's effectively an entire word processor, with support for images, Microsoft Word import and export, and a lot more. You've probably used it before; if you haven't, you can find it by either searching Spotlight for "TextEdit" or by looking in the Applications folder.

The source code to TextEdit comes with the developer tools, and you can find it by going to /Developer/Examples/TextEdit.

1. *Open the TextEdit project.* Double-click the *TextEdit.xcodeproj* file to open it in Xcode.

2. *Run the application.* Click the Run button or press ⌘-R.

    The app will launch. Play around with it by writing some text, and saving and opening some documents.

We'll now use Instruments to examine what TextEdit is doing in memory as it runs.

3. *Quit TextEdit.* You can do this by pressing ⌘-Q or choosing Quit from the TextEdit menu.

4. *Tell Xcode to profile the application.* To do this, choose Profile from the Product menu. You can also press ⌘-I.

    Xcode will rebuild the application, and then launch Instruments. When Instruments launches, it presents a window that lets you choose which aspects of the app you'd like to inspect (Figure 16-1).

5. *Select the Allocations instrument, and click Choose.* Instruments will launch TextEdit, and start recording memory usage information from the application.

    At this point, you're in Instruments proper, so it's worthwhile to stop and take a look around (Figure 16-2).

The Instruments Interface

When you work with Instruments, you're working with one or more individual modules that are responsible for analyzing different parts. Each module is also called an instrument—so, for example, there's the Allocations instrument (for measuring memory performance), the Time Profiler instrument (for measuring runtime performance), the VM Tracker instrument (for measuring memory consumption), and so on.

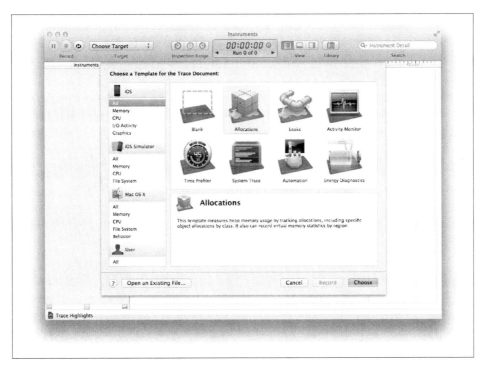

Figure 16-1. The Instruments template chooser

Each instrument is listed in the Instruments pane, on the lefthand side of the window. As an application runs, information from each instrument is shown in the Track pane. If you select an instrument in the Instruments pane, more detailed information is shown in the Detail pane at the bottom of the window. The Track pane is useful for giving you a high-level overview of what information is being reported, but the majority of the useful information is kept in the Detail pane.

The Detail pane shows different kinds of information, depending on the instrument. To choose which information to present, you can use the navigation bar, which separates the window horizontally.

To configure how an instrument collects its data, you can click the *i* button at the right of each row of the Instruments pane. From there, you can set the various options that affect what information the instrument collects.

By default, the Instruments pane and the Detail pane are visible. You can also bring up a third pane, known as the Extended Detail pane. This pane, as its name suggests, displays extended detail information on whatever is selected in the Detail pane. For

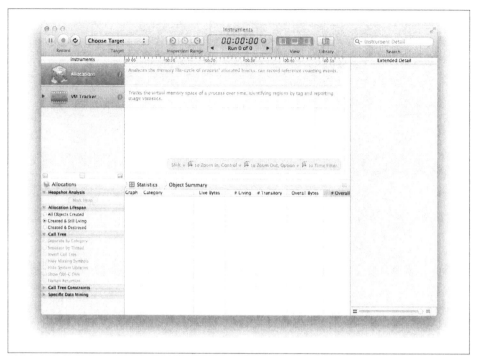

Figure 16-2. The Instruments window

example, if you're using the Allocations instrument, the Detail pane could be showing the objects currently active in your application. You could then select a specific object, and the Extended Detail pane would show exactly where that object was created in your code.

You can also control what Instruments is doing through the Record buttons. The large red button in the center is the main one that we care about—clicking on it will launch the application that's currently under investigation, and start recording data. Clicking it again will quit the application and stop recording, though the data that was collected remains. If you click Record again, a new set of data will be recorded—if you want to see past runs, you can navigate between them by clicking on the arrows in the display in the middle of the toolbar.

To open and close the various panes, click on the view buttons in the toolbar.

Observing Data

We'll now do some work inside TextEdit and watch how the data is collected.

1. *Start recording, if the app isn't open already.* If TextEdit isn't running, hit the Record button to launch it again.

    When the application starts up, it immediately allocates some memory as it gets going. When it needs to store more information, it allocates more. We'll now cause the app to start allocating more memory by adding text to the document.

2. *Enter some text in the document.* Go to the TextEdit window and start typing. Because text isn't very large, we won't see much of a difference in what's being displayed unless we enter quite a lot of text.

    So, to quickly enter lots of text, type something, select it all, copy, and paste. Then select all again, and copy and paste again. Repeat until you've got a huge amount of text in the document.

3. *Observe the memory usage of TextEdit climbing.* Go back to Instruments, and you'll notice that the amount of memory used by the application has increased quite a lot (Figure 16-3).

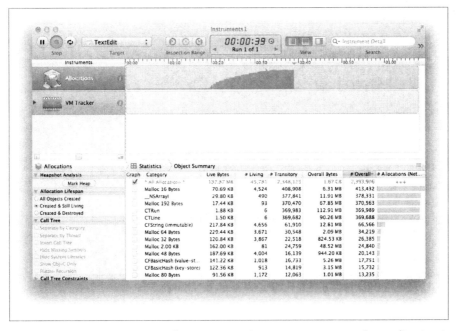

Figure 16-3. Instruments records an increase in memory usage as the application is used

Here, the consumption of memory is OK, because we deliberately stress-tested the application. However, if you see similar spikes in memory usage in your application from regular use, you probably have a problem to solve.

Adding Instruments from the Library

While Instruments provides a selection of templates that you can use to get started (such as the Allocations template we used earlier), you can add more instruments to your trace to help hunt down issues.

To add an instrument to your trace document, select the instrument you want to use from the Library. To open the Library, click the Library button, choose Library from the Window menu, or press ⌘-L (Figure 16-4).

The Library lists all of the available instruments that you can use, as well as information on what each one does. To add an instrument to your trace, drag and drop an instrument into the Instruments pane, or double-click the instrument.

 Not all instruments work on all platforms. For example, the OpenGL ES analyzer instrument only works on iOS.

Combining different kinds of instruments allows you to zoom in on specific problems. For example, if your application is being slow and you think it's because it's loading and processing lots of information at once, you can use a Reads/Writes instrument alongside a Time Profiler. If the slowdowns occur while both of these instruments indicate heavy activity, then your slowdowns are being caused by your application working the disk too hard while using lots of CPU time.

Fixing Problems with Instruments

To demonstrate how to detect and solve problems with Instruments, we'll create an application that has a large memory problem, and then use Instruments to find and fix it.

This iOS application will create and display a large gallery of images and let the user smoothly scroll between them. We'll develop and run it on the iOS Simulator, and then see how well it does on a real device.

The application will consist of a single scroll view, which will have a number of image views added to it. The user will be able to scroll around inside the view to see the different images.

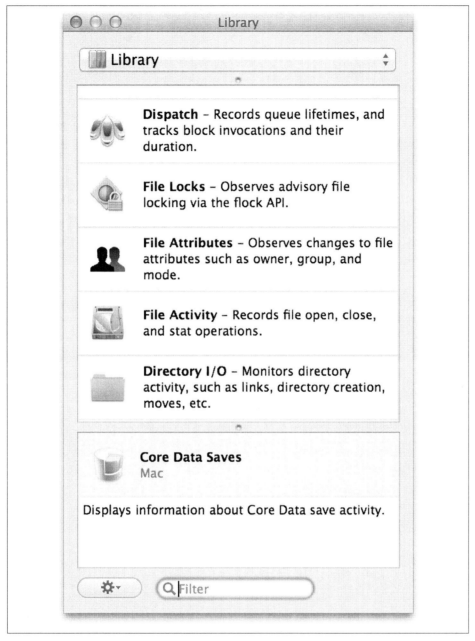

Figure 16-4. The Instruments library

1. *Create a new single-view application for iOS.* Call this application **MemoryDemo**. Make it use storyboards and ARC, and make it run on the iPhone.

2. *Open the main storyboard.* Open *MainStoryboard.storyboard* in the project navigator.

3. *Add a scroll view to the window.* Make it fill the entire screen. While you have it selected, turn Paging Enabled on. This means that the scroll view will behave much like the home screen on the iPhone, where all scrolling snaps to the width of the scroll view.

4. *Connect the scroll view to the view controller class.* Open the assistant, and control-drag from the scroll view into ViewController's interface. Create a new outlet called **imagesContainer**.

5. *Add the code that sets up the application.* Add the following code to *View Controller.m*, and remove the previous implementation of viewDidLoad:

```
- (UIImage*) imageWithNumber:(NSInteger)number {

    CGRect imageRect = self.imagesContainer.frame;

    UIGraphicsBeginImageContext(imageRect.size);

    // Inset the image by 30px so that we can see the rounded corners
    imageRect = CGRectInset(imageRect, 30, 30);

    // Draw a rounded rectangle
    UIBezierPath* path = [UIBezierPath bezierPathWithRoundedRect:imageRect
        cornerRadius:10];

    [path setLineWidth:20];
    [[UIColor blackColor] setStroke];
    [[UIColor scrollViewTexturedBackgroundColor] setFill];

    [path fill];
    [path stroke];

    // Draw the number
    NSString* label = [NSString stringWithFormat:@"%i", number];

    UIFont* font = [UIFont systemFontOfSize:50];
    CGPoint labelPoint = CGPointMake(50, 50);

    [[UIColor whiteColor] setFill];
    [label drawAtPoint:labelPoint withFont:font];

    // Get the finished image and return it
    UIImage* returnedImage = UIGraphicsGetImageFromCurrentImageContext();

    UIGraphicsEndImageContext();

    return returnedImage;
}
```

```objc
- (void) loadPageWithNumber:(NSInteger) number {

    // If an image view already exists for this page, don't do anything
    if ([self.imagesContainer viewWithTag:number])
        return;

    // Get the image for this page
    UIImage* image = [self imageWithNumber:number];

    // Create and prepare the image view for this page
    UIImageView* imageView = [[UIImageView alloc] initWithImage:image];
    CGRect imageViewFrame = [self.imagesContainer bounds];
    imageViewFrame.origin.x = imageViewFrame.size.width * (number - 1);
    imageView.frame = imageViewFrame;

    // Add it to the scroll view
    [self.imagesContainer addSubview:imageView];

    // Mark this new image view with a tag so that we can
    // easily refer to it later
    imageView.tag = number;
}

- (void)viewDidLoad
{
    [super viewDidLoad];

    NSInteger pageCount = 1000;

    for (int i = 1; i < pageCount; i++) {
        [self loadPageWithNumber:i];
    }

    CGSize contentSize;
    contentSize.height = self.imagesContainer.bounds.size.height;
    contentSize.width = self.imagesContainer.bounds.size.width * pageCount;


    self.imagesContainer.contentSize = contentSize;

}
```

6. *Run the application.* The application runs fine on the simulator, but if you try to run it on the device, it seem to hang for a while and finally exit without showing the app.

To find out why this happens, we'll run this inside Instruments.

1. *Set the Scheme to launch on your iOS device.* We want Instruments to run on the device, not the simulator. (If you don't have an iOS device to test on, that's OK—you can still use the simulator, but the numbers won't be representative of how it would work on a real iPhone or iPad.)

2. *Launch the application inside Instruments.* Do this by choosing Profile from the Product menu, or pressing ⌘-I.

3. *Select the Allocations template.* We want to keep an eye on how memory is being used. Select the Allocations template, and click Choose.

4. *When the Instruments window appears, stop the recording.* We want to make some adjustments to how the data is being collected.

 The Allocations template includes two instruments: the Allocations instrument, which keeps track of memory allocations made by your application, and the VM Tracker instrument, which monitors the total usage of memory. Some memory allocations, such as images, don't show up in the Allocations instrument because this memory is handled on the graphics card or in other regions of memory.

Therefore, to keep a close eye on the total amount of memory used by the app, we'll use the VM Tracker instrument. The VM Tracker instrument scans all of the memory used by the app, and reports on how much is being used and where. Normally, the VM Tracker instrument will only scan memory when you explicitly tell it to, because performing a memory scan causes the app to hang for a moment while the scan takes place. Because we want to stay apprised of memory usage as the app launches, we'll instruct the VM Tracker to automatically scan the memory.

5. *Select the VM Tracker in the Instruments pane.* The Detail pane will update to show information gathered by that instrument.

6. *Turn on Automatic Snapshotting and set the Snapshot Interval to 1 second.* This will cause the instrument to scan the memory usage of the app every second.

7. *Start recording.* The application will launch, and the VM Tracker will show how memory is consumed while it starts up.

As the application launches, you'll notice the amount of memory used by the app steadily increase. After a while, the app will start receiving memory warnings (you'll see a bunch of black flags pop up in the timeline), and will then quit.

Clearly, the problem is that the application consumes too much memory. There's an additional problem—the number of images being drawn during startup is causing a huge slowdown. The application is creating and inserting a thousand image views onto the screen. Each image displayed by the image views needs to be kept in memory, which means that the app rapidly runs out of space and is forced to exit.

A better way to handle this is to only display the images that the user is able to see, rather than loading all of them at once. At minimum, there are only three images that need to be present—the one currently being shown, and the two on either side of it. Because of the size of the image views, it's possible for this app to be showing one or two images at the same time, but never three.

To fix the problem, therefore, we need to make the application update the image views while the user is scrolling. If an image view isn't visible by the user, the app should remove it from the screen, which frees up memory.

To do this, we'll add a method that makes sure that the image views for the previous, current, and next pages are present, and then removes all other image views. This method will be called every time the scroll view scrolls, meaning that as far as the user is concerned, every image is on the screen when she needs to see it.

First, we'll set up the view controller to be notified when the scroll view scrolls, and then add the code that checks the image views. Finally, we'll update the `viewDidLoad` method to make it only display the first set of image views.

1. *Open the storyboard and make the scroll view use the view controller as its delegate.*

   Control-drag from the scroll view onto the view controller's icon. Choose "delegate" from the list that pops up.

2. *Open* ViewController.h. We now need to make the class conform to the `UIScroll` `ViewDelegate` protocol. Replace the class's definition with the following line of code:

   ```
   @interface ViewController : UIViewController <UIScrollViewDelegate>
   ```

3. *Add the additional methods to* ViewController.m.

Finally, we'll update the code to update the collection of image views when the scroll view scrolls.

Add the following methods to *ViewController.m*, above the `viewDidLoad` method:

```
- (void) updatePages {
    int pageNumber = imagesContainer.contentOffset.x /
        imagesContainer.bounds.size.width + 1;

    // Load the image previous to this one
    [self loadPageWithNumber:pageNumber - 1];
    // Load the current page
    [self loadPageWithNumber:pageNumber];
    // Load the next page
    [self loadPageWithNumber:pageNumber+1];

    // Remove all image views that aren't on this page or the pages adjacent
    // to it
    for (UIImageView* imageView in imagesContainer.subviews) {
        if (imageView.tag < pageNumber - 1 || imageView.tag > pageNumber + 1)
            [imageView removeFromSuperview];
    }
}

- (void)scrollViewDidScroll:(UIScrollView *)scrollView{
    [self updatePages];
}
```

4. *Replace the* viewDidLoad *method.* Replace the method with the following code:

```
- (void)viewDidLoad
{
    [super viewDidLoad];

    NSInteger pageCount = 1000;

    [self updatePages];

    CGSize contentSize;
    contentSize.height = self.imagesContainer.bounds.size.height;
    contentSize.width = self.imagesContainer.bounds.size.width * pageCount;

    self.imagesContainer.contentSize = contentSize;
}
```

Once you've made these changes, try running the app on the device again. You'll find that its behavior is identical to how it used to run, with the added bonus that the application doesn't run out of memory and crash on launch.

Retain Cycles and Leaks

The Automatic Reference Counting feature built into the compiler is great at reducing problems caused by memory leaks, but it's not foolproof. In this section, we'll look at using Instruments to detect a memory leak.

Automatic Reference Counting releases an object from memory when the last strong reference to that object goes away. However, if two objects have strong references *to each other*, the number of strong references to each object will never be zero, and the objects will stay in memory—even if nothing else in the application has a reference to those objects. This is called a *retain cycle*, so named because if you were to draw a graph showing how each object refers to each other, you'd end up drawing a circle.

You can use Instruments to detect leaked memory, again by using the Allocations instrument. To demonstrate this, we'll build a sample application that has a built-in retain cycle.

This will be a master-detail application that has a custom UIView on the detail view controller. This view uses the view controller as a delegate, whereby it asks which color to use as the background.

1. *Create a new master-detail application for iOS.* Name the application **RetainCycle** and make it use storyboards and ARC.

2. *Create a new file.* Make a new Objective-C subclass, and make it a subclass of UIView. Name it **ExampleView**.

3. *Set up the* ExampleView *class.* Make *ExampleView.h* look like the following code. In this code, we're creating a new delegate protocol for other classes to conform to, and adding a property on the ExampleView class so that it has a delegate.

```
#import <UIKit/UIKit.h>

@class ExampleView;

@protocol ExampleViewDelegate <NSObject>
- (UIColor*)colorForView:(ExampleView*)view;
@end

@interface ExampleView : UIView
@property (strong) IBOutlet id <ExampleViewDelegate> delegate;
@end
```

4. *Make the* ExampleView *class use its delegate when it's loaded.* Add the following method to *ExampleView.m*:

```
- (void)awakeFromNib {
    self.backgroundColor = [self.delegate colorForView:self];
}
```

5. *Add an* ExampleView *to the detail view controller.* Open *MainStoryboard.story board* and remove the label.

   Drag in a new UIView and open its Identity inspector (it's the third button from the left at the top of the Inspector pane).

   Set its class to ExampleView.

6. *Make the* `ExampleView` *use the view controller as its delegate.*

   Control-drag from the `ExampleView` to the view controller's icon, and select "delegate" from the menu that pops up.

   The view will now use the view controller as its delegate, which means we need to make the view controller function as the delegate.

7. *Update DetailViewController.h.* Make the file look like the following code. We've modified it to make it conform to the `ExampleViewDelegate` protocol, which declares that it has a method called `colorForView:` for the `ExampleView` to call.

   ```
   #import <UIKit/UIKit.h>
   #import "ExampleView.h"

   @interface DetailViewController : UIViewController <ExampleViewDelegate>

   @property (strong, nonatomic) id detailItem;
   @property (strong, nonatomic) IBOutlet UILabel *detailDescriptionLabel;

   @end
   ```

8. *Update DetailViewController.m.* All we're doing here is implementing the `colorFor View:` method. Add it to the file:

   ```
   -(UIColor *)colorForView:(ExampleView *)view {
       return [UIColor greenColor];
   }
   ```

Once this is done, we're ready to test it.

9. *Launch the application inside Instruments.* Do this by choosing Profile from the Product menu or pressing ⌘-I.

10. *Select the Allocations template.* We want to keep an eye on how memory is being used. Select the Allocations template and click Choose.

    This application contains a retain cycle. We'll now use Instruments to figure out what's being leaked and where.

11. *Select the Detail row.* A `DetailViewController` will be created and added to the navigation stack.

12. *Search for* `DetailViewController` *in Instruments.* In Instruments, select the Allocations instrument and type **DetailViewController** in the search field at the top-right corner of the screen.

    The list of objects shown in the Detail pane will show only `DetailView Controller` objects. Currently, there's just one.

13. *Tap the back button in the app.* The `DetailViewController` is removed from the screen, and should therefore be removed from memory because nothing else is referring to it.

However, it doesn't go away—it still shows up in the list of objects.

Go back and forth between the detail view controller and the master view controller a few times. Every time you open the detail view controller, a new one is created, and when you close it, it's not being removed from memory.

The `DetailViewController` class is being leaked. The problem lies in this line in *ExampleView.h*:

```
@property (strong) IBOutlet id <ExampleViewDelegate> delegate;
```

The `ExampleView` has a strong reference to the view controller (its delegate) due to the use of the `strong` keyword. The view controller also has a strong reference to the view, because the view controller's view has the `ExampleView` as a subview.

To solve this problem, change the line listed above to this:

```
@property (weak) IBOutlet id <ExampleViewDelegate> delegate;
```

A weak reference means that the `ExampleView` is still able to refer to its delegate, but the view does not own the delegate and doesn't need it to stay in memory. If the delegate does get removed from memory, the reference is set to `nil` to avoid dangling pointers.

Using the Debugger

Xcode includes a source debugger called LLDB. Like all debuggers, LLDB allows you to observe your code as it runs, set breakpoints and watchpoints, and inspect the contents of memory.

The debugger is deeply integrated into Xcode, and Xcode lets you create very specific actions to run when your code does certain things. You can, for example, ask Xcode to speak some text the third time that a specific line of code gets run.

Setting Breakpoints

There are a few ways to set a breakpoint in Xcode. The most common method is to set a breakpoint on a line of code—when execution reaches that point, the debugger stops the program.

To set a breakpoint at a line, click the gray gutter at the left of the code editor. A blue breakpoint arrow will appear (Figure 16-5).

It's easier to add breakpoints, and navigate your code in general, if you turn on line numbers in Xcode. To do this, open Preferences by pressing ⌘-, and open the Text Editing tab. Turn on the Line Numbers checkbox.

```
 99    - (id)init {
100        if ((self = [super init])) {
101            [[self undoManager] disableUndoRegistration];
102
103            textStorage = [[NSTextStorage allocWithZone:[self zone]] init];
104
105        [self setBackgroundColor:[NSColor whiteColor]];
106        [self setEncoding:NoStringEncoding];
107        [self setEncodingForSaving:NoStringEncoding];
108        [self setScaleFactor:1.0];
109        [self setDocumentPropertiesToDefaults];
110        inDuplicate = NO;
```

Figure 16-5. A breakpoint

Once a breakpoint has been added to your code, you can drag the arrow to move the breakpoint. To remove the breakpoint, drag it out of the gutter.

When the program hits a breakpoint, Xcode shows the backtrace of all threads in the debug navigator. From there, you can see how a breakpoint was hit, and what functions were called that led to the program hitting that breakpoint.

Controlling program flow

When the program execution hits a breakpoint, you can choose to simply resume execution, or step through the code line by line.

To control program flow, you use the buttons in the debugger bar. The debugger bar is at the top of the debug area, which you can open and close by clicking the middle segment of the View control, at the top-right of the toolbar (Figure 16-6).

Figure 16-6. The debugger bar

From left to right, the buttons in the debugger bar perform the following actions:

- Close the debug area
- Pause or resume execution
- Step Over (continue to the next line of code)

- Step Into (if the current line of code is a method call, continue into it)
- Step Out (continue until execution leaves the current method)

When you add a breakpoint, it appears in the breakpoints navigator. From there, you can see all of the currently set breakpoints—you can also jump directly to a breakpoint, disable it, or delete it.

Custom breakpoints

Normally, a breakpoint just pauses execution when hit. However, you can customize your breakpoints to perform specific actions.

To customize a breakpoint, right-click the arrow or the breakpoint's entry in the breakpoints navigator, and choose Edit. The Edit Breakpoint window will appear (Figure 16-7).

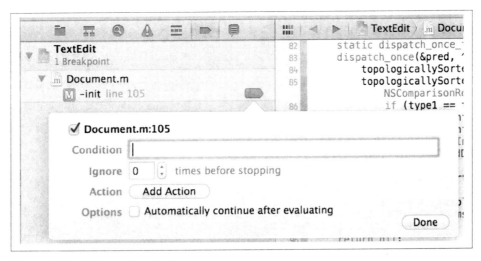

Figure 16-7. Editing a breakpoint

The Edit Breakpoint window allows you to customize when the breakpoint should trigger and what happens when it does. You can also indicate how many times the breakpoint should be ignored, what actions the breakpoint should run, and whether the breakpoint should pause the execution of the program.

Adding actions to a breakpoint allows you to run some AppleScript, speak a line of text, play a sound, or other actions. To add an action, click the "Click to add an action" button and choose the action that should be run.

This is a tremendously flexible feature, as it allows you to get additional information about how your program is running without the program stopping and starting.

Exception and symbolic breakpoints

The breakpoints navigator also allows you to add exception breakpoints and symbolic breakpoints.

An *exception breakpoint* stops the program when an Objective-C or C++ exception is thrown. For example, if you have an NSArray with two items and you try to access the third one, an exception is thrown and your program exits. Normally, Xcode stops the program at the point where the exception is caught, which isn't often the place where it is thrown. This makes it difficult to work out where the problem is. To solve this problem, you can add an exception breakpoint that stops the program at the instant the exception is thrown.

A *symbolic breakpoint* stops the program when a specific, named function or Objective-C method is entered. This is mostly useful when you want to stop execution at a function that you might not have the source code for, and then view the backtrace.

To add an exception or symbolic breakpoint, click the + button at the bottom-left of the breakpoints navigator. You then choose which type of breakpoint you want to add, and Xcode asks you to configure the new breakpoint (Figure 16-8).

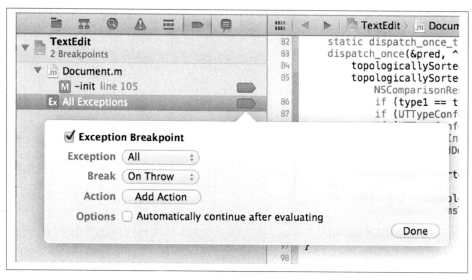

Figure 16-8. Configuring an exception breakpoint

If you're creating an exception breakpoint, you can choose whether you want to stop on Objective-C exceptions, C++ exceptions, or both. You can also choose whether the breakpoint should stop when the exception is thrown or caught.

Inspecting Memory Contents

When the program is stopped in the debugger, you can see the current state of objects and variables in memory.

The variables view is the lefthand section of the debug area. When the program is stopped, the variables view shows the variables that exist at that point.

The variables view shows the value of the variables. If the variables are simple types like integers or BOOLs, their values are shown; if the variables are things like NSStrings or NSArrays, then summary information about them is shown, like the content of the string or the number of items in the array.

If you use the flow control buttons while the program is stopped, the variables view updates to show any changes. If a variable changes, it gets highlighted in blue.

The variables view also allows you to quickly send the description message to any object and see the results. To do this, right-click on a variable and choose Print Description.

Working with the Debugger Console

At the righthand side of the debug area is the console. The console is the command-line interface to the debugger, and allows you to directly access some of the debugger's powerful, lower-level features.

Working with LLDB via the console is a subject large enough to fill its own book, but in this section we'll talk about how to use the console for its arguably most powerful purpose: running custom Objective-C code to work with your program's variables.

Let's assume that the debugger has stopped at a breakpoint in a method. In this method, myArray is an NSArray, and you want to check its contents.

To see how many items are in myArray, you'd type this into the console:

```
print (int)[myArray count]
```

Note the lack of a semicolon. In the console, you don't put a semicolon at the end of lines.

 When you call an Objective-C method in the debugger, you must specify what type of data the method will return. In the above example, count returns an int.

You can send arbitrary Objective-C messages to objects. For example, if you wanted to get the second object in the `myArray` array, you'd do this:

```
print-object [myArray objectAtIndex:1]
```

The `print-object` command takes an Objective-C object and sends it a `description` message. It then returns the string that comes back.

CHAPTER 17

Sharing and Notifications

Just about every app these days deals in some kind of content—whether it's business documents written in an office suite, images created in an image editor, or even high scores earned in a game. Users frequently want to be able to show this content to other people, and while there's a very good established system in place for sharing documents, smaller snippets of content like URLs, individual photos, or other miscellany have fewer well-defined and easy-to-use options.

Starting in OS X 10.8 and iOS 6, the OS provides built-in sharing APIs that let your application send various kinds of content to services that can handle them. For example, online services like YouTube and Vimeo can receive video files and share them over the Internet, the Messages app can send text, photos, and videos, and email can send just about any file.

In addition to sending content to other locations, the OS is also capable of receiving *notifications*. These are short messages sent from a server to an iOS device, which are received regardless of whether the app is running or the phone is awake.

In this chapter, you'll learn how to share data from your application using the built-in sharing APIs, and how to send and receive both push and local notifications.

Sharing

From the user's perspective, the problem of data sharing can be rephrased as, "How can I send this to someone else?" From your application's perspective, however, the problem of data sharing is really the question, "Where can I send this data?"

Different systems are capable of accepting different kinds of data. A video, for example, cannot be sent to a printer, and plain text cannot be sent to a photo-hosting site like Flickr. Fortunately, the sharing systems on both iOS and OS X already know what different data types are supported by the sharing destinations that the OS knows about.

As of OS X 10.8 and iOS 6, the available sharing destinations are the following:

OS X:

- Email: Text, images, videos, and anything that can be copied and pasted
- Messages: Same content as email
- AirDrop: Files
- Aperture: Photos
- iPhoto: Photos
- Flickr: Photos
- YouTube, Vimeo, Tudou, Youku: Videos
- Safari Reading List: URLs
- Setting the Desktop background: Images
- Setting a Twitter profile picture: Images
- Twitter, Facebook, and Sina Weibo: Text, images, videos, and URLs

iOS:

- Email: Text, images, videos, URLs (including URLs pointing to local files)
- Messages: Text
- Twitter, Facebook, Sina Weibo: Text, images, videos, URLs
- Copying to the pasteboard: Text, images, URLs, colors, `NSDictionary` objects
- Saving to the camera roll: Images, videos
- Printing: Text, images, and any of the `UIPrintRenderer` or related printing objects [see "Printing on iOS" (page 240)]
- Assigning to a contact: Images

 Sina Weibo is a social media service, similar to both Twitter and Facebook, based in the People's Republic of China. Youku and Tudou are video hosting services also based in the People's Republic of China.

As you can see, there are a number of different kinds of content that can be given to the various sharing destinations. Fortunately, the method for actually sharing something is rather straightforward:

1. *Make an array containing all of the things you want to share.*

   This array should contain everything that you want to share—text, images, videos, and so on.

2. *Give this array to the sharing system.*

   The OS will figure out which sharing destinations can be used based on what content was provided. The greater the number of different kinds of content you provide, the more sharing destinations will be offered to the user.

   For example, if you provide both text and an image on iOS, both "Save to camera roll" and "Send message" will appear, even though neither service supports both. Only the supported content will be shared by the selected sharing destination.

3. *Let the sharing system actually handle the sharing.*

   Depending on which sharing destination was selected, the user might be prompted to provide a little more information. For example, if the user is posting an image to Twitter, he'll be presented with a Twitter share sheet, which allows him to add some text before sending the tweet.

It's a rather simple and elegant system, and can be a very positive thing for your apps.

To get our hands dirty, we're going to take a look at the different sharing APIs that are available on both iOS and OS X.

Sharing on iOS

Sharing content on iOS is handled by the UIActivityViewController. When you have some content that you want to share—some text stored in an NSString, say—all you need to do is create a new UIActivityViewController and provide it with an array containing that object:

```
NSString* text = @"Hello, world!";
UIActivityViewController* activity = [[UIActivityViewController alloc]
    initWithActivityItems:@[text] applicationActivities:nil];
```

The second parameter, left nil in the previous example, can also take an NSArray of UIActivity subclasses. These can be used if you want your app to provide custom sharing destinations. Note, however, that any custom sharing destinations you include will only show up inside your own app.

Once that's done, you just need to present the view controller modally, just as you would any other modal view controller:

```
[self presentViewController:activity animated:YES completion:nil];
```

From there, the OS takes over, allowing the user to select the sharing destination and completing the share.

To show this in action, we'll build a simple iOS application that supports sharing both text and images.

1. *Create the project.* Create a new single-view iPhone application called **iOSSharing**.

2. *Add an image to share.* Find an image of some sort on your computer, or take one with a camera. Drag it into the project.

3. *Create the interface.*

   - Open *MainStoryboard.storyboard*, and drag a text field into the top of the window.

   - Drag in a UIButton, just beneath the text field. Set its title to **Share Text**.

   - Drag in a UIImageView beneath this button, and set its image to the one that you added earlier.

   - Finally, drag in a second UIButton and place it beneath the image view. Set its title to **Share Image**.

4. *Connect the interface.* There are two actions to add: one for sharing text and one for sharing an image. We're going to connect these two actions to the appropriate buttons; we'll also use the text field and the image view as the sources for the content that will be shared.

   - Open *ViewController.h* in the assistant, and control-drag from the top and bottom buttons into AppDelegate's interface. The two actions you want to create are shareImage and shareText.

   - Once that's done, control-drag from the text field into AppDelegate's interface, and create a new outlet called textView. Then, control-drag from the image view into AppDelegate's interface and create a new outlet called imageView.

   - Finally, because we want the keyboard to go away when the user taps the Return button, control-drag from the text field to the File's Owner in the outline, and choose "delegate" from the menu that pops up.

   The final result should look like Figure 17-1:

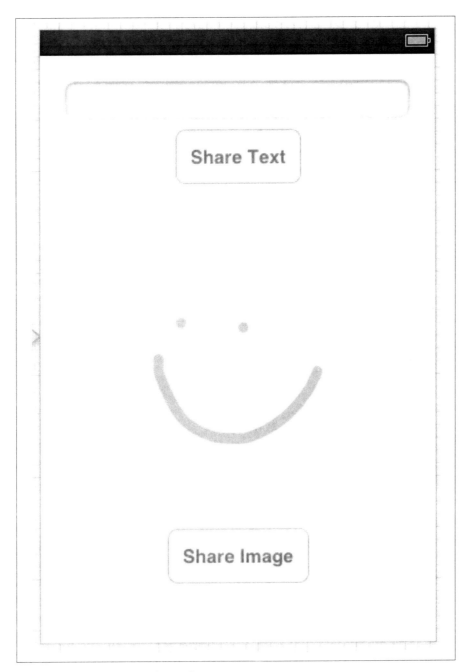

Figure 17-1. The connected interface

The code for this is extremely simple. The two methods that are run when the share buttons are tapped are only two lines each.

5. *Add the image sharing method.* Add the following code to `shareImage:`.

```
UIActivityViewController* activity = [[UIActivityViewController alloc]
    initWithActivityItems:@[self.imageView.image] applicationActivities:nil];
[self presentViewController:activity animated:YES completion:nil];
```

6. *Add the text sharing method.* Add the following code to `shareText:`.

```
UIActivityViewController* activity = [[UIActivityViewController alloc]
    initWithActivityItems:@[self.textView.text] applicationActivities:nil];
[self presentViewController:activity animated:YES completion:nil];
```

7. *Finally, add the code to dismiss the keyboard when the Return button is tapped.* Add the following method to `AppDelegate`'s implementation.

```
- (BOOL)textFieldShouldReturn:(UITextField *)textField {
    [textField resignFirstResponder];
    return NO;
}
```

8. *Run the app.* Try sharing both text and images, and see what sharing services can be used for each.

Sharing on OS X

Sharing content on OS X is very similar to sharing on iOS; the only real difference is in how the list of sharing destinations is presented.

On OS X, you create an `NSSharingServicePicker`, which presents a menu of available sharing destinations depending on what content you provide it. This pattern is very similar to iOS's model.

Creating an `NSSharingServicePicker` looks like this:

```
NSString* text = @"Hello, world!"
NSSharingServicePicker* picker = [[NSSharingServicePicker alloc]
    initWithItems:@[text]];
```

Once the picker has been created, it needs to be presented to the user. Because the picker shows a menu, it needs to know where the menu should appear on screen. This in- for

mation is provided when you call the `showRelativeToRect: ofView: preferredEdge:` method. This method receives an `NSRect` and an `NSView` that the rectangle should be considered to be in the coordinate space of, as well as information indicating which edge of the rectangle the menu should appear on.

For example, if you have an NSView called "myView", you can tell the menu to appear on the far right edge of its bounds rectangle with the following call:

```
[picker showRelativeToRect:myView.bounds
    ofView:myView
    preferredEdge:NSMaxXEdge];
```

The behavior of the picker after this point is identical to UIActivityViewController —the user is invited to choose which sharing service to use, and the OS will ask for additional information as necessary.

Notifications

Notifications are a way for your app to send messages to the user, regardless of whether the application is currently being used or even running. Originally introduced in iOS 3, they've become an indispensable tool for many apps. Starting with OS X 10.8 Mountain Lion, notifications are also available on the Mac.

There are two kinds of notifications: *push notifications* (also known as *remote notifications*) and *local notifications*.

Push Notifications

Every iOS and OS X machine with notifications enabled maintains a permanent connection to Apple's *push notification service*, which delivers short, infrequent messages to applications.

Push notifications work by having a server make an SSL-secured TCP connection to the Apple push notification service. When an application wants to receive push notifications, it calls the registerForRemoteNotificationsOfType: method on the application's global UIApplication or NSApplication object.

When registering for remote notifications, it's important to know about the different kinds that can be delivered. Notifications can:

- Set a badge (that is, a number) on the app's icon, either in the Dock on OS X or on the home screen in iOS
- Play a sound file included in the app (*iOS only*)
- Display an alert (*iOS only*)

All notifications on all platforms may also include additional application-specific information.

What happens when a push arrives

When a remote notification arrives, your application may or may not be running. If it's running, your application delegate receives the `application: didReceiveRemote Notification:` message, which contains as its second parameter an `NSDictionary` containing any additional information in the notification. This is your app's opportunity to do something useful with the notification.

If the application isn't running when the notification arrives, what it's able to do depends on the platform. On OS X, the only thing a notification can do if the app isn't running is to modify the app icon's badge. This is less of a restriction than it seems, since an application that's currently running receives a message sent to its application delegate when the notification arrives, and your application is able to run any code you want when that happens.

On iOS, it's another matter. Because only one app is allowed to be open at the same time [all other apps are allowed to run in the background for a bit, but are eventually suspended or terminated—see "iOS Applications" (page 66)], a notification is more likely to arrive when the app *isn't* running.

An iOS notification is able to contain an alert, which is a string of text that's shown to the user. When the notification arrives, if it contains an alert, that alert text appears on the screen. (The specific presentation depends on the user's preferences, but it's generally a banner at the top of the screen, or a pop-up box if the phone was locked when the notification arrived.) When the user interacts with this alert, the application is launched (or resumed if it was already launched). At this point, your application is informed that it received a notification, and can then respond appropriately.

This is why iOS notifications can contain more than OS X applications—because an iOS app is much less likely to be able to respond to a notification at the moment it arrives, the system steps in to provide some minimal functionality (showing some text, playing a sound, and so on). On OS X, that's not necessary, since the application is much more likely to be running in the background.

Sending Push Notifications

A push notification is nothing more than a JSON-formatted dictionary. When a push notification is created, it can contain any valid JSON data that you want (that is, strings, numbers, arrays, and dictionaries).

 For more information on JSON-formatted data, see "Saving More Complex Data" (page 202) in Chapter 12.

When your application receives the notification, it receives an NSDictionary containing whatever was sent as the push notification.

In addition to the application-specific data that can be included in the JSON dictionary, push notifications also contain a special aps dictionary. This dictionary contains information about how the push notification should be presented: its alert text, the number to display in the application icon's badge, and so on.

For example, here's a sample push notification in JSON form:

```
{
    "aps":{
        "alert":"Hello, world!",
        "badge":1,
        "sound":"hello.wav"
    },
    "foo":"bar"
}
```

This push notification, when delivered to an iOS device, does the following things:

- Displays the alert text "Hello, world!" on the screen
- Sets the badge on the application's icon to 1
- Plays the sound *hello.wav* [which must be inside the application's bundle—see "Working with the Filesystem" (page 154)].

The maximum size for a push notification is 256 bytes, including the aps dictionary. If you try to send a push notification larger than this limit, it won't be accepted by the Apple Push Notification Service.

Additionally, delivery of push notifications is *not guaranteed*. Apple describes it as a "best effort" service, much like SMS. Finally, the delivery mechanism for push notifications cannot be considered secure.

Therefore, your push notifications should never contain any sensitive information, and they shouldn't be used as the primary way for your application to receive data. Instead, use push notifications to let your application know that new data is available; let the application itself do the work of actually retrieving that data.

Additionally, when the *application* receives the notification (either because the notification was opened by the user or the application was running when the notification was received), the NSDictionary that the application receives will contain a value @"bar" for the foo key.

This is a book on Cocoa, not server programming, so we're not going to go into a huge amount of detail on how to set up a server that sends push notifications to Apple. For information on how to do this, see "Apple Push Notification Service" in the *Local and Remote Notification Guide* (*http://bit.ly/WDTjz7*), included in the Xcode developer documentation.

Setting Up to Receive Push Notifications

Applications don't receive push notifications automatically. That's because push notifications are considered a potential intrusion on the user's device—if, as a user, you don't want an app to interrupt you, it shouldn't be able to.

To make your app indicate to the push notification system that it wants to receive notifications, it needs to make a method call to the global `UIApplication` or `NSApplication` object:

```
[[UIApplication sharedApplication]
    registerForRemoteNotificationTypes:UIRemoteNotificationTypeBadge];
```

`registerForRemoteNotificationTypes:` takes a single parameter, which indicates to the system what *types* of notifications to receive. You can pass in the following valid values on iOS and OS X:

iOS:

- `UIRemoteNotificationTypeNone`: No notifications
- `UIRemoteNotificationTypeBadge`: Badges on the app icon
- `UIRemoteNotificationTypeSound`: Sounds
- `UIRemoteNotificationTypeAlert`: Text alerts
- `UIRemoteNotificationTypeNewsstandContentAvailability`: A special notification that lets your application know to download content in the background. This only applies to Newsstand applications, which we don't cover in this book, but see *Newsstand Kit Framework Reference* in the Xcode developer documentation for more information.

OS X:

- `NSRemoteNotificationTypeNone`: No notifications
- `NSRemoteNotificationTypeBadge`: Badges on the app icon

The first time your application ever makes a call to `registerForRemoteNotification Types:`, the OS will present an alert box to the user, asking if he wants to receive notifications. If he chooses not to receive them, your application delegate receives the `application:didFailToRegisterForRemoteNotificationsWithError:` message to let your code know about it:

```
- (void)application:(UIApplication *)application
    didFailToRegisterForRemoteNotificationsWithError:(NSError *)error {

    // Failed to register; the 'error' parameter contains info on why

}
```

Registering for push notifications can also fail if there's no Internet connection, if the push notification service is down, or if your code is running on a platform that doesn't support push notification.

If the user *does* want notifications, the OS contacts the Apple Push Notification service (APNs), which registers the device and application as able to receive notifications. Once this is done, the APNs sends a *device token* back to your application, which is a unique ID that acts as a "telephone number" for push notifications. When a push notification is created, the device token is included and sent to the APNs, which uses it to figure out which of the millions of devices worldwide should receive the notification.

When the application successfully registers for push notifications, it receives the `application:didRegisterForRemoteNotificationsWithDeviceToken:` message, which takes as a parameter an `NSData` object containing the device token:

```
- (void)application:(UIApplication *)application
    didRegisterForRemoteNotificationsWithDeviceToken:(NSData *)deviceToken {

    // Send the device token to a server that can send pushes

}
```

Once you have a device token, it needs to be sent to whatever server will actually be sending the push notifications. Without the device token, it's not possible to indicate which device should receive a push.

 If you don't want to deal with setting up your own push server, there are several existing services that can handle it for you. Most of them are based on usage—that is, the number of push notifications you send per month—and many include a free plan. We've used Urban Airship (*http://urbanairship.com*) and Parse (*http://parse.com*).

Receiving Push Notifications

Remember that a push notification may arrive when your application is open, or when it's not.

When your application is open and a push notification is received, your application delegate receives the `application:didReceiveRemoteNotification:` message:

```
- (void)application:(NSApplication *)application
    didReceiveRemoteNotification:(NSDictionary *)userInfo {

    // Do something with the data contained in 'userInfo'

}
```

This method receives an `NSDictionary` that contains whatever information was contained inside the JSON bundle that was originally sent.

If your application is *not* running and is opened from a push notification, then your application launches and your application delegate receives the `application:didFinishLaunchingWithOptions:` message (on iOS). This is the same message that's sent when an application normally launches, but when opening from a push, the `launchOptions` dictionary contains the contents of the JSON dictionary.

```
- (BOOL)application:(UIApplication *)application
    didFinishLaunchingWithOptions:(NSDictionary *)launchOptions {

    NSDictionary* remoteNotification =
        launchOptions[UIApplicationLaunchOptionsRemoteNotificationKey];

    // remoteNotification now contains the push notification info.

}
```

On OS X, the message received by the application delegate is a little different. On launch, the application delegate receives the `application:didFinishLaunching:` message, which takes an `NSNotification` object as a parameter. The equivalent to the iOS's `launchOptions` dictionary can be accessed thusly:

```
- (void)applicationDidFinishLaunching:(NSNotification *)aNotification {

    NSDictionary* remoteNotification =
        aNotification.userInfo[NSApplicationLaunchRemoteNotificationKey];

    // remoteNotification now contains the push notification info.

}
```

Finally, if your application ever needs to stop receiving push notifications, it can unregister from the Apple Push Notification service by sending the `unregisterForRemoteNotifications` message to the global `UIApplication` or `NSApplication` object:

```
[[NSApplication sharedApplication] unregisterForRemoteNotifications];
```
If you unregister for notifications, you can alway register again later.

Local Notifications

While remote notifications require a complex setup involving a remote computer that communicates with the Apple Push Notification service, *local* notifications are created and presented entirely on the device.

 Local notifications are only available on iOS—the concept doesn't make much sense on OS X.

A local notification looks the same as a remote notification to the user, but its delivery is controlled by the application. Local notifications are represented by the UILocal Notification class.

Local notifications can either be created and presented immediately (if the application is currently running and is in the background), or scheduled to appear at a certain date and time.

To construct a local notification, you simply create, configure, and schedule a UILocal Notification:

```
UILocalNotification* notification = [][UILocalNotification alloc] init];
notification.fireDate = [NSDate dateWithTimeIntervalSinceNow:20];
notification.alertBody = @"Hello, world!";

[[UIApplication sharedApplication] scheduleLocalNotification:notification];
```

This example code creates a local notification that displays the text "Hello world!" in 20 seconds.

When a notification fires and the user chooses to open it, the application delegate receives a message very similar to the one used when a remote notification arrives: appli cation:didReceiveLocalNotification:.

```
- (void)application:(UIApplication *)application
    didReceiveLocalNotification:(UILocalNotification *)notification {

    // 'notification' is a copy of the UILocalNotification that was posted

}
```

Likewise, if the application isn't running when the local notification fires and the user opens the notification, the application is launched, and the launchOptions dictionary contains the notification:

```
- (BOOL)application:(UIApplication *)application
    didFinishLaunchingWithOptions:(NSDictionary *)launchOptions {

    UILocalNotification* localNotification =
        launchOptions[UIApplicationLaunchOptionsLocalNotificationKey];

    // localNotification now contains the local notification object

}
```

A local notification can also be presented immediately in the background. For example, if you have an application that is performing some work in the background and you want to let the user know that the work is complete, you can create a notification to that effect:

```
UILocalNotification* notification = ...
[[UIApplication sharedApplication] presentLocalNotificationNow:notification];
```

Once a local notification has been scheduled, you can cancel it; you can also cancel all scheduled notifications:

```
UILocalNotification* notification = ... // a scheduled notification
[[UIApplication sharedApplication] cancelLocalNotification:notification];
```

or:

```
[[UIApplication sharedApplication] cancelAllLocalNotifications];
```

CHAPTER 18

Nonstandard Apps

For the majority of this book, we've talked about GUI applications designed to run on either OS X or iOS. These applications receive user input via the mouse, keyboard, or touch screen, display information via the screen and are launched by double-clicking them on OS X or tapping them on iOS.

However, not every piece of software that you write is a traditional app. In some cases, you might want to create something that the user doesn't need to see—for example, a background application that periodically talks to the Internet. Another case where you don't want to build a traditional app is when you want to create a preference pane, which the user can access via the System Preferences application.

In this chapter, you'll learn how to build apps for OS X that don't fit the mold of standard applications. Specifically, you'll learn how to build command-line tools (which don't use a GUI), system preference panes, and applications that add an item to the system-wide menu bar.

 This chapter only applies to OS X—on iOS, you can only build apps that the user accesses via the home screen and that display an interface. Command-line tools and daemons aren't supported.

Command-Line Tools

The simplest possible application on OS X is a command-line tool. This kind of app never presents a GUI to the user, but instead sends and receives output via the command line.

The command line is the fundamental method of communication for computer programs; every Unix-based system has one, and since OS X is a Unix OS, your applications can use it.

In fact, this is a feature of the OS that you've already been using—whenever you use NSLog to log some text, that text goes to the command line. (Xcode redirects it so that you can view it in the IDE, but if you were to launch the app via the Terminal, you'd see it there.)

To demonstrate how to build a command-line tool with Objective-C, we'll create a simple app that prints text out to the command line.

1. *Create the project.* Create a new command-line tool project named **CommandLine**. Set the type of the project to **Foundation**.

   Xcode will create a command-line application that uses the Foundation framework and is written in Objective-C.

    There are several types of command-line apps, which vary by the framework that your code uses. If you use Foundation, which is an Objective-C framework, you'll be writing Objective-C. If you create a Core Foundation application, you'll write C.

2. *Add the code.* Replace the main method in *main.m* with the following code:

   ```
   #import <Foundation/Foundation.h>

   int main(int argc, const char * argv[])
   {

       @autoreleasepool {

           for (int i = 10; i > 0; i--) {
               NSLog(@"%i green bottles, standing on the wall", i);
               NSLog(@"%i green bottles, standing on the wall", i);
               NSLog(@"And if one green bottle should accidentally fall");
               NSLog(@"There'll be %i green bottles, standing on the wall\n\n",
               i-1);
           }

       }
       return 0;
   }
   ```

3. *Test the application.* Run the application and note what gets output in the log.

4. *Test the application in the Terminal.*

Open the Terminal application. In Xcode, scroll down to the Products group and open the folder. You'll see the `CommandLine` application. Drag it onto Terminal's icon in the Dock, and watch the program run.

Preference Panes

For the most part, your applications should show their preferences inside the apps themselves. For example, most apps that have preferences you can change have a Preferences window, accessible via the main menu (or by pressing ⌘-,).

However, some software doesn't present a traditional interface where the preferences can be displayed—for example, background applications or device drives. In these cases, you create *preference panes*, which are small programs hosted by the System Preferences application.

Preference panes are designed to allow the user to control features that affect the entire system (as far as the user is concerned). For example, the video codec package Perian adds additional functionality to the built-in QuickTime Player, and therefore doesn't have its own UI. To allow the user to configure how it works, therefore, Perian provides a preference pane.

Preference panes are only available on OS X. On iOS, you use Settings Bundles, which are basically files that describe what settings to show to the user. You don't write any code to display them.

How Preference Panes Work

A preference pane is not a separate application, but is instead a bundle of code loaded by the System Preferences application. The bundle contains code and whatever resources it needs (such as images, nib files, and so on); when the preference pane is installed, System Preferences displays it as an icon in the main window. When the user selects the preference pane's icon, the bundle is loaded, its main nib is displayed, and your code begins running.

The preference pane bundle stays in memory after the user switches to another pane, until the System Preferences application exits.

Because your preference pane is a bundle that's loaded by another application, accessing resources via NSBundle's `pathForResource:ofType:` method or `NSUserDefaults` won't work the same way as in your applications. This is because these methods access the application's bundle and preference domain, not your bundle and preference domain. If you want to set preferences, you need to specifically tell `NSUserDefaults` which domain the preferences should be set in.

Preference Domains

Imagine that two applications exist, both of which set a preference called `favoriteCol` `or`. These applications are by different authors and use the preference in different ways, so each assumes that it's the only one using the *favoriteColor* preference.

To prevent preferences colliding, OS X and iOS separate preferences by *domain*. When you use `NSUserDefault`'s `setValue:forKey:` and `valueForKey:` methods (and related methods like `setBool:forKey:`), it assumes that the preference domain you want to work in is the one with the same name as your application's bundle identifier.

So, to go back to our two example applications, as long as each has a different bundle identifier—and it should, because Apple won't allow it into the App Store unless a unique one is set—the two applications will set and retrieve preferences in their own, separate domains.

When you're building a preference pane, however, the bundle identifier of the application is that of System Preferences. This means that calling methods like `boolForKey:` won't retrieve the settings you want. To solve this problem, you indicate to `NSUser` `Defaults` exactly which preference domain you want to work with.

To retrieve the preferences for a specific domain, you use the `NSUserDefaults` class's `persistentDomainForName:` method. This method takes an `NSString` containing the name of the domain, and returns an `NSDictionary` containing all of the keys and values stored in that domain's preferences.

To set the preferences for this domain, you use the `NSUserDefaults`'s `setPersistent` `Domain:forName:` method. This works in much the same way: it takes an `NSDiction` `ary` containing settings to apply, and an `NSString` containing the name of the domain to set.

This means that, instead of working with preferences on an individual basis, you work with a dictionary that contains all of the settings. When you set the values for a domain, you replace all of the settings at once.

For example, imagine that you want to work with the preferences for the domain `com.oreilly.MyAmazingApplication`.

To get the preferences as a mutable dictionary (so that you can modify it later), you do this:

```
NSDictionary* preferences = [[NSUserDefaults standardUserDefaults]
    persistentDomainForName:@"com.oreilly.MyAmazingApplication"];
NSMutableDictionary* mutablePreferences = [NSMutableDictionary
    dictionaryWithDictionary:preferences];
```

You can then modify that dictionary as you like. When you're done, you set the preferences for the domain by passing in the dictionary:

```
[[NSUserDefaults standardUserDefaults] setPersistentDomain:mutablePreferences
    forName:@"com.oreilly.MyAmazingApplication"];
```

Building a Sample Preference Pane

We'll now build a simple preference pane that displays a single checkbox, which we'll store in the domain com.oreilly.MyAmazingApplication.

1. *Create the project.*

   a. Create a new Preference Pane application for OS X. You'll find the template in the System Plug-in section.

   b. Name the project **PreferencePane**.

2. *Create the interface.*

   a. Open *PreferencePane.xib*. This is the nib file that contains the view that will be shown when the preference pane is selected.

   b. Drag in a checkbox and make its label read whatever you like.

3. *Make the File's Owner of the nib file use the* PreferencePane *class.* By default, the nib file created as part of the project template does not set the File's Owner object to use the main class of the project. We'll change that first.

   a. Select the File's Owner in the Interface Builder, and open the Identity inspector.

   b. Change the class from NSPreferencePane to **PreferencePane** (your class).

4. *Connect the interface to the code.*

   a. Open *PreferencePane.h* in the assistant.

   b. Control-drag from the checkbox into PreferencePane's interface. Create an outlet called **checkbox**.

5. *Add the code that loads the current preference.* We'll first add the code that loads the current value of the setting and turns the checkbox on or off. To do this, replace the mainViewDidLoad method in *PreferencePane.m* with the following code. This method is run when the preference pane finishes loading.

   ```
   - (void)mainViewDidLoad
   {
       NSDictionary* preferences = [[NSUserDefaults standardUserDefaults]
           persistentDomainForName:@"com.oreilly.MyAmazingApplication"];
   ```

```
    self.checkbox.state =
        [[preferences objectForKey:@"isChecked"] boolValue];
}
```

6. *Add the code that sets the preference when the pane is closed.*

   Add the following method to *PreferencePane.m*. This method is called after the preference pane has stopped being shown by the user—such as when the System Preferences pane quits or the user clicks the Back, Forward, or Show All button.

   ```
   - (void)didUnselect

   {
       NSDictionary* preferences = [[NSUserDefaults standardUserDefaults]
           persistentDomainForName:@"com.oreilly.MyAmazingApplication"];

       NSMutableDictionary* mutablePreferences = [NSMutableDictionary
           dictionaryWithDictionary:preferences];

       [mutablePreferences setObject:[NSNumber
           numberWithBool:self.checkbox.state] forKey:@"isChecked"];

       [[NSUserDefaults standardUserDefaults]
           setPersistentDomain:mutablePreferences
           forName:@"com.oreilly.MyAmazingApplication"];
   }
   ```

7. *Test the application.*

    You can't test preference panes like you can other applications, because preference panes aren't run like normal applications. Instead, you build the application and load it into the System Preferences application.

   a. Build the preference pane by pressing ⌘-B or choosing Build from the Product menu.

   b. Launch the System Preferences application.

   c. Open the Products group in the project navigator. Drag the *PreferencePane.pre fPane* file onto the System Preferences application in the Dock. System Preferences will ask how you want to install the preference pane.

Play around with the preference pane. If you check the checkbox, quit System Preferences, and come back to your preference pane, the checkbox will remain checked.

Status Bar Items

Another example of applications that don't present themselves with traditional GUIs are applications that exist as *status items*—items that live in the top-right corner of the screen. OS X has a number of built-in applications that live like this, such as the volume changer and clock.

Status items can display any text, image, or view when clicked, and can display either a menu or a custom view. You create a status item by asking the system's status bar to create one for you; you then customize the status item by setting its title text, image, or view, and providing it with an NSMenu or other view to display when it's clicked.

```
NSStatusItem* statusItem = [[NSStatusBar systemStatusBar]
    statusItemWithLength:NSVariableStatusItemLength];

statusItem.title = @"Test";
statusItem.menu = aMenu; // an NSMenu that contains the items you want to show
statusItem.highlightMode = YES; // should it change color when clicked?
```

 You must keep a reference to the NSStatusItem object that you get from the NSStatusBar class. If you don't, the object will be released from memory and removed from the status bar.

Status items allow you to work with an application's features without requiring the application be the foreground application. For example, Twitter for Mac shows a status item while the application is running that changes color when new messages arrive.

You can also create an application that *only* displays a status item. Such applications are generally background utility apps such as Dropbox, which use the status item to indicate the app's current status and provide an easy way to access basic settings, as well as a means to access a more complete settings UI for controlling the application.

If you're writing an application that only shows a status item, you likely don't want to show the dock icon. To implement this, set the "Application is agent (UIElement)" value in the application's *Info.plist* file to **YES**, and the app will not show a dock icon.

Building a Status Bar App

We'll now demonstrate how to build a status bar application that doesn't show a dock icon.

1. *Create the application.* Create a Cocoa application named **StatusItem**.

2. *Create the interface.* This application will have neither a menu bar nor a window to show. The only UI will be the status item.

   a. Open *MainWindow.xib* and delete both the main menu and the main window.

   b. Drag in an NSMenu. It will contain three items—delete the second and third.

   c. Make the single menu item's label read **Quit**.

3. *Connect the interface to the code.*

   a. Open *AppDelegate.h.*

   b. Control-drag from the menu into AppDelegate's interface, and create a new outlet called **menu**.

   c. Control-drag from the Quit menu item into AppDelegate's interface, and create an action named **quit**.

4. *Add the variable and code.* Next, we'll create the status item and prepare it. We'll also add the code that gets run when the Quit menu item is chosen.

   a. We'll also need to add a class extension that has an instance variable that stores the NSStatusItem object. Without this variable, the status item would be removed from memory, and therefore the status item would disappear, immediately after it was added.

   b. Make *AppDelegate.m* look like the following code:

```
#import "AppDelegate.h"

@interface AppDelegate () {
    NSStatusItem* statusItem;
}

@end

@implementation AppDelegate

@synthesize window = _window;
@synthesize menu = _menu;

- (void)applicationDidFinishLaunching:(NSNotification *)aNotification
{
    statusItem = [[NSStatusBar systemStatusBar]
    statusItemWithLength:NSVariableStatusItemLength];

    statusItem.title = @"Test";
    statusItem.menu = self.menu;
    statusItem.highlightMode = YES;
}
```

```
- (IBAction)quit:(id)sender {
    [[NSApplication sharedApplication] terminate:nil];
}
@end
```

5. *Make the application an agent.* Finally, we'll make the application not show a dock icon. The status item will remain visible no matter which application is currently active, so there's always a way to access it.

   a. To do this, you modify the application's *Info.plist* file and indicate that it's an *agent.* "Agent" is Apple's term for a background application that doesn't present a dock icon.

   b. Select the project at the top of the project navigator. Open the Info tab at the top of the main editor.

   c. Add a new entry into the property list that appears: **Application is agent (UIElement)**. Set the value of this entry to **YES**.

6. *Run the application.* Nothing will appear in the dock, but the word "Test" will appear at the top of the screen in the menu bar. You can open this menu and choose to quit the app.

CHAPTER 19

Working with Text

Both OS X and iOS have tremendously powerful tools for working with text. Whether it's working with multiple languages, converting data into human-readable forms, or detecting information in text, Cocoa and Cocoa Touch contain a wide variety of useful tools for working with strings, text, and language.

In this chapter, you'll learn how to use the system's built-in internationalization and localization features to easily translate strings in your code to whatever language the user is running on. You'll also learn how to use NSFormatter and its subclasses to format data into strings, and how to use data detectors to detect URLs and dates in arbitrary text.

Internationalization and Localization

Your primary language may not be the one spoken by your end user. When you write strings embedded in your code for the user to see, those strings are hardcoded into the compiled executable—so if something is written in English, then the user will see it in English, even if she doesn't necessarily read English.

To address this problem, Cocoa has support for *localized text*, which is text that is replaced at runtime with versions appropriate for your user. In your code, you use placeholder strings, and store the translated versions for every language that you support in a separate file. When the code that displays the text runs, it checks to see which language the user is using, and replaces the placeholder text with the appropriate version.

Strings Files

A *strings file* maps internal representations of text to localized representations. Strings files look like this:

```
"welcome message" = "Welcome to OS X!";
"quit message" = "Goodbye! Come back soon!";
```

Strings files let you keep the text used in your application separate from your code. This becomes especially useful when the text used in your application changes—for example, when running in another language.

Strings files can be localized, which means that Xcode will create multiple versions of the file based on language; at runtime, the application will use only the version of the file appropriate to the user's choice of language. If an appropriate version doesn't exist, the application will load the best one it can find.

Creating a Sample Localized Application

To demonstrate how localization works in Cocoa, we'll build an application that makes use of strings files to translate its interface.

1. *Create the project.* Create a new Cocoa application named **Localized**.

2. *Create the interface.* Open *MainWindow.xib* and drag a label into the window.

3. *Connect the interface to the code.* Open *AppDelegate.h* in the assistant. Control-drag from the label into AppDelegate's interface. Create a new outlet for the label called **languagesLabel**.

4. *Add the code.* Replace the applicationDidFinishLaunching: method with the following code:

   ```
   - (void)applicationDidFinishLaunching:(NSNotification *)aNotification
   {
       NSString* currentLanguage = [[[NSUserDefaults standardUserDefaults]
           objectForKey:@"AppleLanguages"] objectAtIndex:0];

       NSString* labelFormat = NSLocalizedString(@"main language: %@", nil);

       self.languageLabel.stringValue = [NSString stringWithFormat:labelFormat,
           currentLanguage];

   }
   ```

5. *Run the application.* The label will display the current language you're using.

The NSLocalizedString function and its sibling functions load text from the Local ized.strings file—specifically from the localized version of that file that fits the user's current language.

To localize this application, we'll create the strings file, and then add both English and French localizations.

6. *Add the strings file.* Create a new file in the project: a strings file. You'll find this in the Resource section of the file templates.

   Name the file *Localizable.strings.*

 It's important to use this filename, since this file is the one the app will look for if you don't specify another name.

7. *Add the English and French versions of the strings file.* Select *Localizable.strings.* Open the File inspector and scroll down to Localizations.

   Click the + button. The default localization will be added, which is English.

   Click the + button again. This time, a menu will appear. Choose French.

   Now two copies of the strings file appear—one for English and one for French.

8. *Add the English text.*

   Open *Localizable.strings (English)* and add the following text:

   ```
   "main language: %@" = "The main language is %@";
   ```

9. *Add the French text.*

   Open *"Localizable.strings (French)* and add the following text:

   ```
   "main language: %@" = "La langue principale est %@";
   ```

10. *Run the application.* Now that the localized strings files have been written, test the application in English mode.

    The text of the label will change to the better-written English text.

Next, we'll test the French version. To avoid having to change the language of the entire system, we'll make Xcode launch the application with an overridden `AppleLanguages` preference.

To do this, we'll edit the current scheme and add a parameter that is passed to the application at start time.

1. *Make the application launch using the French language.* Click on the Scheme at the top-left of the window. (It's the drop-down list just to the right of the Stop button.)

   Choose Edit Scheme... from the menu that appears.

   Make sure that the Run Localized.app option is selected. Open the Arguments panel.

   Click the + button at the bottom of the Arguments Passed on Launch list.

   Add the following argument:

```
-AppleLanguages "('fr')"
```

2. *Run the application like a Frenchman.*

   Run the app again. Note that the text appears in French. *Quelle surprise!*

   You can continue adding more localized strings and more localizations to your application. The more languages supported by your app, the more potential users you have.

Formatting Data with NSFormatter

Many useful pieces of information need conversion to text before a human can read them. Additionally, different people expect information to be presented in different ways depending on where they live. For example, dates store date and time information, but dates and times are displayed differently depending on the country. The differences could be as simple as the order of numbers and punctuation—dates are written "MM-DD-YY" in the US, and "DD-MM-YY"[1] in Australia. However, sometimes the differences are radical—your user could be using the Muslim calendar, in which case the same point in time has a completely different date representation.

To solve this and other problems, Cocoa separates dates from their presentation. When you want to work with date and time information, you use the NSDate class. When you want to create text to display a representation of that date to the user, you use the NSDateFormatter class.

Dates aren't the only things that can be formatted. Numbers have different representations in different cultures, as well as different representations in different contexts.

For example, in the US, the decimal marker is a period (.), while in many European countries the marker is a comma (,). If you're writing an application that displays monetary figures, it's common to display negative figures in parentheses (()). Additionally, the locale that your user is in will very likely have a different currency symbol than $.

NSNumberFormatter takes localization into account, and creates strings that suit what your user expects to see and what your application needs to display.

Formatting Dates with NSDateFormatter

To demonstrate how formatters work, we'll create a simple application that displays the current date to the user using NSDateFormatter.

---

1. The authors, who are Australian, contend that this is superior.

---

1. *Create the application.* Create a new Cocoa application called **TodaysDate**.

2. *Create the interface.* The interface for this application will be as simple as the previous one—we'll simply show a label that renders the user's current date.

   Open *MainWindow.xib* and add a label to the main window. Resize the label to make it fit the window's width, and set its alignment to centered.

3. *Connect the interface to the code.* Open *AppDelegate.h* in the assistant.

   Control-drag from the label into `AppDelegate`'s interface. Create an outlet for the label called **dateLabel**.

4. *Write the code.*

   Replace the `applicationDidFinishLaunching:` method with the following code:

```
- (void)applicationDidFinishLaunching:(NSNotification *)aNotification
{

    NSDateFormatter* dateFormatter = [[NSDateFormatter alloc] init];

    [dateFormatter setTimeStyle:NSDateFormatterNoStyle];
    [dateFormatter setDateStyle:NSDateFormatterLongStyle];

    NSString* dateString = [dateFormatter stringFromDate:[NSDate date]];


    self.dateLabel.stringValue = [NSString stringWithFormat:
        @"The current date is %@", dateString];

}
```

 Creating an `NSDateFormatter` is a rather expensive operation. If you need to format a large number of dates, create one and keep it around, rather than creating a new one for every time you need to format a date.

5. *Run the application.* The date will appear in the application, correctly formatted for your user's locale.

   You can set the style of both the time and date in the formatter. Both `setTimeStyle:` and `setDateStyle:` accept any of the following options (note that the precise format will change depending on the user's locale—read on if you want total control!).

   `NSDateFormatterNoStyle`
   　　Dates and times don't appear at all.

`NSDateFormatterShortStyle`

A brief style. Usually, only numbers appear.

Dates appear like "10/24/86" and times appear like "5:05pm."

`NSDateFormatterMediumStyle`

Slightly more detail appears in the medium style.

Dates appear like "Oct 24, 1986." Times appear like the short style.

`NSDateFormatterLongStyle`

With the long style, almost every detail appears. Month names, for example, are fully spelled out.

Dates appear like "October 24, 1986" and times appear like "5:05:23pm."

`NSDateFormatterFullStyle`

Every detail is presented in the full style, including era and time zone information.

Dates appear like "Friday, October 24, 1986 AD" and times appear like "5:05:23pm AEDT."

`NSDateFormatter` also allows you to format dates with your own format string. A format string defines which components of the date and time should appear.

For example, to render an `NSDate` to look like this: "17:05 October 24, 1986" (regardless of locale), you do this:

```
NSDateFormatter* dateFormatter = [[NSDateFormatter alloc] init];
[dateFormatter setDateFormat:@"HH:mm, MMMM d"];

NSString* dateString = [dateFormatter stringFromDate:[NSDate date]];
```

All the different letters in the format string define what parts of the date and time appear, and the number of times the symbol is repeated changes the format of the component.

For full details on the format patterns that can be used, see the Unicode specification TR35 (*http://bit.ly/YAibhW*), which is used by both OS X and iOS.

Detecting Data with NSDataDetector

As far as the system is concerned, text that it receives can be literally anything. However, text frequently contains information that's useful to both the user and to the app you're writing. For example, posts to Twitter often contain links to websites, and it's a useful feature for a Twitter app to be able to quickly open a link in the tweet's text. Another example is date and time information: an email could contain the date for a meeting, and an app may want to extract that.

To extract information from text, you use the `NSDataDetector` class. This class reads through a string and looks for whatever data you tell it to keep an eye out for.

You can use data detectors to detect the following kinds of data in strings:

- Dates
- Addresses
- Links
- Phone numbers
- Transit information (like flight information)

When you create an `NSDataDetector`, you provide it with the kinds of information that you're looking for. You then provide a string to the data detector, and get back an `NSArray` that contains `NSTextCheckingResult` objects. Each `NSTextCheckingResult` contains additional information about what type each result is—a date, URL, or other kind of detectable data.

For example, if you were looking for URLs, you'd do this:

```
NSError *error = nil;
NSDataDetector *detector = [NSDataDetector
    dataDetectorWithTypes:NSTextCheckingTypeLink error:error];
```

Once the detector has been prepared, you can pass a string through it and get the number of matches it finds. You also provide the range of the string that you want to check—if you have a large string, you might want to search in sections.

```
NSString* string = @"Here is a link: http://oreilly.com!"
NSInteger numberOfMatches = [detector numberOfMatchesInString:string
    options:0
    range:NSMakeRange(0, [string length])];

// numberOfMatches is 1
```

You can use this technique to get a quick count of the number of detected items in a string. If you want to get the detected results themselves, you do this:

```
NSArray *matches = [detector matchesInString:string
    options:0
    range:NSMakeRange(0, [string length])];
```

For each `NSTextCheckingResult` object in the returned array, you can get the relevant information.

Testing a Data Detector

To demonstrate data detectors, we'll build a simple application that allows users to type in anything they want, and see what the data detector finds.

The application will present a text field and a button. When the button is clicked, the text will be checked and the results will be presented in a label.

1. *Create the project.* Create a new Cocoa application. Call it **DataDetectors**.

2. *Create the interface.* Open *MainWindow.xib*.

   Drag in a multiline text field and place it in the top half of the window.

   Drag in a button and place it under the text field. Change its label to Check.

   Drag in a second multiline text field. Place it under the button, in the bottom half of the window.

3. *Connect the interface to the code.* Open *AppDelegate.h* in the assistant.

   Control-drag from the top text field into AppDelegate's interface. Create an outlet called **inputTextField**.

   Control-drag from the bottom text field into AppDelegate's interface. Create an outlet called **outputTextField**.

   Control-drag from the button into AppDelegate's interface. Create an action called **check**.

4. *Add the code.* Replace the check: method with the following code:

```
- (IBAction)check:(id)sender {
    NSDataDetector* detector = [NSDataDetector
        dataDetectorWithTypes:NSTextCheckingAllTypes error:nil];

    NSString* inputString = self.inputTextField.stringValue;
    NSMutableString* resultsText = [NSMutableString string];

    NSArray* matches = [detector matchesInString:inputString
        options:0
        range:NSMakeRange(0, inputString.length)];

    for (NSTextCheckingResult* match in matches) {
        switch (match.resultType) {
            case NSTextCheckingTypeLink:
                [resultsText appendFormat:@"Found a link: %@\n", match.URL];
                break;
            case NSTextCheckingTypeDate:
                [resultsText appendFormat:@"Found a date: %@\n", match.date];
                break;
            case NSTextCheckingTypePhoneNumber:
                [resultsText appendFormat:@"Found a phone number: %@\n",
                    match.phoneNumber];
                break;
            case NSTextCheckingTypeAddress:
                [resultsText appendFormat:@"Found an address: %@\n",
                    match.addressComponents];
                break;
            default:
                break;
        }
    }
```

```
    }
        self.outputTextField.stringValue = resultsText;
    }
```

5. *Run the application.* Type in text like this:

Apple's doing an event at 4pm tomorrow!

and click the Check button. The app will display the date and time it detected.

iCloud

Introduced in iOS 5, iCloud is a set of technologies that allow users' documents and settings to be seamlessly synchronized across all the devices that they own.

iCloud is heavily promoted by Apple as technology that "just works"—simply by owning a Mac, iPhone, or iPad, your documents are everywhere that you need them to be. In order to understand what iCloud is, it's worth taking a look at Apple's advertising and marketing for the technology. In the ads, we see users working on a document, and then just putting it down, walking over to their Macs, and resuming work. No additional effort is required on the part of the user, and users are encouraged to think of their devices as simply tools that they use to access their omnipresent data.

This utopian view of data availability is made possible by several very large data centers that Apple constructed in the early 2010s, and a little extra effort on the part of you, the developer.

In this chapter, you'll learn how to create applications that use iCloud to share settings and documents across the user's devices.

What iCloud Stores

Simply put, iCloud allows your applications to store files and key-value pairs on Apple's servers. Apps identify which file storage container or key-value pair database they want to access, and the operating system takes care of the rest.

In the case of files, your application determines the location of a container folder, the contents of which are synced to the network. When you copy a file into the container or update a file that's already in the container, the operating system syncs that file across all other applications on devices that have access to the same container.

For settings, you access an instance of NSUbiquitousKeyValueStore, which works almost identically to NSUserDefaults with the exception that it syncs to all other devices.

The word "ubiquitous" appears a lot when working with iCloud. So often, in fact, that it's used instead of the marketing term "iCloud." This is intended to reinforce what iCloud should be used for—it's not a storage space on the Internet, like Box.net or similar "cloud file storage" services, but rather a tool for making users' data ubiquitous, so they can access it from anywhere.

Users are limited in the amount of data they can store. By default, iCloud users get 5GB of space for free, and can pay for more. There aren't any per-application limits on the amount of data that your application can store, but the user isn't allowed to exceed their total limit (though they can purchase more space). For the key-value store, you can store 64KB of information per application.

This means that when you're working out how iCloud fits into your application, you have to choose where you're going to put the data. Storing files in an iCloud container is a good option if your application works with documents—image editors or word processors are good examples. Files are also useful for storing more structured information, such as to-do lists or saved game files. If you want to store simple, application-wide state, such as the most recently opened document, then the key-value store works well.

More than one application can access the same iCloud container or key-value store. All that's required is that the same developer writes both, and that the bundle IDs have the same team prefix.

 iCloud does not work in the iOS Simulator. It does work on the Mac and on iOS devices. If you want to make an app for the iPhone or iPad that uses iCloud, you'll need to have a device that you can test on.

Setting Up for iCloud

In order to use any of Apple's online services, an application needs to identify itself and the developer who created it. This means that if you want to work with iCloud, you must have a paid developer account for each platform that you want to develop on. So if you want to make iCloud apps for the Mac, you need a paid Mac developer account. And if you want to make iOS apps at all, of course, you need a paid iOS developer account.

To access iCloud, your application's bundle ID (the unique application identifier that looks like this: com.oreilly.MyiCloudApp) must be registered with Apple as one that is enabled for iCloud. To get ready to build an iCloud app for the Mac, we're going to set up an application ID that's ready for iCloud.

Let's get started. For this example, we're going to assume that you've already set up your certificate and have registered your computer as a development device.

1. Go to the Mac Dev Center (*http://bit.ly/RbMsjY*).

2. Sign in with your account.

3. Open the Developer Certificate Utility.

4. Click Register Mac App ID.

5. Provide your app ID. This needs to be a string that looks like a reverse domain name. For example, the app ID that we've made here is `com.oreilly.LearningCo coa.iCloudMac`. Take a domain name, reverse it, and add your application name to the end. You're also asked to give the app ID a name; name it whatever you like.

6. The new app ID will appear in the list, and will appear as configurable for iCloud. Click Configure.

7. Check the Enable for iCloud box.

The developer portal will notify you that any new provisioning profiles you make with this app ID will be enabled for iCloud, but that if you want to make existing provisioning profiles use iCloud, you need to manually regenerate them. This only matters if you're adding iCloud to an existing app.

8. Next, create a provisioning profile for this app ID by clicking Provisioning Profiles.

9. Click Create Profile. Create a new development provisioning profile that uses the new app ID.

10. Download the new provisioning profile and drag it onto Xcode's icon in the dock to add it.

Once you've done this, Apple knows that an application with the bundle identifier you provide is allowed to access the iCloud services. When you create your application, its bundle identifier needs to be the same as the one you just registered and the application must be code-signed. If it's not, it won't be allowed to use iCloud.

We'll now set up the project in Xcode. To tell the OS that the application wants to use iCloud, we need to create an Entitlements file that indicates exactly what in iCloud we want to access. This file is created and managed for us by Xcode.

1. Create a new Cocoa application and name it what you like. When you create the application, make its bundle identifier the same as the app ID you created earlier.

2. Once Xcode has finished creating the application, select the project at the top of the project navigator. In the application's Summary tab, scroll down to Entitlements.

3. Choose Enable Entitlements. An Entitlements file will be created in the project.

To access iCloud storage and store files, you indicate which iCloud container your application should use. The examples in this chapter will cover both the key-value store and iCloud file containers, and both are identified with the same style of identifier.

4. We need to add an iCloud container ID. Click the + button, and a new container will be added.

5. We also want access to the iCloud key-value store, so check the iCloud Key-Value Store checkbox and make sure that its name is the same as the iCloud container ID.

The application is now set up to use iCloud. To get started working with the system, we'll first make sure that everything's working as it's supposed to.

Testing Whether iCloud Works

In order to determine whether the application has access to iCloud, we'll run a quick test to make sure that our setup is working. To do this, we'll ask the `NSFileManager` class for the "ubiquity container" URL. This is the location on the filesystem that is used for storing iCloud files; if the system returns the URL, we're in business. If it returns `nil`, then the app hasn't been set up for iCloud properly.

To add the test, replace `applicationDidFinishLaunching:` in *AppDelegate.m* with the following code:

```
- (void)applicationDidFinishLaunching:(NSNotification *)aNotification
{
    NSLog(@"Ubiquity Container URL: %@", [[NSFileManager defaultManager]
        URLForUbiquityContainerIdentifier:nil]);
}
```

Run the application. Take a look at the console output. If you see a URL, then iCloud is configured correctly. If the app reports that the ubiquity container URL is `nil`, then iCloud isn't set up correctly, and you should double-check your code signing and settings.

Storing Settings

The first thing that we'll do is use the key-value store to cause a setting to be stored in iCloud, which will be accessible via both an iOS application and a Mac application.

The key-value store, accessed via `NSUbiquitousKeyValueStore`, works very much like the `NSUserDefaults` object. You can store strings, numbers, arrays, and dictionaries in the store. As we mentioned before, the total amount of data that you can store in the key-value store is 64KB, and each item can be no larger than 64KB.

In this example, we're going to start by storing a single string in iCloud. First, we'll update the `AppDelegate` object to store and retrieve this value from the key-value store.

1. Open *AppDelegate.h* and add the following code to `AppDelegate`'s `@interface` section:

```
@property (strong) NSString* cloudString;
```

We'll now create the setters and getters. Unlike other properties, which store their content in instance variables, for this property we'll create our own setter and getter methods that store and fetch the data from iCloud.

2. Open *AppDelegate.m* and add the following code to the start of `AppDelegate`'s `@implementation` section:

```
@dynamic cloudString;
```

This directive tells the compiler that you're going to handle creating the setter and getter methods, and that it shouldn't worry about creating an instance variable for the property.

3. Create the setter and getter methods by adding the following methods to *App Delegate.m*:

```
- (NSString *)cloudString {
    return [[NSUbiquitousKeyValueStore defaultStore]
        stringForKey:@"cloud_string"];
}

- (void)setCloudString:(NSString *)cloudString {
    [[NSUbiquitousKeyValueStore defaultStore] setString:cloudString
        forKey:@"cloud_string"];
    [[NSUbiquitousKeyValueStore defaultStore] synchronize];
}
```

The first method, `cloudString`, asks the default `NSUbiquitousKeyValueStore` object for the value stored in iCloud associated with the key `cloud_string`. The second method, `setCloudString:`, takes a string and puts it in iCloud under the same key. It then immediately syncs the local copy of the key-value store to disk.

This method here works fine when we're the only application accessing the data, but the whole point of iCloud is that it's designed for multiple applications accessing the same data. It's therefore possible that, while the application is running, another instance of the application (perhaps running on another device that the user owns) changes the same value. Our application needs to know that the change has taken place, so that both apps show the same information.

When the key-value store is changed externally—that is, by another application—the notification NSUbiquitousKeyValueStoreDidChangeExternallyNotification is posted. So to be informed of these changes, we'll make the AppDelegate class receive this notification, and then let the rest of the application know that the cloudString property changed (which will in turn make the UI update).

First, we'll register for the notifications, and then we'll add the method that gets run when the key-value store is changed.

4. Add the following code to the end of applicationDidFinishLaunching::

```
[[NSNotificationCenter defaultCenter] addObserver:self
    selector:@selector(keyValueStoreDidChange:)
    name:NSUbiquitousKeyValueStoreDidChangeExternallyNotification
    object:[NSUbiquitousKeyValueStore defaultStore]];
```

5. Add the following method to *AppDelegate.m*:

```
- (void) keyValueStoreDidChange:(NSNotification*)notification {
    [self willChangeValueForKey:@"cloudString"];
    [self didChangeValueForKey:@"cloudString"];
}
```

We're now done with the code. It's time to create the interface, which will consist of a text field that's bound to the application delegate's cloudString property. This way, whenever the user changes the contents the text field, the setCloudString: method will be run, which stores the new string in iCloud. Additionally, because we'll be using bindings, the fact that the keyValueStoreDidChange: method calls the willChange ValueForKey and didChangeValueForKey methods to indicate a change in the "cloud String" property will cause the text field to update if another application makes a change.

1. Open *MainWindow.xib*, and open the window.

2. Drag in an NSTextField.

3. With the text field selected, open the Bindings inspector, which is the second tab to the right at the top of the Utilities pane.

4. Open the Value property and choose App Delegate in the Bind To drop-down menu. Set the Model Key Path to **self.cloudString**.

We're all set—the interface is prepared and will show the value stored in iCloud. Go ahead and run the app: you can enter text, and it will be saved.

This is all well and good, but iCloud only gets impressive when there's more than one device that has access to the same information. We'll now create an iOS application that shows what you type in the Mac application; the app will also allow you to make changes, which will automatically show up in the Mac app.

A reminder: the iOS Simulator doesn't support iCloud, and you'll need to use a real iPhone, iPod touch, or iPad to test iCloud with.

To make an iOS app that uses iCloud, you need to create an application ID for it that's registered to use the iCloud service, just like with the Mac app.

1. Open the iOS Developer Center (*http://developer.apple.com/ios*).
2. Click iOS Provisioning Portal.
3. Create a new app ID by following the same steps you did for the Mac app ID. The layout of the web app is different, but the steps are the same.

You can't use the same app ID for your iOS application as you did for your Mac app, but that's OK—as long as your team ID remains the same, they'll be able to access the same data.

When you're done, you should have a new app ID that can use iCloud.

To keep the project manageable, we're going to make the iOS app be an additional part of the Mac app's project. Instead of creating a new project, we'll create a new *target* for the iOS app. This will keep everything in the same window, and has some additional advantages like making it easier to share source code between the two apps.

4. Create a new target by choosing File→New→Target.
5. Make the new target a single-view iOS application. Make sure the bundle identifier is the same as the app ID that you just created for the iOS application.

When the project is created, the application needs to be configured to use iCloud, just like the Mac application. Specifically, the iOS app must be configured to use the same iCloud resources as the Mac app, which will make it possible for the two apps to share data.

6. Select the project at the top of the project navigator. Open the Summary tab.
7. Scroll down to Entitlements and turn on Use Entitlements.
8. Turn on iCloud Key-Value Store. Make the store identifier the same as the one used for the Mac application.
9. Add an iCloud container. Again, make the identifier the same as the Mac application.

The iOS application is now ready to work with iCloud, just like the Mac app. We'll now set up its interface, which will consist of a single text field.

In order to be notified of when the user is done editing, we'll make the view controller used in this iOS application a UITextFieldDelegate. When the user taps the Return key (which we'll convert to a Done button), the application will store the text field's contents in iCloud.

10. Open *MainStoryboard.storyboard*. Drag in a UITextField and place it near the top of the screen.

11. Select the text field and open the Attributes inspector. Scroll down to the "Return key" drop-down, and choose Done.

The interface is done, but we still need to make the view controller be notified when the user taps the Done button.

12. Control-drag from the text field to the view controller, and choose "delegate" from the pop-up menu that appears.

13. Open *ViewController.h* in the inspector.

14. Control-drag from the text field into ViewController's @interface section. Create a new outlet called **textField**.

15. Make the class conform to UITextFieldDelegate by changing its @interface line to look like this:

```
@interface ViewController : UIViewController <UITextFieldDelegate>
```

Now we can make the application draw its data from iCloud. We'll do this by setting the text of the textField to whatever's in the iCloud key-value store when the view loads.

We'll also register the ViewController class as one that receives notifications about when the key-value store is updated externally.

 iCloud updates its contents both when the application is running and when it's not. This means that if you make a change to a setting in the key-value store on your iPhone and then later open the same app on your iPad, the data will have likely already arrived.

16. Update the viewDidLoad method to use the following code:

```
- (void)viewDidLoad
{
    [super viewDidLoad];

    [[NSNotificationCenter defaultCenter] addObserver:self
        selector:@selector(keyValueStoreDidChange:)
        name:NSUbiquitousKeyValueStoreDidChangeExternallyNotification
        object:[NSUbiquitousKeyValueStore defaultStore]];
```

```
        self.textField.text = [[NSUbiquitousKeyValueStore defaultStore]
            stringForKey:@"cloud_string"];
}
```

Next, we'll add the method that runs when the user taps the Done button. This works because the class is the delegate of the text field; `textFieldShouldReturn:` is called by the text field to find out what happens when the Return button is tapped.

In this case, we'll make the keyboard go away by making the text field resign first-responder status, and then store the text field's contents in iCloud.

17. Add the following method to `ViewController`:

```
(BOOL)textFieldShouldReturn:(UITextField *)textField {
    [self.textField resignFirstResponder];
    [[NSUbiquitousKeyValueStore defaultStore] setString:self.textField.text
        forKey:@"cloud_string"];
    return NO;
}
```

Finally, we'll add the method that runs when another application updates the key-value store. All it will do is get the latest value from the key-value store and make the text field display it.

18. Add the following method to `ViewController`:

```
- (void) keyValueStoreDidChange:(NSNotification*)notification {
    self.textField.text = [[NSUbiquitousKeyValueStore defaultStore]
        stringForKey:@"cloud_string"];
}
```

We can now see this in action! Run the iOS app and the Mac app together. Change a value on one of the apps and watch what happens.

 Be patient—it might take a few seconds before the change appears on the other device.

iCloud Storage

Storing keys and values in iCloud is extremely useful for persisting user preferences across all their devices, but if you want to make the user's files just as ubiquitous, you need to use iCloud storage.

In this section, we'll make an app that allows the user to store stuff in iCloud storage. The Mac app will let you add items to iCloud and list everything in storage. Its iOS counterpart will be simpler and will show a list of files currently in iCloud storage, which updates as files are added or removed.

Before we can get to work, we need to give the Mac application permission to access the user's files. By default, when you enable iCloud, Xcode helpfully marks the application as sandboxed.

Sandboxing an application restricts what it's allowed to access. Before sandboxing, all applications were allowed to access any file that belonged to the user, which caused problems if the app was compromised by a remote attacker. Apple requires any application that's submitted to the Mac App Store to be sandboxed. (All iOS applications are sandboxed—it's a requirement of running on the device.)

By default, the application will be sandboxed to the point where it can't access any user files at all. Because we're making an application that lets the user take files and move them into iCloud, we'll need access to those files.

1. Open the project settings for the Mac application and scroll down to Entitlements.
2. Make sure that Enable App Sandboxing is turned on, and then scroll down to User Selected File Access. Set this to Read/Write Access.

With that out of the way, we can begin working with iCloud storage in the Mac app.

The way that our implementation will work is this: we'll have a property on the App Delegate class that is an NSArray containing NSStrings of each path of the files in the storage container. This array will be displayed in a table view so that you can see what's included. We'll also add a button that, when clicked, will prompt the user for a file to move into iCloud storage.

In real life, you'd likely do something more interesting with the files than just show that they're there, but this will get us started.

3. Open *AppDelegate.h* and add the following code to AppDelegate's @interface section:

```
@property (strong) NSArray* filesInCloudStorage;
```

4. Open *AppDelegate.m* and add the following code to AppDelegate's @implementation section:

```
@synthesize filesInCloudStorage = _filesInCloudStorage;
```

Next, we'll create and set up the table view that displays the list of files. To keep things simpler, we'll use bindings to make the table view show its content.

5. Open *MainWindow.xib* and drag in an NSTableView into the main window. Make it fill the rest of the window.

6. Select the table view and make it have one column.

7. Drag in an NSButton and change its label to **Add File**….

With the interface laid out, we can begin to connect it to the code. We'll start by making the button run an action method when clicked, and then bind the table view to the application. Because we're working with an array, we'll use an array controller to manage the link between the array of files stored in the app delegate and the table view.

8. Open *AppDelegate.h* in the assistant.

9. Control-drag from the button into AppDelegate's @interface section, and create a new action called **addFile**.

We'll now bind the table to the app delegate via an array controller.

10. Drag an array controller into the outline.

11. Select the array controller and open the Bindings tab.

12. Open the Content Array property, and choose App Delegate from the Bind To drop-down menu.

13. Set the Model Key Path to *self.filesInCloudStorage*.

14. Select the table view column, and bind its Value to the Array Controller. Set the controller key to **arrangedObjects** and the model key path to **description**.

We're using description since it's a convenient way to simply display a string version of the contents of the array.

Next, we need to load the list of files that are in iCloud into the array, and then keep an eye out for new things arriving. To check the contents of the iCloud container, we first get its URL with this code:

```
NSURL* documentsDirectory = [[[NSFileManager defaultManager]
    URLForUbiquityContainerIdentifier:nil]
    URLByAppendingPathComponent:@"Documents" isDirectory:YES];
```

The ubiquity container is the folder that contains all of the information that's synced to iCloud. Inside this is another folder called Documents, which is where your application should put all synced documents. It's technically possible to store information outside this folder, but the advantage of using the Documents folder is that, on iOS, the user is able to delete individual documents in order to free space, whereas anything outside that folder is considered internal data and can't be individually deleted by users—they can only remove it by deleting the entire iCloud container.

To work out what's inside the iCloud container and to be informed of when its contents change, we use the `NSMetadataQuery` class. This class, once configured with information about what you're looking for, runs continuously and sends notifications whenever its contents change.

To use this, we'll add an instance variable to store the query object, and when the application launches, we'll configure and start the query.

15. Open *AppDelegate.m* and modify the class extension at the top of the file so that it looks like the following:

    ```
    @interface AppDelegate () {
        NSMetadataQuery* metadataQuery;
    }
    @end
    ```

16. Add the following code to the end of the `applicationDidFinishLaunching:` method:

    ```
    metadataQuery = [[NSMetadataQuery alloc] init];
    [metadataQuery
      setSearchScopes:
        [NSArray arrayWithObject:NSMetadataQueryUbiquitousDocumentsScope]];

    [metadataQuery setPredicate:
        [NSPredicate predicateWithFormat:@"%K LIKE '*'",
          NSMetadataItemFSNameKey]];

    [[NSNotificationCenter defaultCenter] addObserver:self
        selector:@selector(queryDidUpdate:)
          name:NSMetadataQueryDidUpdateNotification object:metadataQuery];
    [[NSNotificationCenter defaultCenter] addObserver:self
        selector:@selector(queryDidUpdate:)
          name:NSMetadataQueryDidFinishGatheringNotification object:metadataQuery];

    [metadataQuery startQuery];
    ```

This code starts by creating the metadata query object, and instructs it to limit its results to only include items found inside the Documents folder in the ubiquity container. We also give it a *predicate*, which is a description of what to look for—in this case, we're saying "find all objects whose filenames are anything," which translates to "all files in the Documents folder."

We then register the app delegate to receive notifications whenever the metadata finishes its initial sweep of the folder, and also whenever the folder changes contents. In both cases, the same method will be called.

Finally, the query is started.

We now need to add the `queryDidUpdate:` method, which will prepare the `filesIn`
`CloudStorage` property and fill it with the paths that it found.

17. Add the following method to `AppDelegate`:

```
- (void) queryDidUpdate:(NSNotification*)notification {
    NSMutableArray* files = [NSMutableArray array];

    for (NSMetadataItem* item in metadataQuery.results) {
        NSURL *filename = [item valueForAttribute:NSMetadataItemPathKey];
        [files addObject:filename];
    }

    self.filesInCloudStorage = files;
}
```

This code loops over every result in the query and retrieves the path for it. The paths
are then stored in an array, which is used to update the `filesInCloudStorage` property.
Because we're using bindings, the act of updating this property will update the contents
of the table view.

Next, we add the method that actually adds an item to iCloud storage. This method
presents a file-open panel that lets the user choose which item to move into storage.

The process of moving a file into storage is the following. First, you work out the URL
of the file you want to move. Then, you ask the `NSFileManager` to generate a destination
URL. Finally, you perform the move by asking the file manager to make the file ubiquitous, passing in the source and destination URLs.

 Moving files into storage is just that—moving the file. If you want to
copy a file into storage, duplicate it and move the copied file.

18. Add the following method to `AppDelegate`:

```
- (void)addFile:(id)sender {
    NSOpenPanel* panel = [NSOpenPanel openPanel];
    [panel beginSheetModalForWindow:self.window
    completionHandler:^(NSInteger result) {
        if (result == NSOKButton) {
            NSURL* containerURL = [[NSFileManager defaultManager]
                URLForUbiquityContainerIdentifier:nil];
            containerURL = [containerURL
                URLByAppendingPathComponent:@"Documents" isDirectory:YES];
            NSURL* sourceURL = panel.URL;
            NSURL* destinationURL = [containerURL
                URLByAppendingPathComponent:[panel.URL lastPathComponent]];
```

```
                    NSError* error = nil;
                    if ([[NSFileManager defaultManager] setUbiquitous:YES
                        itemAtURL:sourceURL
                        destinationURL:destinationURL
                        error:&error] == NO) {
                        NSLog(@"Couldn't make the file ubiquitous: %@",
                            [error localizedDescription]);
                    }

                }
            }];
        }
```

Run the app. You can now add stuff to iCloud.

Now we'll make the same thing work on iOS. First, we'll update the UI to include a text field that displays the list of files, and then we'll add the same NSMetadataQuery that lets the app know what's in the container.

1. Open the main storyboard and add a text view. Make it not editable.

2. Open *ViewController.h* in the assistant.

   Control-drag from the text field into ViewController's @interface section, and connect it to a new outlet in ViewController called **fileList**.

Now we'll make the code work. This is almost identical to the Mac version—we create the metadata query, prepare it, and set it running. When the query finds files, we'll update the text field and display the list of items.

3. Replace the viewDidLoad method with the following code:

```
- (void)viewDidLoad
{
    [super viewDidLoad];

    [[NSNotificationCenter defaultCenter] addObserver:self
        selector:@selector(keyValueStoreDidChange:)
        name:NSUbiquitousKeyValueStoreDidChangeExternallyNotification
        object:[NSUbiquitousKeyValueStore defaultStore]];

    self.textField.text = [[NSUbiquitousKeyValueStore defaultStore]
        stringForKey:@"cloud_string"];

    metadataQuery = [[NSMetadataQuery alloc] init];
    [metadataQuery setSearchScopes:[NSArray
        arrayWithObject:NSMetadataQueryUbiquitousDocumentsScope]];

    [metadataQuery setPredicate:[NSPredicate
        predicateWithFormat:@"%K LIKE '*'", NSMetadataItemFSNameKey]];
```

```
[[NSNotificationCenter defaultCenter] addObserver:self
    selector:@selector(queryDidUpdate:)
    name:NSMetadataQueryDidUpdateNotification
    object:metadataQuery];

[[NSNotificationCenter defaultCenter] addObserver:self
    selector:@selector(queryDidUpdate:)
    name:NSMetadataQueryDidFinishGatheringNotification
    object:metadataQuery];

[metadataQuery startQuery];

self.fileList.text = @"";
}
```

This code is pretty much identical to the Mac version. The only difference is that we're directly updating the text view instead of using bindings.

Next, we'll add the method that updates when the metadata query finds files.

4. Add the following method to ViewController:

```
- (void) queryDidUpdate:(NSNotification*)notification {
    NSMutableArray* files = [NSMutableArray array];

    for (NSMetadataItem* item in metadataQuery.results) {
        NSURL *filename = [item valueForAttribute:NSMetadataItemPathKey];
        [files addObject:filename];
    }

    self.fileList.text = [files description];
}
```

Now run the app, and add a file to iCloud via the Mac app. It'll appear in the iOS app.

It's important to note that items that show up in the iCloud container aren't necessarily fully downloaded, particularly if the file is large. Likewise, an item that's uploading to iCloud might take some time.

You can determine the status of a file at a given URL by using NSURL's valueForAttri bute: key. For example, to work out if a file is completely available, you do this:

```
// anURL is an NSURL pointing at an item in the ubiquity container
BOOL isDownloaded = [[anURL
    valueForAttribute:NSMetadataUbiquitousItemIsDownloadedKey]
    boolValue];
```

In order to be a good citizen in iCloud, there are a number of things that your application should do in order to provide the best user experience:

- Don't store some documents in iCloud and some outside. It's easier for users to choose to store all their data in iCloud or to not store anything there.

- Only store user-created content in iCloud. Don't store caches, settings, or anything else—iCloud is meant for storing things that cannot be re-created by the app.

- If you delete an item from iCloud, the file is removed from *all* the user's devices and computers. This means that you should confirm a delete operation with the user before performing it, since users might not understand the implications and may think that they're only deleting the local copy of the file.

Index

Symbols

* (asterisk), 41
: (colon), 24
@ (at sign), 39, 49
[ ] (square brackets), 25

A

absolute paths, 64
Acrobat Reader (Adobe), 69
actions
    connecting views to code, 75
    creating, 16
    defined, 16, 79
    outlets and, 80
    sending messages to nil, 26
    target-action relationship, 79
Adobe Acrobat Reader, 69
alerts, scheduled, 244
animation (see Core Animation)
APIs, undocumented, 72
app-scoped bookmarks, 161
Apple Developer Forums, 2
Apple ID, 2
application delegates (see NSApplicationDele-
    gate protocol)
application sandboxes
    about, 69
    enabling, 159

    open and save panels, 160
    restrictions for, 70–72, 159
    security-scoped bookmarks and, 161
applications, 59
    (see also document-based applications)
    about, 59
    background, 66, 68
    building for events, 247–252
    building with nibs and constraints, 82–84
    bundle IDs for, 5
    buttons in, 79
    compiled binary in, 61
    composition of, 61–63
    connecting code in, 16–18
    creating, 6, 14
    designing interfaces for, 15–15, 74
    entitlements for, 71, 161
    favicon example, 98–100
    finding resources in, 63
    foreground, 66
    frameworks and, 61
    inactive, 66
    iOS structure, 70
    lifecycle for iOS, 66–69
    lifecycle for OS X, 64–65
    multitasking, 67–69
    OS X structure, 71
    photo, 140–141
    private APIs and, 72

We'd like to hear your suggestions for improving our indexes. Send email to index@oreilly.com.

run loop in, 65
security considerations, 69
suspended, 67
viewing structure of, 61–63
array controllers, 168
arrays
  about, 43–45
  fast enumeration and, 46
  mutable, 46
ASCII encoding, 52
assign property, 28
asterisk (*), 41
at sign (@), 39, 49
Attributes inspector, 15
audiovisual content
  about, 129
  AV Foundation and, 129–130
  playing sound with AVAudioPlayer, 135–137
  playing video with AVPlayer, 130–135
  working with photo library, 137–143
automatic reference counting
  about, 5, 32
  blocks and, 93
  strong references and, 267
autosaving feature, 198
autosizing masks model, 81
AV content (see audiovisual content)
AV Foundation, 129, 129
AVAudioPlayer class
  about, 135
  currentTime property, 137
  delegation and, 57
AVAudioPlayerDelegate protocol, 57
AVCaptureInput class, 137
AVCaptureOutput class, 137
AVCaptureSession class, 137
AVPlayer class
  about, 130
  play method, 130
  video player example, 131–135
AVPlayerLayer class
  about, 131
  playerLayerWithPlayer: method, 131
  video player example, 131–135
awakeFromNib: message, 64, 80

B

background applications, 66, 68
Berkeley sockets API, 215

bindings
  about, 163
  complex app example, 169–174
  to controllers, 167
  NSTableView class and, 189
  simple app example, 164–167
  views to models, 164
Bindings inspector, 172, 314
__block keyword, 95
blocks
  about, 89–90
  calling, 89
  lifecycles for, 92–93
  memory management and, 92, 94
  parameters and, 91, 93
  syntax for, 90
Bonjour protocol, 220
BOOL parameter, 91, 94
bounds rectangles, 109
breakpoint navigator, 13, 272
breakpoints
  customizing, 271
  exception, 272
  setting, 269–272
  symbolic, 272
breakpoints button, 11
build configurations, 11
bundle IDs, 5
bundles, defined, 59, 63
buttons
  about, 79
  adding, 15

C

CALayer class
  about, 85, 131
  video player example, 132
calendars
  accessing, 245
  events and, 243
  privacy considerations, 252
capitalization in strings, 40
CATransaction class
  about, 86
  begin met hod, 86
  commit method, 86
cell tower lookups, 225
CGContextRef type, 126
CGContextRestoreGState function, 122

CGContextSaveGState function, 122
CGContextSetShadowWithColor function, 122
CGFloat structure, 119
CGPoint structure, 41
CGRect structure, 108
Clark, Josh, 73
class extensions, 30–31
class methods, 22, 24
class prefixes, 5
classes
    conforming to protocols, 29
    container, 49
    defined, 22
    implementing, 23
    inheritance and, 23
    interfaces and, 23
    model-view-controller paradigm and, 55–56
    property list, 202
CLGeocoder class, 230
CLLocation class
    about, 230
    horizontalAccuracy property, 227
CLLocationManager class
    about, 225
    locationManager:didFailWithError: method, 226
    locationManager:didUpdateToLoca-
        tion:fromLocation: method, 231
    startUpdatingLocation method, 226
    stopUpdatingLocation method, 226
CLLocationManagerDelegate protocol
    about, 228
    locationManager:didUpdateToLoca-
        tion:fromLocation: method, 226
CMMotionManager class
    about, 234
    accelerometerData property, 234
    deviceMotion property, 234
    gyroData property, 234
    startAccelerometerUpdates method, 234
    startDeviceMotionUpdates method, 234
    startGyroUpdates method, 234
Cocoa Touch, defined, 61
Cocoa, defined, 61
coding, defined, 53
collection views
    about, 190
    data sources and delegates, 175
    defined, 175

UICollectionView class, 190–193
colon (:), 24
com.apple.security.files.bookmarks.app-scope
    entitlement, 161
command-line tools, 289–291
compiled binary in applications, 61
concurrency with operation queues, 95–97
Connections inspector, 189
constraints
    about, 80
    building apps with, 82–84
    implicit, 81
    viewing for objects, 81
constraints menu (Interface Builder), 82
container classes, 49
context, defined, 103
controller classes, 56
controller objects, 167, 168
controllers
    array, 168
    binding to, 167
    defined, 55
    MVC pattern and, 55, 74
    object, 168
    table view, 178
    view, 74, 76–78, 79
coordinate space, 105
copy property, 28
Core Animation
    about, 84, 85
    iOS platform and, 87
    layers in, 85, 131
    OS X platform and, 86
Core Location
    about, 223, 225–229
    geocoding and, 230–232
Core Motion, 223, 233–238
count property, 44
CTM (current transformation matrix), 119, 126
custom breakpoints, 271
custom paths, 114–116
custom views
    about, 110
    creating custom paths, 114–116
    creating projects, 110
    filling with solid color, 110–112
    gradients in, 122–124
    multiple subpaths, 117–118
    shadows in, 118–122

transforms, 126–127
working with paths, 113

D

data management
   about, 50
   deserialization process, 52–54
   detecting data, 304–307
   loading data from files and URLs, 50
   serialization process, 52–54
data sharing, 275–281
data source protocol, 176
data sources
   collection views and, 190
   defined, 176
   objects as, 178
   table view controllers and, 178
databases, defined, 196
dates, formatting, 302–304
debug area (Xcode window), 13
debug navigator, 12
debuggers
   about, 269
   debugger console, 273
   inspecting memory contents, 273
   setting breakpoints, 269–272
decoding, defined, 53
default value, 152
defaults object
   accessing preferences, 153
   defined, 152
delegates
   collection views and, 190
   table views and, 176, 181
delegation design pattern, 56
deserialization process, 52–54
design patterns
   about, 54
   delegation, 56
   key-value observing, 57
   model-view-controller, 55–56
designated initializers, 34
developer programs
   about, 1
   Apple supported, 1
   registering, 2
device motion, 223, 233–238
dictionaries, 47–49
digital signing certificates, 2

directories
   creating, 158
   deleting, 158
dirty rectangle, 108
document objects, 196, 197
document-based applications
   about, 195
   document objects in MVC, 196
   iOS platform and, 206–213
   kinds of documents, 196
   NSDocument class and, 196
   OS X platform and, 198–206
   role of documents, 197
   saving complex data, 202–206
   saving simple data, 200–202
   UIDocument class and, 196
document-scoped bookmarks, 161
documents
   printing, 239–242
   representing on disks, 196
   representing with NSDocument, 199
   representing with UIDocument, 206–213
   role of, 197
   viewing previous versions, 199
downloading Xcode, 3
drawing graphics
   about, 103–104
   building custom views, 110–127
   gradients, 124
   pixel grid, 105–107
   shadows, 120–120
   in views, 108–109
@dynamic directive, 28

E

editor (Xcode window), 8
EKCalendar class, 243
EKCalendarItem class, 244, 246
EKEvent class, 243
EKEventStore class
   about, 243
   calendarsForEntityType: method, 245
   EKEventStoreChangedNotification, 245, 247
   event-finding predicates, 246
   initWithAccessToEntityTypes: method, 244
   predicateForEventsWithStartDate:end-
      Date:calendars: method, 246
EKSpan class, 246
encapsulation, 22

entitlements, application, 71, 161
Event Kit, 243
Event Kit event store, 243
event-finding predicates, 246
events
    about, 243, 246
    accessing, 245
    building applications for, 247
    privacy considerations, 252
    repeating, 244
exception breakpoints, 272

F

factory methods, 34
fast enumeration, 46
favicon application example, 98–100
file packages, 196
file: scheme, 217
files
    copying, 158
    creating, 158
    deleting, 158
    flat, 196
    loading data from, 50
    moving, 158
    storing, 155, 159, 309
    strings, 299
filesystem
    NSFileManager class and, 156–159
    storing files, 159
    user access to, 195
    working with, 154
filing paths, 104
Finder
    looking inside applications, 60
    opening, 4
flat files, 196
foreground applications, 66
formatting text, 302–304
Foundation framework
    about, 37
    arrays, 43–47
    container classes, 49
    data management, 50–54
    design patterns, 54–57
    dictionaries, 47
    immutable objects, 37
    mutable objects, 37
    strings, 38–43

frame rectangles, 108
frameworks, 60
freeze-dried objects, 64, 75

G

geocoding, 230–232
getter methods, 26
GLKit controller, 77
GPS devices, 224
gradients, 122–124
graphical images
    about, 103
    building custom views, 110–127
    drawing, 103–104
    drawing gradients, 124
    drawing in views, 108–109
    drawing shadows, 120–120
    pixel grid, 105–107
graphical user interfaces
    about, 73
    building apps with nibs and constraints, 82–84
    constructing, 80–82
    Core Animation, 84–87
    in iOS, 73
    MVC and application design, 74
    nib files and, 74–80
    in OS X, 73

H

.h file extension, 23
header files, 23
heads-up display (HUD) windows, 76
heap, defined, 92
HTTP (HyperText Transfer Protocol), 216
http scheme, 216
HUD (heads-up display) windows, 76
HyperText Transfer Protocol (HTTP), 216

I

iCloud
    about, 145, 309–310
    setting up for, 310–312
    storing key-value pairs, 317–324
    storing settings, 312–317
    testing, 312
    working with, 154

Identity inspector, 191
identity matrix, 126
immutable objects, 37
@implementation directive, 24, 30
implementation files, 23
implementation, defined, 23
implicit animations, 86
implicit constraints, 81
importing QuartzCore framework, 86
inactive applications, 66
index paths, 177
Info.plist file
    about, 61
    iOS applications, 66
    OS X applications, 64
inheritance, defined, 23
init method, 65
inspector (utilities pane), 13
installing Xcode, 3
instance methods
    about, 24
    setter and getter, 26
instance variables
    defined, 22
    setter and getter methods and, 27
    storing blocks as, 93
instances, defined, 22
Instruments
    about, 255
    adding from library, 260
    fixing problems with, 260–266
    getting started with, 256–258
    observing data, 259
Interface Builder
    about, 74
    connecting views to code, 75
    constraints menu, 82
    outlet collections and, 16
    table views and, 180
    views and, 74
    windows supported, 76
@interface directive, 23, 140
interfaces, 16
    (see also graphical user interfaces)
    connecting code to, 16–18
    defined, 16, 23
    designing for applications, 15–15, 74
    good design practices, 14
internationalization, 299

Internet Explorer 6 (Microsoft), 69
invocation operations, 96
invocation, defined, 26
invoke message, 92
iOS developer program, 1, 2
iOS platform
    animations on, 87
    application lifecycle, 66–69
    application sandboxes, 69–72
    approach to applications, 59–64
    bindings and, 163
    connecting code between interfaces and
        apps, 16–18
    creating applications for, 6
    data sharing and, 276, 277–280
    designing interfaces for, 15–15
    document-based applications and, 206–213
    drawing gradients on, 124
    drawing shadows on, 121
    graphical user interfaces in, 73
    multitasking on, 67–69
    printing documents, 240–242
    setting up to receive push notifications, 284
    transforms on, 126
    UICollectionView class and, 190–193
    UITableView class and, 176–184
    video player example, 131–135
    views and, 108
iOS Simulator, 10, 18–19, 234
issue navigator, 12
iTunes App Store
    bundle IDs and, 5
    developer programs and, 1
    private APIs and, 72
iTunes libraries, shared, 220–222

J

JavaScript Object Notation (JSON), 202, 282
Jobs, Steve, 74
JSON (JavaScript Object Notation), 202, 282

K

key-value coding, 145–147
key-value observing
    about, 145, 148
    binding support, 164
    design patterns for, 57
    notifying observers of changes, 150

registering for change notifications, 148
key-value pairs, storing, 317–324

L

layer property, 85
layers (Core Animation), 85, 131
layout objects, 190
library (utilities pane), 13
Linux platform, applications on, 59
LLDB debugger
    about, 269
    debugger console, 273
    inspecting memory contents, 273
    setting breakpoints, 269–272
local notifications, 281, 287
localized text, 299–302, 302
location awareness
    about, 223
    Core Location and, 223, 225–229
    geocoding and, 230–232
    hardware considerations, 224
    privacy and, 232
log navigator, 13

M

.m file extension, 23
Mac App Store
    application sandboxes and, 70
    bundle IDs and, 5
    developer programs and, 1
    private APIs and, 72
Mac developer program, 1, 2, 2
    (see also OS X platform)
main queue, 96
memory leaks, 92, 266–269
memory management
    about, 31
    automatic reference counting, 5, 32, 93
    blocks and, 92, 94
    inspecting memory contents, 273
    memory leaks, 92, 266–269
    OS X applications, 64
    reference counting, 32
    retain cycles and, 32, 266–269
    suspended applications and, 68
messages
    about, 25
    awakeFromNib:, 64, 80

invoke, 92
    sending to nil, 26
methods, 24
    (see also specific types of methods)
    block parameters and, 93
    calling, 25
    defined, 22, 24
    overriding, 23
    setter and getter, 26
Microsoft Internet Explorer 6, 69
model classes, 56
model-view-controller (MVC) pattern
    about, 55–56
    application design and, 74, 79
    document objects in, 196, 197
models
    autosizing masks, 81
    binding to views, 164
    controllers and, 168
    defined, 55
    document objects as, 197
    MVC pattern and, 55, 74
    springs and struts, 81
motion, device, 223, 233–238
multimedia content (see audiovisual content)
multitasking applications, 67–69
mutable arrays, 46
mutable objects, 37
MVC (model-view-controller) pattern
    about, 55–56
    application design and, 74, 79
    document objects in, 196, 197

N

navigation controllers, 77
navigator (Xcode window), 12
networking
    building networked applications, 218
    discovering nearby services, 220–222
    making conections, 215
    NSHTTPURLResponse class and, 218
    NSURL class and, 216
    NSURLConnection class and, 218
    NSURLRequest class and, 217
    NSURLResponse class and, 218
.nib file extension, 74
nib files
    about, 64, 74, 74–75
    building apps with, 82–84

document-based applications, 199
loading, 80
structure of, 75–78
nonatomic property, 28
notifications
    defined, 150, 275
    kinds of, 281
    local, 281, 287
    NSNotification class and, 150
    push, 281–287
    registering for, 148
NS prefix, 5
NSApplication class
    application:didRegisterForRemoteNotifica-
        tionsWithDeviceToken: method, 285
    registerForRemoteNotificationTypes: meth-
        od, 281, 284
    unregisterForRemoteNotifications method,
        286
NSApplicationDelegate protocol
    applicationDidBecomeActive: method, 65,
        66
    applicationDidFinishLaunching: method, 65,
        134, 171
    applicationDidFinishLaunching:withOp-
        tions: method, 66
    applicationDidResignActive: method, 65
    applicationWillBecomeActive: method, 65
    applicationWillResignActive: method, 65, 66
    applicationWillTerminate: method, 65, 67
NSArray class
    about, 37, 43, 46
    defaults object and, 153
    geocoding example, 230
    indexOfObject: method, 45
    indexOfObjectEqualTo: method, 45
    isEqualToArray: method, 42
    key-value observing and, 149
    objectAtIndex: method, 38, 44
    pointing to folder items, 157
    as property list class, 202
    subArrayWithRange: method, 45
NSArrayController class, 168, 171
NSAttributedString class, 169
NSBezierPath class
    bezierPathWithRect: method, 111
    bezierPathWithRoundedRect:xRadius:yRa-
        dius: method, 113
    closePath method, 118

creating custom paths, 115
curveToPoint: method, 118
drawing shadows, 120
lineToPoint: method, 118
NSBundle class
    finding resources in applications, 63
    pathForResource:OfType: method, 291
NSButton class, 132, 239
NSCoding protocol
    about, 53
    encodeWithCoder: method, 53
    initWithCoder: method, 53
NSCollectionView class, 190
NSColor class
    colors for shadows, 119
    constructing gradients, 123
    filling views with solid colors, 111
NSCopying protocol, 45
NSData class
    about, 38, 50
    dataWithContentsOfFile method, 22
    defaults object and, 153
    document-based applications and, 198
    flat files and, 197
    writeToFile:atomically: method, 52
NSDataDetector class, 304–307
NSDate class
    about, 302
    dateByAddingTimeInterval: method, 250
    defaults object and, 153
NSDateComponents class, 250
NSDateFormatter class, 302–304
NSDictionary class
    about, 49
    defaults object and, 152, 153
    key-value observing and, 149
    objectForKey: method, 48, 146
    pointing to attributes, 157, 158
    as property list class, 202
    push notifications and, 282
NSDocument class
    about, 196
    dataOfType:error: method, 199, 201
    document-based applications and, 198
    method supported, 196
    readFromData:ofType:error: method, 199,
        201
    representing documents with, 199
    role of documents and, 197

windowControllerDidLoadNib: method, 201
windowNibName method, 199
NSDocumentController class, 198
NSError class, 157
NSFileManager class
  about, 156–157
  contentsOfDirectoryAtURL:includingPro-
    pertiesForKeys:options:error: method,
    157
  copying files, 158
  creating directories, 158
  creating files, 158
  deleting files, 158
  iCloud storage and, 321
  moving files, 158
  ubiquity container URL, 312
  URLsForDirectory:inDomains: method, 159
NSFileWrapper class, 198
NSFormatter class, 302–304
NSGradient class
  about, 122
  initWithColorsAndLocations: method, 123
NSGraphicsContext class
  restoreGraphicsState method, 120, 122
  saveGraphicsState method, 119, 122
NSHTTPURLResponse class, 218
NSImageView class, 218
NSIndexPath class, 177
NSJSONSerialization class, 202, 203
NSKeyedArchiver class
  about, 53
  encodeFloat:forKey: method, 53
  encodeInteger:forKey: method, 53
  encodeObject:forKey: method, 53
NSKeyValueCoding protocol
  setValue:forKey: method, 147
  valueForKey: method, 147
NSKeyValueObserving protocol
  addObserver:forKeyPath:options:context:
    method, 149
  didChangeValueForKey: method, 150
  observeValueForKeyPath:ofOb-
    ject:change:context: method, 149
  willChangeValueForKey: method, 150
NSLocalizedString function, 300
NSLog class, 290
NSMenu class, 295
NSMetadataQuery class, 320

NSMutableArray class
  about, 37, 46
  addObject: method, 38, 46, 47
  bindings app example, 171
  controller objects and, 168
  insertObject:atIndex: method, 46
  network services example, 222
  objectAtIndex: method, 38
  removeObject: method, 47
  removeObjectAtIndex: method, 47
  replaceObjectAtIndex:withObject: method,
    47
  sortUsingDescriptors: method, 189
NSMutableData class, 50
NSMutableDictionary class, 49
NSMutableString class, 38
NSMutableURL class, 216
NSMutableURLRequest class
  about, 217
  setHTTPMethod: method, 217
NSNetService class, 220
NSNetServiceBrowser class, 220, 220
NSNetServiceBrowserDelegate protocol, 220,
  222
NSNetServiceDelegate protocol, 220, 222
NSNotFound constant, 45
NSNotification class, 66, 150
NSNotificationCenter class, 150
NSNull class, 44
NSNumber class
  about, 49
  defaults object and, 152, 153
  as property list class, 202
NSNumberFormatter class, 302
NSObject class
  about, 33
  alloc method, 33
  dealloc method, 34
  defaults object and, 152, 153
  init method, 34
  retain and release messages, 34
NSObjectController class, 169
NSOpenPanel class, 160
NSOperation class, 96
NSOperationQueue class
  about, 96
  addOperationWithBlock: method, 96
NSPredicate class, 245
NSPreferencePane class, 293

NSRange structure, 41
NSRect structure, 108, 113
NSSavePanel class, 160
NSShadow class
    about, 119
    drawing shadows, 120
    set method, 119
NSSharingServicePicker class, 280
NSSize structure, 119
NSSortDescriptor class, 188
NSStatusItem class, 295, 296
NSString class
    about, 38, 38
    application example, 182
    class extensions and, 30
    creating strings, 39
    dataUsingEncoding: method, 38
    defaults object and, 153
    designated initializers, 34
    initWithData:encoding: method, 50
    isEqualToString: method, 42
    printing documents, 240
    as property list class, 202
    rangeOfString:options: method, 43
    stringWithContentsOfFile:encoding:error:
        method, 52
NSStringEncoding enumeration, 50
NSTableColumn class, 184
NSTableView class
    about, 184–188, 190
    application example, 82, 171
    bindings and, 189
NSTableViewDataSource protocol
    application example, 187
    numberOfRowsInTableView: method, 187
    tableView:sortDescriptorsDidChange: meth-
        od, 188
NSTableViewDelegate protocol
    application example, 187
    tableView:viewForTableColumn:row: meth-
        od, 184, 187
NSTextField class, 314
NSTextView class, 239
NSUbiquitousKeyValueStore class
    about, 310, 312
    NSUbiquitousKeyValueStoreDidChangeEx-
        ternallyNotification, 314
NSURL class
    about, 216

fileURLWithPath: method, 217
iCloud storage and, 323
pointing to folder items, 157
pointing to sound files, 136
resourceValuesForKeys:error: method, 157
startAccessingSecurityScopedResource:
    method, 162
stopAccessingSecurityScopedResource:
    method, 162
URLByAppendingPathComponent: method,
    159
URLWithString: method, 216
NSURLConnection class, 218, 219
NSURLRequest class
    about, 217
    requestWithURL: method, 217
    requestWithURL:cachePolicy:timeoutInterv-
        al: method, 217
NSURLResponse class, 218
NSUserDefaults class
    about, 151, 167
    objectForKey: method, 153
    persistentDomainForName: method, 292
    preference panes and, 291
    registerDefaults: method, 152
    setBool:forKey: method, 292
    setObject:forKey: method, 154
    setPersistentDomainForName: method, 292
    setValue:forKey: method, 292
    standardUserDefaults: method, 151
    valueForKey: method, 292
NSUserDefaultsController class, 167
NSUTF8StringEncoding constant, 52
NSValue class, 49, 152
NSView class
    about, 108
    arrays and, 44
    building custom views, 110
    CALayer class and, 85
    drawRect: method, 110, 239
    print: method, 239

0

object controllers, 168
Object Library, 80
object-oriented programming
    about, 21
    class extensions in, 30–31
    inheritance in, 23

interfaces and implementations in, 23
memory management and, 31–33
messages in, 25
methods in, 24
NSObject lifecycle and, 33
objects in, 22
properties in, 26–28
protocols in, 29
Objective-C language
about, 21
class extensions in, 30–31
interfaces and implementations in, 23
memory management and, 31–33
messages in, 25
methods in, 24
NSObject lifecycle and, 33
object-oriented programming and, 21–31
objects in, 22
properties in, 26–28, 150
protocols in, 29
objects
about, 22, 41
arrays and, 43
binding to views, 163
as data sources, 178
document, 196, 197
freeze-dried, 64, 75
immutable, 37
interfaces and, 23
layout, 190
mutable, 37
nib files and, 74
property list, 153
rehydrated, 64, 75
viewing constraints on, 81
observing data, 259
operation queues
concurrency with, 95–97
defined, 89, 96
NSOperation class and, 96
performing work on, 97
options dictionary, 66
OS X platform
animations on, 86
application lifecycle, 64–65
application sandboxes, 69–72
approach to applications, 59–64
binding support, 163
data sharing and, 276, 280

document-based applications and, 198–206
downloading Xcode, 3
graphical user interfaces in, 73
Mac developer program and, 1, 2
NSTableView class and, 184–190
printing documents, 239
setting up to receive push notifications, 284
views and, 108
outlet collections, 16
outlets
actions and, 80
connecting views to code, 75
creating, 16
defined, 16, 79
overriding methods, 23
owning references, 33

P

packages
defined, 59
determining location of, 63
file, 196
page controllers, 77
panel windows, 76
paths
absolute, 64
creating custom, 114–116
custom views example, 113
defined, 104
filling, 104
index, 177
multiple subpaths, 117–118
stroking, 104
photo library
about, 137, 142
building photo apps, 140–141
capturing photos and video from cameras,
138–139
pixel grid
about, 105
Retina displays, 105–106
screen points and, 107
.pkg file extension, 59
polling technique, 57
Powerbox, 160
predicates, event-finding, 246
preference domains, 292
preference panes
about, 291, 291

building sample, 293–294
preference domains and, 292
preferences
about, 151
accessing, 153
registering default, 152–153
setting, 154
Print Simulator, 242
print-object command, 274
printing documents, 239–242
privacy, location and, 232, 252
private APIs, 72
program flow, debugger and, 270
project navigator, 12
project templates, creating, 4
projects
compiling, 60
creating, 3–7, 110
storyboards and, 15
targets and, 11
viewing in Xcode, 7–14
properties
accessing, 26
constraint considerations, 81
declaring, 27–28, 150
defined, 23
property attributes, 27
@property directive, 27, 150
property list classes, 202
property list objects, 153
protocols
classes conforming to, 29
declaring, 29
defined, 29
push notification service, 281, 283
push notifications
about, 281
receiving, 286
sending, 282
setting up to receive, 284–285

Q

QuartzCore framework, 86
queues
operation, 89, 95–97
reuse, 179
threads and, 97

R

readonly property, 28
readwrite property, 28
reference counting, 32
registering
for change notifications, 148
default preferences, 152–153
for developer programs, 2
rehydrated objects, 64, 75
release messages, 32
reminders in events, 244
remote notifications (see push notifications)
resolving service, 220
resources, finding in applications, 63
retain cycles, 32, 266–269
retain messages, 32
Retina displays, 105–106
reuse queues, 179
reverse geocoding, 230
rows in table views, 177
Run button, 10
run loop in applications, 65

S

sandboxes (see application sandboxes)
scheduled alerts, 244
schemes, defined, 11
screen points, 107
search navigator, 12
searching strings, 43
sections in table views, 177
security, application sandboxes and, 69, 159–162
security-scoped bookmarks, 161–162
selector, defined, 25
serialization process, 52–54
service, resolving, 220
setter methods, 26
shadows
about, 118–119
drawing, 120–120
saving and restoring graphics contexts, 119
sharing data, 275–281
simulators (see iOS Simulator)
sort descriptors, 188
sorting table views, 188
sound content (see audiovisual content)
Spotlight, opening, 4

springs and struts model, 81
square brackets [ ], 25
stack, defined, 92
status bar items, 295–297
Stop button, 10
storing
    files, 155, 159, 309
    key-value pairs, 317–324
storyboards, projects and, 15
string literals, 39
strings
    capitalization in, 40
    comparing, 42
    creating, 39
    defined, 38
    finding substrings, 40–42
    searching, 43
    working with, 39–42
strings files, 299
stroking paths, 104
strong property, 27
strong references, 33, 267
structures
    defined, 41
    iOS applications, 70
    of nib files, 75–78
    OS X applications, 71
    viewing for applications, 61–63
subclasses, defined, 23
subpaths
    about, 117
    multiple, 117–118
substrings, finding, 40–42
subviews, 108
superclasses, 23
superviews, 108
suspended applications, 67
symbolic breakpoints, 272
symbols navigator, 12
@synthesize directive, 28

T

tab bar controllers, 77
table view cells, 176, 178–181
table view controllers, 178
table views
    about, 176
    data sources and delegates, 175
    defined, 175

implementing, 182–184
Interface Builder and, 180
NSTableView class and, 184–190
sections and rows, 177
sorting, 188
UITableView class and, 176–184
target-action relationship, 79
targets
    defined, 11
    target-action relationship, 79
testing
    iCloud, 312
    unit tests, 5
text
    detecting data, 304–307
    formatting, 302–304
    localized, 299–302, 302
textured windows, 76
threads, queues and, 97
toolbar (Xcode window)
    about, 9
    breakpoints button, 11
    editor selector, 11
    Run button, 10
    scheme selector, 11
    status display, 11
    Stop button, 10
    view selector, 11
transactions
    creating, 86
    defined, 86
transforms, 126–127
typedef keyword, 94

U

ubiquity container URL, 312
UIActivity class, 277
UIActivityViewController class, 277, 281
UIAlertView class, 18
UIApplication class
    about, 56, 66
    application:didRegisterForRemoteNotifica-
        tionsWithDeviceToken: method, 285
    applicationDidEnterBackground: method,
        56, 67
    applicationWillEnterBackground: method,
        100
    applicationWillEnterForeground: method, 68

registerForRemoteNotificationTypes: method, 281, 284

UIApplicationDidEnterBackgroundNotification, 151

unregisterForRemoteNotifications method, 286

UIBarButtonItem class, 241

UIBezierPath class, 111

UIButton class, 140, 278

UICollectionView class, 190–193

UICollectionViewCell class, 190

UICollectionViewController class, 191

UICollectionViewDataSource protocol, 193

UICollectionViewLayout class, 190

UIColor class, 111

UIDocument class
about, 196, 206
methods supported, 196
representing documents with, 206–213
role of documents and, 197

UIImage class, 50, 240

UIImagePickerController class
about, 138
building photo apps, 140
isCameraDeviceAvailable: method, 139
isSourceTypeAvailable: method, 139
sourceType property, 142

UIImagePickerControllerDelegate protocol
building photo apps, 140
imagePickerController:didFinishPickingMediaWithInfo: method, 138, 142
imagePickerControllerDidCancel: method, 139

UIImageView class, 140, 218, 278

UILabel class, 192

UILocalNotification class, 287

UINavigationBar class, 241

UINavigationControllerDelegate protocol, 140

UIPrintFormatter class, 240

UIPrintInteractionController class, 240

UIPrintPageRenderer class, 240

UIPrintRenderer class, 276

UIScrollViewDelegate protocol, 265

UISimpleTextPrintFormatter class, 240

UITableView class
about, 176, 190
application example, 182–184
sections and rows, 177
table view cells and, 178–181

table view controllers, 178

UITableViewCell class
detailTextLabel property, 180
imageView property, 180
textLabel property, 180

UITableViewController class, 176, 182

UITableViewDataSource protocol
about, 178
application example, 98
numberOfSectionsInTableView: method, 183
tableView:cellForRowAtIndexPath: method, 178–181, 183
tableView:numberOfRowsInSection: method, 178, 183

UITableViewDelegate protocol
about, 181
application example, 98
tableView:didSelectRowAtIndexPath: method, 181, 184

UITextFieldDelegate class, 316

UITextView class, 207, 241

UITextViewDelegate protocol, 211

UIView class
about, 108
animateWithDuration:animations: method, 87
CALayer class and, 85
drawRect: method, 108

UIViewController class
about, 178
application example, 182
dismissViewControllerAnimated:completion: method, 139
presentViewController:animated:completion: method, 138

Unicode standard, 52

unit tests, 5

URLs (Uniform Resource Locators)
about, 216
absolute paths and, 64
loading data from, 50
ubiquity container, 312

user constraints, 82

user preferences (see preferences)

UTF-8 encoding, 52

utilities pane (Xcode window)
about, 13
Attributes inspector, 15

V

video content (see audiovisual content)
view controllers
    about, 74, 76–78
    target-action relationship, 79
View Effects inspector, 132
views, 176
    (see also table views)
    binding to models and, 164
    binding to objects, 163
    bound rectangles in, 109
    building custom, 110–127
    collection, 175, 175, 190–193
    connecting code to, 75
    constraints in, 80
    controllers and, 168
    data source protocol, 176
    defined, 55
    drawing in, 108–109
    frame rectangles in, 108
    Interface Builder and, 74
    MVC pattern and, 55, 74, 79

W

weak property, 27
weak references, 33

WiFi base station lookups, 224
windows
    constraints in, 80
    defined, 73
    Interface Builder supported, 76
    sandboxes and, 160
    size considerations, 78
    target-action relationship, 79
Windows platform, applications on, 59

X

Xcode application
    about, 1, 3
    compiling projects, 60
    downloading, 2, 3
    installing, 3
Xcode window
    debug area, 13
    editor component, 8
    getting around in, 3–7
    navigator section, 12
    toolbar section, 9–11
    utilities pane, 13
    viewing projects in, 7–14
.xib file extension, 74

About the Authors

Jon Manning is the co-founder of Secret Lab, an independent game development studio based in Hobart, Tasmania, Australia. He's worked on apps of all sorts, ranging from iPad games for children to instant messaging clients. He's a Core Animation demigod, and frequently finds himself gesticulating wildly in front of classes full of eager-to-learn iOS developers. Jon is the world's biggest Horse_ebooks fan (*https://twitter.com/Horse_ebooks*), and can be found on Twitter as @desplesda.

Paris Buttfield-Addison is the other co-founder of Secret Lab, which remains an independent game development studio based in Hobart, Tasmania, Australia. He's also worked on all sorts of apps, ranging from one of the most popular iPad cooking apps to home-automation tools. He's a OS X developer from the very beginning, and has an surprisingly deep knowledge of Australian taxation law. Paris can be found on Twitter as @parisba. Secret Lab can be found at *http://www.secretlab.com.au* or on Twitter as @thesecretlab.

Colophon

The animal on the cover of *Learning Cocoa with Objective-C*, Third Edition, is an Irish setter. Bred as a sporting dog in the 19th century, the Irish setter's agility and energy made it a prime companion for pheasant and quail hunters. By the 1890s, the dog's attractive, silky red coat and elegant build boosted its popularity as a show dog. For the past century, breeders have created a larger dog with a longer coat, with deep chestnut red or patches of red and white hair. The Irish setter is also popular as a family dog. Described as loyal, gentle, energetic, and happy, this breed gets along well with children. Some hospitals, nursing homes, and rehabilitation centers also adopt the Irish setter as a therapy dog.

The cover image is a 19th-century engraving from the Dover Pictorial Archive. The text font is Adobe Minion Pro; the heading font is Adobe Myriad Condensed; and the code font is Dalton Maag's Ubuntu Mono.

Get even more for your money.

Join the O'Reilly Community, and register the O'Reilly books you own. It's free, and you'll get:

- $4.99 ebook upgrade offer
- 40% upgrade offer on O'Reilly print books
- Membership discounts on books and events
- Free lifetime updates to ebooks and videos
- Multiple ebook formats, DRM FREE
- Participation in the O'Reilly community
- Newsletters
- Account management
- 100% Satisfaction Guarantee

Signing up is easy:

1. **Go to: oreilly.com/go/register**
2. **Create an O'Reilly login.**
3. **Provide your address.**
4. **Register your books.**

Note: English-language books only

To order books online:
oreilly.com/store

For questions about products or an order:
orders@oreilly.com

To sign up to get topic-specific email announcements and/or news about upcoming books, conferences, special offers, and new technologies:
elists@oreilly.com

For technical questions about book content:
booktech@oreilly.com

To submit new book proposals to our editors:
proposals@oreilly.com

O'Reilly books are available in multiple DRM-free ebook formats. For more information:
oreilly.com/ebooks

O'REILLY®

Spreading the knowledge of innovators

oreilly.com

CPSIA information can be obtained at www.ICGtesting.com
Printed in the USA
LVOW051703030113

314244LV00007B/249/P

9 781449 318499